PROSPERO'S CELL

and

REFLECTIONS ON A MARINE VENUS

Prospero's Cell

and

Reflections on a Marine Venus

BY

LAWRENCE DURRELL

ILLUSTRATED

E. P. DUTTON & CO., INC.
New York   1960

Library of Congress Catalog Card Number: 60-12104

PROSPERO'S CELL

*A guide to the landscape
and manners of the island of
Corcyra*

by

LAWRENCE DURRELL

FOUR
OF THE CHARACTERS
IN THIS BOOK
ARE REAL PEOPLE
AND APPEAR HERE
BY THEIR OWN CONSENT.
TO THE FOUR OF THEM
THEODORE STEPHANIDES
ZARIAN
THE COUNT D.
AND MAX NIMIEC
IT IS DEDICATED BY THE AUTHOR
IN LOVE AND ADMIRATION

Acknowledgements

Acknowledgements for material used in this book must be made to:

Dr. Theodore Stephanides, R.A.M.C., who has placed five unpublished monographs at my disposal containing the fruits of ten years' research; Mr. Jean Tricoglou of Cairo for illustrations and other matter; Mr. Theodore Moschonas for valuable suggestions; and to Miss Y. Cohen for invaluable aid in copying out manuscripts.

'A Greekish isle, and the most pleasant place that ever our eyes beheld for the exercise of a solitary and contemplative life. . . . In our travels many times, falling into dangers and unpleasant places, this only island would be the place where we would wish ourselves to end our lives.'—ANTHONY SHERLEY, *His Persian Adventure 1601*.

Contents

Illustrations

Prospero's Cell

I

Divisions upon Greek Ground

'No tongue: all eyes: be silent.'
The Tempest

Somewhere between Calabria and Corfu the blue really begins. All the way across Italy you find yourself moving through a landscape severely domesticated—each valley laid out after the architect's pattern, brilliantly lighted, human. But once you strike out from the flat and desolate Calabrian mainland towards the sea, you are aware of a change in the heart of things: aware of the horizon beginning to stain at the rim of the world: aware of *islands* coming out of the darkness to meet you.

In the morning you wake to the taste of snow on the air, and climbing the companion-ladder, suddenly enter the penumbra of shadow cast by the Albanian mountains—each wearing its cracked crown of snow—desolate and repudiating stone.

A peninsula nipped off while red hot and allowed to cool into an antarctica of lava. You are aware not so much of a landscape coming to meet you invisibly over those blue miles of water as of a climate. You enter Greece as one might enter a dark crystal; the form of things becomes irregular, refracted. Mirages suddenly swallow islands, and wherever you look the trembling curtain of the atmosphere deceives.

Other countries may offer you discoveries in manners or lore or landscape; Greece offers you something harder—the discovery of yourself.

10.4.37

It is a sophism to imagine that there is any strict dividing line between the waking world and the world of dreams. N. and I, for example, are confused by the sense of several contemporaneous lives being lived inside us; the sensation of being mere points of

11

reference for space and time. We have chosen Corcyra perhaps because it is an ante-room to Aegean Greece with its smoke-grey volcanic turtle-backs lying low against the ceiling of heaven. Corcyra is all Venetian blue and gold—and utterly spoilt by the sun. Its richness cloys and enervates. The southern valleys are painted out boldly in heavy brush-strokes of yellow and red while the Judas trees punctuate the roads with their dusty purple explosions. Everywhere you go you can lie down on grass; and even the bare northern reaches of the island are rich in olives and mineral springs.

25.4.37

The architecture of the town is Venetian; the houses above the old port are built up elegantly into slim tiers with narrow alleys and colonnades running between them; red, yellow, pink, umber—a jumble of pastel shades which the moonlight transforms into a dazzling white city built for a wedding cake. There are other curiosities; the remains of a Venetian aristocracy living in overgrown baronial mansions, buried deep in the country and surrounded by cypresses. A patron saint of great antiquity who lies, clad in beautifully embroidered slippers, in a great silver casket, apt for the performance of miracles.

29.4.37

It is April and we have taken an old fisherman's house in the extreme north of the island—Kalamai. Ten sea-miles from the town, and some thirty kilometres by road, it offers all the charms of seclusion. A white house set like a dice on a rock already venerable with the scars of wind and water. The hill runs clear up into the sky behind it, so that the cypresses and olives overhang this room in which I sit and write. We are upon a bare promontory with its beautiful clean surface of metamorphic stone covered in olive and ilex: in the shape of a *mons pubis*. This is become our unregretted home. A world. Corcyra.

5.5.37

The books have arrived by water. Confusion, adjectives, smoke, and the deafening pumping of the wheezy Diesel engine. Then the

Divisions upon Greek Ground

caique staggered off in the direction of St. Stephano and the
Forty Saints, where the crew will gorge themselves on melons and
fall asleep in their coarse woollen vests, one on top of the
other, like a litter of cats, under the ikon of St. Spiridion of Holy
Memory. We are depending upon this daily caique for our provisions.

6.5.37

Climb to Vigla in the time of cherries and look down. You will
see that the island lies against the mainland roughly in the form
of a sickle. On the landward side you have a great bay, noble and
serene, and almost completely landlocked. Northward the tip of
the sickle almost touches Albania and here the troubled blue of
the Ionian is sucked harshly between ribs of limestone and spits
of sand. Kalamai fronts the Albanian foothills, and into it the
water races as into a swimming-pool: a milky ferocious green when
the north wind curdles it.

7.5.37

The cape opposite is bald; a wilderness of rock-thistle and melancholy asphodel—the drear sea-squill. It was on a ringing spring day
that we discovered the house. The sky lay in a heroic blue arc as
we came down the stone ladder. I remember N. saying distinctly
to Theodore: 'But the quietness alone makes it another country.'
We looked through the hanging screen of olive-branches on to the
white sea wall with fishing-tackle drying on it. A neglected balcony. The floors were cold. Fowls clucked softly in the gloom where
the great olive-press lay, waiting its season. A cypress stood motionless—as if at the gates of the underworld. We shivered and sat on
the white rock to eat, looking down at our own faces in the
motionless sea. You will think it strange to have come all the way
from England to this fine Grecian promontory where our only
company can be rock, air, sky—and all the elementals. In letters
home N. says we have been cultivating the tragic sense. There is
no explanation. It is enough to record that everything is exactly
as the fortune-teller said it would be. White house, white rock,
friends, and a narrow style of loving: and perhaps a book which
will grow out of these scraps, as from the rubbish of these old

13

Venetian tombs the cypress cracks the slabs at last and rises up
fresh and green.

We are lucky in our friends. Two of them seem of almost mythological quality—Ivan Zarian and the arcane professor of broken
bones Theodore Stephanides. Zarian is grey, eminent and impos-
ing with his mane of hair and his habit of conducting himself as
he intones his latest love-song; he claims to be Armenia's greatest
poet with a firmness and modesty that completely charm. He has
spent nearly two years here intoning his work to anyone who
would listen, and making an exhaustive study of the island wines.
He has managed to convert the top floor of the St. George Hotel
into a workroom—indeed a wilderness of manuscript and paintings. Here, looking out upon the blunt fortifications of the Eastern
Fort, and pausing from time to time to relish a glass of wine, he
compiles his literary column for some new world Armenian news-
papers. On Friday, the 8th of March, he sent me a friendly
message reading:

> Dear Durrell: we miss you but most your beautiful wife. Dear,
> boy, yes, certainly I have immortalized you this week. I have
> written this epoch of our lives. Great love from Zarian.

Zarian walks as if he wears a heavy cloak. A copious and extravagant figure it was he who instituted our literary meetings once a
week at the 'Sign of the Partridge', off the main square of the
town. Zarian possesses an extraordinary typewriter which enables
him, by simply revolving the bed of type, to write in French and
Italian as well as in Armenian and Russian. At these weekly meetings he rises to his feet and, in a beautifully controlled voice, recites
the 'to be or not to be' speech from Hamlet, first in French, and
then in Armenian, Russian, Italian, German and Spanish. He
scorns to learn English properly.

From my notebook   *12.5.37*

For Theodore's portrait: fine head and golden beard: very
Edwardian face—and perfect manners of Edwardian professor.

Divisions upon Greek Ground

Probably reincarnation of comic professor invented by Edward Lear during his stay in Corcyra. Tremendous shyness and diffidence. Incredibly erudite in everything concerning the island. Firm Venezelist, and possessor of the dryest and most fastidious style of exposition ever seen. Thumbnail portrait of bearded man in boots and cape, with massive bug-hunting apparatus on his back stalking across country to a delectable pond where his microscopic world of algae and diatoms (the only real world for him) lies waiting to be explored. Theodore is always being arrested as a foreign agent because of the golden beard, strong English accent in Greek, and mysterious array of vessels and swabs and tubes dangling about his person. On his first visit to Kalamai house he had hardly shaken hands when sudden light came into his eye. Taking a conical box from his pocket he said 'excuse me' with considerable suppressed excitement and advanced to the drawing-room wall to capture a sand-fly exclaiming as he did so in a small triumphant voice 'Got it. Four hundred and second.'

17.5.37

Gulls turning down wind; to-day a breath of sirocco and the sea grinding and crushing up its colours under the house; the town gardens steaming in their rotten richness. The Duchess of B. abroad in a large hat, riding in a horse-carriage. Shuttered mansions with the umbrella pines rapping at the windows. On the great southern shelf you can see the road running white as a scar against the emerald lake; the olives are tacking madly from grey to silver, and behind the house the young cypresses are like drawn bows. Nicholas who was standing firm and square before us on the jetty a minute ago is now that speck of red sail against the mountains. Then at night it dies down suddenly and the colour washes back into the sky. At the 'Sign of the Partridge' Zarian gives a discourse on landscape as a form of metaphysics. 'The divine Plato said once that in Greece you see God with his compasses and dividers.' N. maintains Lawrence's grasp of place against an English boy who declares all the Lawrentian landscapes to be invented not described; while Theodore surprises by asking in a small voice for a glass of wine (he does not drink) and adding in an even smaller voice: 'What is causality?'

Divisions upon Greek Ground

18.5.37

Causality is this dividing floor which falls away each morning when I am back on the warm rocks, lying with my face less than a foot above the dark Ionian. All morning we lie under the red brick shrine to Saint Arsenius, dropping cherries into the pool— clear down two fathoms to the sandy floor where they loom like drops of blood. N. has been going in for them like an otter and bringing them up in her lips. The Shrine is our private bathing-pool; four puffs of cypress, deep clean-cut diving ledges above two fathoms of blue water, and a floor of clean pebbles. Once after a storm an ikon of the good Saint Arsenius was found here by a fisherman called Manoli, and he built the shrine out of red plaster as a house for it. The little lamp is always full of sweet oil now, for St. Arsenius guards our bathing.

22.5.37

At evening the blue waters of the lagoon invent moonlight and play it back in fountains of crystal on the white rocks and the deep balcony; into the high-ceilinged room where N.'s lazy pleasant paintings stare down from the walls. And invisibly the air (cool as the breath from the heart of a melon) pours over the window-sills and mingles with the scent of the exhausted lamps. It is so still that the voice of a man up there in the dusk under the olives disturbs and quickens one like the voice of conscience itself. Under the glacid surface of the sea fishes are moving like the suggestion of fishes—influences of curiosity and terror. And now the stars are shining down frostblown and taut upon this pure Euclidian surface. It is so still that we have dinner under the cypress tree to the light of a candle. And after it, while we are drinking coffee and eating grapes on the edge of the mirror a wind comes: and the whole of heaven stirs and trembles—a great branch of blossoms melting and swaying. Then as the candle draws breath and steadies everything hardens slowly back into the image of a world in water, so that Theodore can point into the water at our feet and show us the Pleiades burning.

28.5.37

At such moments we never speak; but I am aware of the brown

MAÏOTPO
N.N.W. WIND

Borea
N.N.E. WIND

ALBANIA

Ship of
Ulysses

Karusades

Kasuppi
P. St.
Stefano

Koulouru

L. Butrinto

White
House

Butrinto

AUOTPO
toxpNTHS
WIND

1055

Skripero
Dukades

Ypso

Big &
Fauns

St. Angle

Paleokastrizza

Lakos

Govino Bay

Valle di Ropa

△ Vido

Corfu

TPoxMONTAPA
WIND

P. St. Giorgio

Myrtiotissa

Hermones

Sinarades

Pelleka

Analog-itas

L. Khalichiopoulo

Canone

Achilleion

Benizza

Sturo

SIPOKO

SOUTH WIND

Khamos

Lefkimo
Point

ZOVEYTOS
WEST WIND

C. di Karissio

C. Bianco

CORFU

Best Dancing
Fiestas ★

Best Costumes ♛

Best Wines ❀

Best
Beaches ◆

Best Views ○

W ─── E

S

arms and throat in the candlelight and the brown toes in the sandals. I am aware of a hundred images at once and a hundred ways of dealing with them. The bowl of wild roses. The English knives and forks. Greek cigarettes. The battered and sea-stained notebook in which I rough out my poems. The rope and oar lying under the tree. The spilth of the olive-press which will be gathered for fuel. The pile of rough stone for the building of a garden wall. A bucket and an axe. The peasant crossing the orchard in her white head-dress. The restless cough of the goat in the barn. All these take shape and substance round this little yellow cone of flame in which N. is cutting the cheese and washing the grapes. A single candle burning upon a table between our happy selves.

4.6.37

I have preserved the text of Theodore's first communication. It arrived on Sunday by the evening boat and was delivered at the door by Spiro the village idiot. Since it was superscribed URGENT I made the messenger the gift of a drachma.

'*I learn with considerable joy from our mutual friend Z that you are intending a written history of the isle. It is a project which I myself have long contemplated but owing to the diffuseness of my interests and lack of literary talent I have always felt myself unequal to the task. I hasten however to place all my material at your service, and on Tuesday will send you (a) my synoptic history of the island, (b) my facts about St. Spiridion, (c) my fresh-water biology of Corcyra, (d) a short account of the geology of the island of Corcyra. This should interest you. It is only the beginning. Yours sincerely, Theodore Stephanides.*'

It is on the strength of this that I have entered into a correspondence characterized on my part by flights of deliberately false scholarship, and on his by the unsmiling and fastidious rectitude of a research worker. Our letters are carried to and fro by the island boats. It is, as he says, only a beginning.

7.6.37

At night the piper sometimes plays, while his grazing sheep walk upon the opposite cape and browse among the arbutus and scrub. We lie in bed with our skins rough and satiny from the salt and listen. The industrious and rather boring nightingales are abashed by the soft liquid quartertones, the unearthly quibbles of the flute. There is form without melody, and the notes are emptied as if drop by drop on to the silence. It is the wheedling voice of the sirens that Ulysses heard.

9.6.37

We have been betraying our origins. N. has decided to build a garden on the rock outside the house. We will have to bring the soil down in sacks, and employ the Aegean technique of walled boxes and columns. The design is N.'s and its execution is in the hands of John and Nicholas, father and son, who are the best masons in the village. The father builds slightly lopsided because, he says, he is blind in one eye; and his son comes silently behind him to rectify his errors and admire his facility in pruning the mountain stone into rough blocks. John is most comfortable squatting on his haunches in the shadow cast by his wide straw hat and talking scandal; he moves along the wall in a series of hops like a clipped magpie. His son is a fresh-faced dumb youth with a vivid smile and excellent manners. He dresses in the hideous cloth cap and torn breeches of the European workman, while his father still wears pointed slippers. It is worth perhaps recording the traditional island costume, now seldom seen except at festivals and dances.

Blue embroidered bolero jacket with black and gold braid and
   piping.
A white soft shirt with puffed sleeves.
Baggy blue breeches called Vrakes.
White woollen gaiters.
And pointed Turkish slippers with no pom-pom.
Either a soft red fez with a blue tassel
Or a white straw hat.

11.6.37

The straw from the packing-cases will go to cover the floor of the magazine where the goat is tethered. The rooms look lovely and gracious with their white-washed walls, and the few bright paintings and books. The windows give directly on to the sea, so that its perpetual sighing is the rhythm of our work and our sleep-

18

ing. By day it runs golden on the ceilings, reflecting back the bright peasant rugs—a ship, a gorgon, a loom, a cypress-tree; reflecting back the warm crude pottery of our table; reflecting back N. now brown-skinned and blonde, reading in a chair with her legs tucked under her. Calm eyes, calm hair, and clear white teeth like those of a young carnivore. As Father Nicholas says: 'What more does a man want than an olive-tree, a native island, and woman from his own place?'

13.6.37

The man and his wife are fine creatures. He is called Anastasius and she Helen. It is obvious from their children that the marriage was a marriage of love rather than convenience. She is most delicately formed in a deep silken olive-colour; their hair has that deep black which shines out in sudden hints of blue—the simile of the Klepthic poems says 'hair like the wing of a raven'. Beautifully formed eyebrows above their dark eyes, clear and circumflex. Only their hands and feet—like those of all peasants—are blunt and hideous: mere spades grown upon the members through a long battle with soil, ropes, and wood. Their daughters are called Sky and Freedom.

17.6.37

'Formal geology', writes Theodore in his treatise, 'will still find features of interest in Corcyra; and if the form of the island in general is conditioned by its limestone features, there are many interesting configurations worth the mature attention of field-workers.'

Southward the land falls gently away to the white cape, luxuriant and steaming; every curve here is a caress, a nakedness to the delighted eyes, an endearment. Every prospect is contained in a frame of cypress and olives and brilliant roofs. Inlets, lakes, islands lead one slowly down to the deserted salt-pans beyond Lefkimi.

Two great ribs of mountain enclose this Eden. One runs from north to south along the western ranges; while from east to west the dead lands rise sheer to Pantocrator. It is in the shadow of this mountain that we live. Here little vegetation clings to the rock; water, harsh with the taste of iron and ice cold, runs from the ravines; the olive-trees are stunted and contorted in an effort to maintain a purchase on this crumbling gypsum territory. Their roots, like the muscles of wrestlers, hang from the culverts. Here the peasant girls lounge on the hillside—flash of colour like a bird —with a flower between their teeth, while their goats munch the tough thistle and ilex.

'All epochs from the Jurassic are represented here. In the north the configurations of certain caves suggest volcanic origins, but this has not yet been proved.' The grottoes at Paleocastrizza are ribbed with jewels which smoulder purple and yellow and nacre in the reflected light of the intruding sea. Grapes from this mountain region yield a wine that bubbles ever so slightly; an undertone of sulphur and rock. Ask for red wine at Lakones and they will bring you a glass of volcano's blood.

20.6.37

Zarian sends me a poem about the island in Armenian to which he adds an English translation. Writing of Corcyra he says: 'The gold and moving blue have stained our thoughts so that the darkness is opaque, and we see in our dreams the world as if in some great Aquarium. Exiles and sharers, we have found a new love. This is Corcyra, the chimney-corner of the world.'

Since I have nothing else I reciprocate with my poem on Manoli, the landscape painter of Greece: 'After a lifetime of writing acrostics he took up a brush and everything became twice as attentive. Trees had been simply trees before. Distinctions had been in ideas. Now the old man went mad, for everything undressed and ran laughing into his arms.'

Theodore promises 'Maps, Tables, and Statistics'. I am making no attempt to control all this material. If I wrote a book about Corcyra it would not be a history but a poem.

World of black cherries, sails, dust, arbutus, fishes and letters from home.

24.6.37

Fragment from a novel about Corcyra which I began and destroyed: 'She comes down through the cloud of almond-trees like a sentence of death, all dressed in white and leading her flock

20

to the very gates of the underworld. Our hearts melt in us at the candour of her smile and the beauty of her walk. Soon she is to marry Niko, the fat moneylender, and become a stout shrew drudging out to olive-pickings on a lame donkey, smelling of garlic and animal droppings.'

25.6.37

N. has been away for three days in the town, trying to buy a few odds and ends of furnishings for the house. The silence here is like a discernible pulse—the heart-beat of time itself. I am all day alone on the great rock; the sea is cold—its chill hurts the back of the throat like an iced wine; but blue as the grave, while the sun is blazing. To-night a letter by boat from her. 'I have bought us a twenty-foot cutter, carvel built, and Bermuda rigged. I am terribly excited—the whole world seems to be open before us. But O how wine-darkly she rides. Bringing her out to-morrow with Petros. Wait for me at the point.'

26.6.37

The problem of water for the garden is serious. The only spring is on the highroad a quarter of a mile up the ravine. All our water is carried down on the backs of womenfolk in huge earthen jars. We had Nick the douser down with his hazel-twig, but after walking backwards and forwards grumbling under his breath for a quarter of an hour, he pronounced the water 'too deep'—over five metres. As the house stands at sea-level we could not afford to dig and have the well turn brackish on us. It must be a mountain spring or nothing. Meanwhile my two erudites send their suggestions by water—each a model of its kind. Zarian suggests a machine that a friend of his invented for turning salt water into fresh; he forgets how it works but he will write to America at once for particulars. It costs rather a lot but would save trouble; we would simply put one end of the pump in the sea and spray the garden with fresh water. Theodore, on the other hand, suggests something more practical. In the droughty summer the natives of Macedonia construct themselves ice-boxes by pulping quantities of prickly pear which they bury in a hole to the depth of about two metres. The hole is filled with fine pebbles or stones, and when the rains

21

come the absorbing pulp of the prickly pear sups up the water and retains it in its pores. He suggests that we should adopt this scheme for our walled garden-boxes. 'Be careful', he adds, 'to pulp the tree well. Count V. tried this in his country house garden on my advice but omitted to pulp the prickly pear so that by some unfortunate chance he found it growing up through his flower-beds. This, as you can imagine, was a catastrophe and he has not spoken to me since.'

3·7·37

The conventions of our weekly meeting at 'The Partridge' are charming; we share our food, our criticism, and even our mail. When Zarian gets a letter from Unamuno or Celine it is read out and passed round the table; and when I get one of Henry Miller's rambling exuberant letters from Paris the company is delighted. This is the real island flavour; our existence here is in this delectable landscape, remote from the responsibilities of an active life in Europe, have given us this sense of detachment from the real world. Over the smoking copper pans the face of Paul, the Cretan manager of the tavern, looms strangely. He watches over the dishes, pausing to wipe the sweat out of his great brown moustaches; his manner is that of one who has dealt with epicures for a lifetime. Later Luke, the blind guitarist, arrives, led by his small son —a child of great beauty and pallor. Its face is the face of a Byzantine ikon. Stiffly the old red-faced man sits down on a chair, and strikes his instrument; the small expressionless face of the boy is cocked over his cheap violin as he tunes it. Then they strike up one of the familiar Greek jazz songs—inevitably a tango; yet the words haunt, and the refrain is taken up to the accompaniment of knife and fork by the roystering Zarian, Peltours the lean Russian painter, Veronica and John, Nimiec, Theodore. The narrow white-washed room with its ugly tables and cheap advertisements rings.

'Loneliness, Loneliness,
You are bitter company to us.'

Afterwards we walk down in the warm night to the dark slip-way, and, as the moon is rising, shake out the jib of the *Van Norden*, start her engine, and put our noses northward into the night.

Divisions upon Greek Ground

Lights move on the darkness hardly grazing the surface of the consciousness. From the receding shore, clear on the water, we can hear Zarian still contending some majestic literary theme. N. curls in a rug and dips her grapes over the side in the shining sea. And hollow over the harbour, speeding us with the promise of a safe arrival, St. Spiridion strikes the hour of midnight.

4·7·37

We breakfast at sunrise after a bathe. Grapes and Hymettos honey, black coffee, eggs, and the light clear-tasting Papastratos cigarette. Unconscious transition from the balcony to the rock outside. Lazily we unhook the rowboat and make for the point where the still blue sea is twisted in a single fold—like a curtain caught by a passing hand. A shale beach, eaten out of the cliff-point, falling to a row of sunken rocks. A huge squat fig-tree poised like a crocodile on the edge of the water. Five fathoms directly off the point so that sitting here on this spit we can see the dolphins and the steamers passing within hail almost. We bathe naked, and the sun and water make our skins feel old and rough, like precious lace. Yesterday we found the foetus of an octopus, colourless ball of gelatine, which throbbed invisibly in the palm of the hand; to-day the fisherboys have found our beach. They have written Angli ("Ἄγγλοι') in charcoal on one of the rocks, we have responded with 'Hellenes' which is fair enough. We have never seen them. N. draws a little head in a straw hat with a great nose and moustache.

5·7·37

Yesterday was a fisherman's holiday; first a great glistening turtle was washed up on the beach at the cliff edge. It was quite dead and its heavy yellow eyelids were drawn down over its eyes giving it a sinister and reptilian air of being half asleep. It must have weighed about as much as the dinghy. I expected the fishermen to make some use of the meat but nobody has touched it—except the village dogs which have been worrying its flippers.

More exciting was the killing of the eel. We were unhooking the boat when a small boy who was helping us cast off pointed to something in the water and exclaimed 'Zmyrna'. I was about to

23

probe about with an oar—for I could see nothing in the shadow of the great rock—when Anastasius came running like a flash from the carpenter's shop. He held two heavy four-pronged tridents. For a moment or two he stared keenly down into the water; we could see nothing beyond the movements of marine life, the swaying of the seaweed fronds and the strange flickering passage of small fish. Then Anastasius lowered a piece of wood—simply the unshod shaft of a trident—into the darkest patch of the shadow. There was a small audible snap—as of a rat-trap closing—and his shoulders became rigid; maintaining his pressure on the wood he picked up a trident and lowering the point slowly into the water suddenly struck home at an angle. There was a sudden convulsion among the seaweed and the head of the eel emerged; it seemed to our terrified eyes about the size of a dog's head and infinitely more senseless and wicked. The trident had pierced the skull and while it was still dazed from the blow Anastasius strove to dislodge it from its perch. Help, too, was at hand. Old Father Nicholas came racing down with a couple of sharpened boat-hooks and these were driven into the meaty shoulders of the eel.

It took three of them to lug it on to the rock, and for a quarter of an hour on dry land it fought savagely, with two tridents piercing its brain and two more in its sides. I can hear the dry snapping of its jaws on the stick as I write. It had muscle on it like a wrestler, and its tail tapered into a great finned bolster of brown gristle— a turbine; altogether the whole fish looked more like an American invention than anything from the water-world; and it had the ferocity and determination of Satan. It was interesting to see how *afraid* its evil aspect made one; long after it was dead the peasants were driving their tridents into it with imprecations; and everyone gave it a wide berth until it stiffened with an unmistakable rigor.

Another reflection of this anxiety: Helen was given a terrific scolding because she was in the habit to poking about in the rocks at low tide barefooted. 'And if such an animal got you?' Anastasius kept repeating. 'And if such an animal got you?'

The children stood like carvings by the sea in their red flannel frocks, never taking their eyes off the dead eel. They all had their thumbs in their mouths. Then Sky removed her thumb with a

THE EASTERN ADRIATIC
*drawn by Bernard J. Palmer after a copy of a late Portolano engraved in Italy
by Lucini for Robert Dudley, 1646*

little sigh and said: 'Let's go,' and they trotted off up among the olive-trees.

To-night we shall have eel-meat with red sauce for supper.

6.7.37

At night the fishing-boats put out; they carry great carbide-flares to attract the fish to the nets, and the dark bulk of the Albanian shadow opposite is studded with their jewelled fires. Dark red and smoky, occasional fires glow on the hills themselves; yellow and small along the sealine shine the lights of the solitaries who hunt alone in boats with tridents. I must record the method and the instruments employed in carbide fishing—but to-night my mind is full of a story which Nicholas has been telling me. It concerns two lovers in Corcyra during the occupation of the Turks. He was an Albanian Moslem and she a Greek. During a political crisis he was banished from the island and she was kept guarded in a country-house on the coast; before he left they agreed to signal to each other by lighting fires—he on the tip of Cape Stiletto and she at Govino on the second Sunday of every month. For three years these fire-messages passed telling each of them that the other was well. Then one night the girl died and her attendants forgot to light the accustomed fire. The fire on the Cape, however, burned at the accustomed time. But when her Albanian lover saw no response to his message he knew that something serious was afoot and crossed over to the island to try and visit her. He was caught and murdered. Yet ever since then on the second Sunday of every month there is a fire alight on the end of Cape Stiletto; it burns brackishly for a few hours and then goes out. Sometimes it shows a greenish flame. It is *not* a carbide-fisher as there is no shallow beach off the cape; it is *not* a scrub-fire because on this bare promontory there is nothing but rock. It is, says Nicholas, the Albanian sending his message—a message to which there is never any answer, for Govino headland lies dark and unresponsive to the west, under the hump of shadow from the mountains.

7.7.37

The boat rides beautifully. N. has christened her the *Van Norden*. Now in the still weather we keep her anchored close under the balcony; she is smart in her black paint with brass fittings and a white awning. Yesterday we took her out in a fresh north-easterly wind up as far as the Forty Saints. I wanted to conquer my timidity about a following wind. But she ran before it like a knife. The wood around the lead keel however is puffed and cankered; she must come out and be painted against worms. I notice that we speak about her in the compassionate and familiar way that people speak about their pets. The young schoolmaster Niko is full of envy, and in order to show off we invited him for a sail in the evening. He handles her much more sensitively than either of us; with roughness and determination, with an unerring sense of what to ask her. She turns upwind like a dancer and falters into the still water under the house like a vessel of silk.

II

The Island Saint

The island is really the Saint: and the Saint is the island. Nearly all the male children are named after him. All the island craft carry his tintype—mournful of beard and brow—nailed to their masts of unseasoned cypress wood. To use his name in an oath is to bind yourself by the most solemn of vows, for St. Spiridion is still awake in Corcyra after nearly two thousand years on earth. He is the Influence of the island.

In the chapel of the church of his name he lies, looking a trifle misanthropic but determined, as befits one who has seen most sides of life on earth, and who is on equal terms with heaven. The sarcophagus is deeply lined and comfortable; he lies in hibernating stillness in his richly wrought casket, whose outer shell of silver is permanently clouded by the breath of the faithful who stoop to kiss it. The darkness swims with chalices and banners—all the garishness of Byzantine church-decoration. A style of art which is literal rather than figurative: the saint has a real nimbus of silver let into the canvas round his haunted oval face. Eyes of black olive stare unrepenting down from every wall.

Here in the church of St. Spiridion, Venice and Turkey compete in silver and brass, in bronze and iron; and under this tortured inlay-work and colour the dark pagan eyes still stare with their fleshly hunger—reminding you how close the old pantheon is, locked in this narrow ritualism.

Light, dammed up by the obtuse walls, bursts fiercely through the great porches and explodes like butter over the scarves and head-dresses, the beards and lips and clothes of the peasants.

The saint lies quite composed in his casket. He is a mummy, a small dried-up anatomy, whose tiny feet (clad in embroidered slippers) protrude from a vent at the bottom of his sarcophagus.

The Island Saint

If you are one of the faithful you may stoop and kiss his slippers. He will answer your prayers.

Who is Spiridion? His life is an amusing study in myth. He was born and lived as a shepherd in the mountains of Cyprus. When his wife died he buried his unhappiness between the four walls of a monastery, becoming immediately remarkable for his fineness of spirit and fidelity to God. As a bishop he took part in the great council of Nicea, where he gave miraculous testimony of the then disputed doctrine of the Trinity by casting a brick (which he must have secreted about his person) to the ground, where it immediately gushed fire and water in one.

A long life, many good works, and not a few miracles contributed to his subsequent popularity, so that when he died, this humble Bishop of Trymithion (he was well over ninety years old) had become revered almost as a saint.

He was buried: but the restless virtue in him could not waste in the earth—and now exhalations of sweetness from his coffin began to trouble the orthodox. A spray of red roses broke from his tomb —to-day still to be seen in Cyprus. These combined omens persuaded the religious to dig his body up—and no sooner was this done than Spiridion justified his resurrection by a miracle, entering, so to speak, into his posthumous life and career from the refuge of God Himself.

He had hardly a chance to settle down for when Cyprus fell to the Saracens his relics were removed to Constantinople; and when Constantinople itself was threatened by the locust hordes of the Moslem world he was once more forced to change his country of operations.

At this time the Saint was in private ownership. A Greek, recorded as having been both priest and wealthy citizen, and whose name survives as Kalocheiritis, preserved him equally against the unbelieving Moslems and incipient decomposition. This Greek appears to have had some traffic in saints since at the same time he possessed the embalmed body of another saint—a lady of virtue —Saint Theodora Augusta.

Kalocheiritis packed his two saints (very much as a pedlar packs his apparatus) in two shapeless sacks. He slung them, one on each side of his mule, and telling the curious that they contained animal

The Island Saint

fodder, crossed one fine spring morning into the enchanted land-scapes of Greece.

The long conversations held between Augusta and Spiridion as they jolted over the bare mountain tied in sacks, are not recorded by the hagiographers—and indeed have aroused the curiosity of none besides myself. I cannot believe however that such a long journey can have been passed without some exchange of theological pleasantries—though I do not claim the least gallantry or any such immodesty for Spiridion; but they could not have gone on together, day by day, roped like carrion in their stifling sacks, without feeling the necessity for speech. They must have smelt together the bruised rawness of the sage even above the clinical richness of the embalming fluids. The air must have sharpened as they reached the pine-belted slopes of the Epirus mountains; the incessant halts must have been intolerable to the dead man and woman, who had need of neither food nor sleep, but jolted on in darkness rich only in a knowledge of God.

Paramythia in Epirus gave them refuge until 1456 when they were brought across the blue waters of the gulf to Corcyra, and laid in the chapel of Michael the Archangel.

Here, it appears they decided to stay, the two saints. Perhaps the fecundity and beauty of the island appealed to them as much as the merry laziness of the natives. At all events here they have both withstood fire, siege and famine for several hundred years. When the Turks appeared with their menacing hordes it was the Saint who dispersed them disguised as a south-westerly squall; when epilepsy struck down the Armenian quarter it was Theodora who expelled it; and when the great plague of Naples selected Corcyra as a theatre of operations Spiridion is said to have sent it off to Naples with one contemptuous invocation, in the shape of a frightened black cat.

Owing to the rights of possession the Saint has passed through many hands. The three sons of Kalocheiritis, for example, inherited nothing beyond the two embalmed figures of their father. The two eldest were given a half share each in Spiridion, while the youngest was forced by law to accept Theodora entire. He was obviously not content with this arrangement since he very soon relinquished the lady to the community. Spiridion, however, was a source of revenue as well as awe. By 1489 his two half shares were united in the possession of Philip the grandson—who made an attempt to carry off the relic to Venice, obviously to increase his turnover. This suggestion threw the island into a ferment, and he was forced to allow the tears and entreaties of the Corcyreans to prevail. Spiridion stayed but it was not till 1598 that he got his own church.

With the next generation the Saint became a dowry—for Philip's daughter Asimeni had little beyond her beauty, and marriages were as much forms of financial arrangement then as they are to-day.

The Saint was, so to speak, married into the Boulgaris family, and in their possession he has remained until to-day, universally loved and respected throughout the Ionian.

To the little figure in its casket the faithful bring posies of flowers and trinkets—but chiefly candles to back up their prayers. In the shady market-place outside the church there is a stall brimming with candles of all sizes, and here those who wish may buy anything from the smallest dip to a huge Chandler's Masterpiece, as long and thick as a man's arm. These candles give a strange impression, reminding one of stumps of human limbs smouldering in the dimness before the altar.

I must not forget to add that among the decorative motifs of the church is a wealth of Douanier-like paintings of shipwrecks, left as testimonials by thankful sailors whom the Saint helped into harbour in bad weather; there are also several pairs of unsolicited but accepted crutches. But the Saint is chiefly the patron of sailors, though his dominion can be extended in cases of need. Little children find him often in their dreams, a grim little figure of a man (not unlike General Montgomery) who knows exactly how to deal with croup, diphtheria, or lice.

Four times a year is the Saint's casket borne on a triumphal procession round the town; while on Christmas Eve and at Easter he is placed on a throne in the church and accessible to all comers. But the processions are something more than empty form. From early morning the streets are crowded with the gay scarves and head-chiefs of peasants from outlying districts who have come in to attend the service; every square is alive with hucksters' stalls sell-ing nuts, ginger-beer, ribbons, sweetmeats, carpet-strips, buttons, lemonade, penholders, bootlaces, toothpicks, lucky charms, ikons, wood carvings, candles, soap and religious objects. You will see the piled coiffures of Gastouri under their raving head-cloths of rose, yellow and blue; you will see the staid blue and white of the northern womenfolk, so like magpies; kilted Albanians in embroidered boleros, and woollen cross-gartered stockings—their womenfolk jingling in bracelets of coins; you will see the verminous Abbots of Fano and points north, and you will see the woollenvested sailors of the opposite coast with their goathide belts and knives, and their moustache ends drawn back round their ears.

The sun shines brightly and the air sparkles with the Albanian snow-caps opposite; wild duck curve and scatter outside the gulf, and sails of madder, rose, bitumen, violet, are all trimmed in the direction of the old fort whose guns belch a salute in honour of the Saint.

The procession is led by the religious novices clad in blue cassocks and carrying gilt Venetian lanterns on long poles; they are followed by banners, heavy and tasselled, and rows of candles crowned with gold and trailing streamers. These huge pieces of wax are carried in a leather baldric—slung, as it were, at the hip. After them comes the town band—or rather the two municipal bands, bellowing and blasting, with brave brass helmets of a firebrigade pattern, glittering with white plumes. Now troops in open order follow, backed by the first rows of priests in their stove pipe hats, each wearing a robe of unique colour and design—brocade of roses, maize, corn, grass-green, kingcup-yellow. It is like a flower bed moving.

At last the archbishop appears in all his pomp, and since he is the signal for the Saint to appear, all hands begin to make the sign of the cross and all lips to move in prayer.

The Saint is borne by six sailors under an old canopy of crimson and gold, supported by six silver poles and flanked by six priests. He is carried in a sort of sedan-chair, and through the screen his face appears to be more than ever remote, determined, and misanthropic. At the sight of him, however, warmth and happiness comes to every face. Radiantly happy the peasants turn from the procession to spend the long day dawdling over coffee or lemonade;

or bargaining over olives and livestock to take back with them on the island boats at nightfall. His brief appearance has qualified once more the terrors and ardours of living, and reminded them that he is there, still indefatigably on the job.

For the curious, St. Spiridion's Legendary will afford details of his adventures against the forces of heaven and earth—and his triumphs against them. For the contemporary sceptic there is a little booklet (sold for three drachmae at the steps of the church) in which one may read of more recent miracles. A policeman cured of epilepsy; the evil eye averted; an old man cured of the distressing gift of tongues.

Theodora Augusta, however, is now a barely distinguishable figure in the romance of Corfiot Saints; and to a large extent her powers have been taken over by a female saint—no less than St. Corcyra herself—with which modern hagiographers will have to deal. She is infinitely less interesting than Spiridion; and devotes most of her energies to causing dreams about buried treasure.

Spiridion is a formalist in his line; it is nearly always catastrophes to the community at large that he averts; yet he does not scorn the personal petition. Sit in the darkness of his church at midday and watch his petitioners; the deep shadow of the oak pews will hide you as you watch the reverence done and the waxen dip placed in the great brass quiver in which other candles are already burning.

Prayer is a form of bargaining; you will see at once that the psychological attitude to the Saint is one of rough familiarity. The tone of voice (that is to say the internal tone of voice—for the prayer is silent though the lips move) is the tone that one would adopt to a recalcitrant child. There is no question of humble pleading, and a foregone acceptance of refusal; the petitioner, whatever his request, assumes that it is most likely to be granted, and that it is consonant with the most elementary logic. It is what one could call 'a winning style', and it demands an equally resilient psychological attitude on the part of the Saint. Often such petitions are not only not granted—but other burdens as well are suddenly placed on the head of the unlucky petitioner. Thus Karamanos, the ugly boatbuilder of Nisaki, tried to obtain a cure for his epilepsy by prolonged prayer and the offering of numerous

The Island Saint

candles. Not only did his epilepsy get worse, but he contracted meningitis also and nearly died. His wife explained this by saying that the Saint had seen through him—and detected in him a loose-liver and foul-mouthed man. As he was the most moderate, faithful, just and hard-working character in the village one can only conclude that the Saint saw deeper than the rest of us—or else had confused him with his brother Basil who answered faithfully enough to this description.

At all events the Saint holds the island in his power; the boats that set out nightly for fishing or daily for foreign ports of call, all travel in his benign shadow; and it is he who welcomes you to port on the days when the deep-trenched north wind blanches the sea, and when the ironclads by the Venetian fort turn slowly on the leash to face it. It is he who guards your spirit when the wind screams down the ravines of Pantocrator. And when you are washed up in the dead calm of dawn, entangled like a sculpture in your broken boat and sprung nets—it is in his image and shadow that your soul finds rest. To him belongs the lovely greeting: Ὁ Ἅγιος Σπυρίδων μαζὶ σου.

III

Ionian Profiles

25·7·37

The sea's curious workmanship: bottle-green glass sucked smooth and porous by the waves: vitreous shells: wood stripped and cleaned, and bark swollen with salt: a bead: sea-charcoal, brittle and sticky: fronds of bladder-wart with their greasy marine skin and reptilian feel: rocks, gnawed and rubbed: sponges, heavy with tears: amber: bone: the sea.

Our life on this promontory has become like some flawless Euclidean statement. Night and sleep resolve and complete the day with their *quod erat demonstrandum*; and if, uneasily stirring before dawn, one stands for a moment to watch the morning star, which hangs like a drop of yellow dew in the east, it is not that sleep (which is like death in stories, beautiful) has been disrupted: it is the greater for this noiseless star, for the deep scented tree-line and the sea pensively washing and rewashing one dreams. So that, confused, you wonder at the overlapping of the edges of dream and reality, and turn to the breathing person in whose body, as in a sea-shell—echoes the systole and diastole of the waters.

Nights blue and geometric; endearing and seducing moon; the sky's curvature like an impress of an embrace while she rises—as if in one's own throat, so pure and glittering. When you have stared at her until she chills you, the human proportions of your world are reasserted suddenly. Suddenly the man crosses the orchard to the seawall. Helen walks with a lighted candle across the grass to tend the goat. Abstract from the balcony Bach begins to play—absorbed in his science of unknown relations, and only hurting us all because he implies experience he cannot state. And because paint and words are useless to fill the gap you lean forward and blow out the lamp, and sit listening, smelling the dense pure odour of the wick, and watching the silver rings play on the ceiling. And so to bed, two enviable subjects of the Wheel.

34

Ionian Profiles

Yesterday we awoke to find an Aegean brigantine anchored in the bay. She wore the name of *Saint Barbara* and two lovely big Aegean eyes painted on her prow with the legend Θεὸς ὁ Δίκαιος ('God the Just'). The reflected eyes started up at her from the lucent waters of the lagoon. Her crew ate melons and spoke barbarically—sounding like Cretans. But the whole Aegean was written in her lines, the great rounded poop, and her stylish rigging. She had strayed out of the world of dazzling white windmills and grey, uncultured rock; out of the bareness and dazzle of the blinding Aegean into our seventeenth-century Venetian richness. She had strayed from the world of Platonic forms into the world of Decoration.

Even her crew had a baked, dazed, sardonic look, and sought no contact with my chattering, friendly islanders. The brig put out at midday and headed northward to the Forty Saints in a crumple of red canvas. Like a weary dancer to the Forty Saints and the Albanian peaks, to mirror herself in some deserted and glassy bay like a mad butterfly. We could not bear to see her go.

My material is rapidly getting out of control once more. Theodore has been to stay for a few days. Characteristic of his shy heart he sends us presents. For N. a box of Turkish delight with pistachio-nuts in it; for me a flute made of brass, with the word Μοναξιὰ ('Loneliness') engraved upon it. It is impossible to get a note out of it so I have asked the peasants to find me the shepherd boy to teach me.

Theodore has recorded the latest miracle of St. Spiridion with sardonic humour. An old man from a country village appeared at the X-ray laboratory with what was diagnosed as an incurable cancer of the stomach; medicine having washed its hands of him, the old man and his family made a mass-petition to the Saint. Within three weeks he reappeared before the doctors. The cancer had been reabsorbed. Theodore is professionally downcast, but secretly elated to find that the Saint has lost none of his art. It gives him the opportunity for a long disquisition upon natural resistance. It appears that the peasants can stand almost any physical injury which can be seen; but that a common cold may carry off a patient from sheer depression and terror. He gives an instance of a peasant who had a fight with his brother and whose head was literally cloven with an axe. Tying the two pieces of his skull together with a handkerchief the wounded man walked three miles into town to visit a doctor. He is still alive, though feeble-minded.

Zarian has contributed a wonderful piece of natural observation for our notebooks. He observed last Tuesday that the four clock-faces of the Saint's church all registered different times of day. Intrigued, he asked permission to examine the phenomenon, scenting an ecclesiastical mystery. But it turns out that the clock-hands are made of the flimsiest material and that the pressure of the wind upon the clock. . . . Therefore when the north wind blows the northern clock-face is slowed up considerably, while when the south wind takes up its tale the southern clock-face shows a loss of time.

Not that time itself is anything more than a word here. Peasant measurement of time and distance is done by cigarettes. Ask a peasant how far a village is and he will reply, nine times out of ten, that it is a matter of so many cigarettes.

30.7.37

It is important, when writing about the peasants, not to falsify them with sentimental humour. It is very much the fashion to represent them as comic and quaint abstractions attached to picturesque names like Paul and Socrates and Aristotle. The fact that they dress oddly seems to drive city-bred writers into a frenzy of romantic admiration. But really the average Balkan peasant is quite commonplace, as venal, cunning, or admirable, as a provinical townsman. And the sentiment which attaches to the pastoral life of these picturesque communities (which treasure amulets against the devil and believe in a patron saint), has been very much overdone. Anthropologists are only just beginning to visit the suburbs of our greater cities with their apparatus. Their findings should establish a greater sense of connection between the peasant and the townsman.

Ionian Profiles

3.8.37

Theodore has one particular friend who is a so-called lunatic. He sits with the others most of the time under the trees outside the whitewashed asylum building, looking at his own fingers; but at times an abrupt desire to talk seizes him, and when it does he unerringly selects for audience the so-called sane who pass along the dusty white road outside the railings. His name is Basil and he has yellow dilated eyes and a deep voice. Theodore often pauses on his way out of town to greet him, rattling his stick against the railings to draw his attention, and shifting the great green bag of tree-spore and seed which he carries about him on his walks. The lunatic sticks his head through the bars and smiles artfully. He says:

'They say I am mad.'

'Yes,' says Theodore gravely.

'And here I am.'

'Yes,' says Theodore.

'I am fed and clothed and do not have to work.'

'Yes.'

'Well—am I mad, or are the people outside mad?'

This is in the purest vein of Ionian logic and is to be commended to students of sociology. Basil's dossier lists him as a melancholic. A novice in a nearby monastery he early showed a gift for casuistry —that melancholy science. But he dips his fingers into Theodore's little paper bag of sweets with a transfiguring smile of happiness before he goes back to his place on the garden bench among the others.

6.8.37

'If you had an opportunity to put a question to Socrates what would it be?' writes Zarian. 'I would ask him if he was a happy man. I am sure that greater wisdom imposes a greater strain upon a man.' At the 'Partridge' this view is contested bitterly by Peltours and N. Wisdom, they say, teaches the ratiocinative faculty how to rest, to attain a deeper surrender of the whole self to the flux of time and space. Theodore recalls Socrates' epileptic fits while I find myself thinking of a line from Donne prefixed to 'Coryat's Crudities': 'When wilt thou be at full, Great Lunatique?'

Ionian Profiles

Fishing demands the philosophic attitude. We have been waiting a week for propitious nights to use the carbide lamp and the tridents and at last the wish has been granted: deep still water and a waning moon which will not rise until late.

After dinner I hear the low whistle of the man by the sea and I go out on to the balcony. He is shipping his basket and tridents and screwing his carbide-lamp to the prow. To-night I am to try my hand at this peculiar mode of fishing. The tridents are four in number and varying in size; besides them we ship the octopus hook—attached to a staff about the size of a billiard cue—for octopus is not stabbed direct but coaxed: whereas squid and fish are victims of a direct attack.

Small adjustments are made. He removes his coat which smells of glue and wood shavings and bales some of the water out from under the floor-boards. Then we cast off and move slowly out into the darkness. The night is deep and clean-smelling and utterly silent. Far out under the Albanian hills glow the little flares of other carbide-fishers. Anastasius circles in the margin of rocks below the house and begins to talk quietly, explaining his practice. Midges begin to fly into our faces and we draw down our sleeves to cover our arms. He rows standing up and turning his oars without breaking the surface—since it is into this spotless mirror that we must gaze, and the least motion of wind smears all vision.

Presently the carbide lamp is lit and the whole miraculous underworld of the lagoon bursts into a hollow bloom—it is like the soft beautiful incandescence of a gas-mantle lighting. Transformed, like figures in a miracle, we gaze down upon a sea-floor drifting with its canyons and forests and families in the faint undertow of the sea—like a just-breathing heart.

Now hoarse in the darkness beyond the point the Brindisi packet-boat brays once; and nearer a grampus gives a Blimp-like snort. Then we are alone again.

Anastasius talks quietly. When I am tired I must not hesitate to tell him, he says. He himself is indefatigable and in good weather fishes half the night. But he is not really talking to me; he is talking himself into the receptive watchfulness of the hunter—the unreasoning abstraction which will allow him to anticipate the movement of fish; he is like a chess player combining possibilities in his own mind and testing them, so to speak, upon futurity.

We move in a concave ripple. Deep rock-surfaces, yellow and green and moving like a human scalp with marine fucus. Fishes, a school, the silver-white of σπάρος dawdle to the entrance of a cave and goggle at us. Each wears a black dapple on the back, and they look, in their surprise, like a row of semiquavers. Then, as if frightened by some purely marine event they disappear with the suddenness of a thrown switch. An eddy of wind purls the surface and Anastasius dips his twig of almond into the bottle of olive oil hanging at the prow. He scatters a few drops before us and the water clears again and steadies. I catch my breath, for there, crouching on a patch of reddish sand is the famous and eatable σκορπειὸς (I take him to be the sea-scorpion) with his bulldog head flattened upon a stone. Anastasius gets him squarely through the body at the first lunge and soon he is fluttering and ebbing in the darkness at my feet—a small dying pulse, uncomfortably tapping against the dry wood. Twice I put him in the basket and twice he leaps out and beats against the wood like the pulse of a dying bird.

We do not speak now, but proceed slowly along the edge of the lagoon in silence, surveying the haunted underworld which seems so like a panorama of the moon's surface. We stop where the fig-trees overhang and he tells me to look down. I can see nothing. Gingerly he lowers the trident and strikes; it is buried in a small white shape which begins to flutter madly. The small frightened eyes of the squid. As it breaks surface it spits a mouthful of ink over his face and arms and begins to wheeze like a sick kitten. Cursing softly and laughing he scrapes it off the trident against the gunwale and lets it drop into the basket where the contact of its fluttering hardly dead body suddenly rouses the stiffened body of the Scorpion to a small fluttering gasp of life. The air is cold to-night, and the sudden chill is fruitful, for within an hour we have several squid and two unnameable white fish besides the scorpion.

Anchored in a tiny bay we smoke a cigarette and Anastasius breaks off a piece of dry bread in his teeth. The air makes one hungry. The lamp is guttering and he charges it again with rock carbide. Once more the underworld flares into bloom. It is time, says Anastasius, for us to land an octopus, and to this end he ships the tridents and lets down his hooked staff, with its floating decoy of parsley training dispiritedly from it. He begins probing gently under rocks, turning this way and that. From the darkness of the cliff-edge above us a fir-cone falls with a little plop into the water. 'Look,' says Anastasius suddenly between his teeth, and I lean down. From under a rock, lazily moving, is something which looks like a snake. He is touching it very gently with the sprig of parsley, flirting with it. The tentacle plays softly with the leaves and is joined coyly by a second tentacle: then a third. They make playful passes at the sprig of green which conceals the waiting hook. Presently the ugly gas-mask head of the octopus comes into view, peering with moronic concentration at the decoy. And the moment has come. Anastasius slips the hook under the hood and tugs. There is a sudden strain and convulsion. The tentacles of the beast become rigid, but it is too late. Up it comes, writhing and grovelling, carrying two small boulders in its paws which it drops into the boat with a tremendous clatter, alarming us both. He now grips it firmly, and the hideous thing wraps itself round his arm, fighting back strongly. His object is to find the critical central bone, and he gives a sudden movement of the wrists, turning the hood inside out and plunging his teeth into a certain place in order to break it. A convulsion, and the whole mechanism seems to falter and fall to pieces. The tentacles still frantically suck and writhe, but they are now attached to a paralysed and shattered brain which gives them no directions for escape. Thrown dully to the bottom of the boat, they suck along the wood with the dull tearing noise that medical tape makes when it is being torn from human flesh.

Anastasius laughs softly and washes his hands in sea-water to dry them on the edge of his coat. A fish is a fish, but squid and octopus are a delicacy for him.

We take up the hunt in a desultory way and I manage, under his tuition, to spear yet another squid, and to miss a red mullet.

It is past midnight, and a small wind has sprung up, forcing us to use more and more olive oil to still the surface. We retrace our path slowly indulging in afterthoughts: looking under rocks which we have missed, and probing the larger caves in the hope of rousing an eel. Soon we are back at the davits, slinging the boat. Helen is there to meet us with bread and wine. I lend her my torch and she exclaims proudly over the catch in the happy vein of a person whose lunch and dinner for the morrow has been provided for.

By now a thin slice of moon is up, and early morning winds are beginning to curl up and lie on the surface of the water for a minute at a time before disappearing. The cypresses stretch for a moment from their romance stillness, like tired and cramped human models. I pause irresolute at the still edge of the bay, wondering whether the water is too cold for a bathe. The taste of the Greek cigarette is light and heady.

To-morrow I am to be instructed in the art of fishing with the shoulder net—called δείχτι. This has a span of about six feet, and is loaded at the edge with lead. It is carried folded in a certain way on the left shoulder and is used to trap fish in shallow water. The throwing of it demands a special skill.

And so, confused by these shallow veins of thought, to the balcony and the bedroom. The *Van Norden* lies at anchor twenty feet from the house, her tall spars rigid and consciously beautiful on the lacquer of the sea.

Sleep, in this cool, still room, is like entering a cave.

10.8.37

The Albanian smuggler has been over again from the Forty Saints. He is a fierce old ruffian, evil of manner and with no sense of humour. In his great sack he brought tobacco leaf, which we are buying for next to nothing. Anastasius teaches me how to strip each leaf of veins and lay them one on top of the other. Then we put them out to dry for a while, and finally to rest in the great magazine with its dry musty air and its rows of tomatoes drying on strings. Here after a while we roll and press the leaf and cut it finely with a razor blade. It is probably the coolest and richest pipe tobacco in the world, pure leaf and heavy. Anastasius loads his own cigarettes with it.

11.8.37

Took the *Van Norden* up in the direction of the Forty Saints in a strong western wind, but became totally becalmed in the lea of the headland, and lay off the Stephano lighthouse, watching a party refuel the lamp. It was strange to lie in this well of still water while not more than two hundred yards off the wind crisped the sea, and the air was wild with herring gulls. One of the lighthouse men tried to engage us in amiable conversation but at that range we could not understand a word he said, so we had to be content to wave to each other.

Zarian and his wife had arrived when we got back for tea, to stay a couple of days. Zarian says he has read somewhere that Nelson once drafted a plan to take the Old Fort (considered impregnable in his time) by running a frigate aground by the seawall, and boarding her from the masts. From every point of view a bad plan for there is a sea ramp which would have grounded the ship before her boarding crews were within reach of the lower battlements.

A letter from Zarian's wife in the south of the island.

'. . . You say I am your cruellest critic. I have been afraid when you seemed about to submit the island to the contamination of "fine writing"—but I need not have been. You will never touch it, my dear boy. Has the chapter upon Corcyra's perpetual spring been finished? I had it so much in mind that this walk southward with Theodore and the child has been like wandering through your book ahead of you. But how can you do it—how can anybody? There is as you say, no sense of season for the small ones. I have thrown away my paint box. Soon you will be throwing away your typewriter. All the summer children like iris and anemone, are out again—glades of them falling away to the White Cape, revived by the first autumn rains. Here it is your own underworld. My sketchbooks are fuller of notes than any Theodore could make it: speedwell, iris stylosa (?), marigolds, cranesbill, buttercup and pimpernel. Even the beady blue drops of grape hyacinth—how?

'You should do a sort of ballet of fruits and flowers; chorus the rough blue of sea, the staple olive-tone washed in rotation by the wild pearfoam, and the lands under Spartila by peachmist and asphodelcloud. It is too much. Mist of plum, pear, almond.

'Now we camped for the night in an orchard where nespoles in golden knots—but why go on? You must come and see for your-

self. Utterly silent and out of prehistory lay a little olive grove
shelving into the sea on a beach carpeted with brown dry seaweed.
We have been cooking from a friendly cottage with an earth floor,
the garden of it crammed with wistaria, carnation and stock—
drunk-making and rich.

'High up above me when I look up from this pad I see two
villages with cypresses on crags above us; where the ancient temple
was is now a small white-washed church—nothing has really
changed as you said. And the crags are alive with golden broom.
Kestrels hover and shriek over the blue gulf. A girl minds her
sheep and is friendly. Here it is the habit to keep a flower dangling
in the teeth—to set off the wonderful flashing smile.

'This morning when we went down for a bathe we found the
abbot of a local monastery sitting on a rock fishing for dear life.
He accepted a sandwich with great politeness and exchanged it
for a cigarette which he took from his stove-pipe hat, which meant
that he untidied his hair; he had to comb it out again and restore
the bun at the back.

'So you see how terribly unearthly we are becoming, just three
days in this haunted grove. And of course we have given your love
to everyone here.'

13.8.37

Father Nicholas is a great mythological character. He is a big-
boned rosy-faced old man of close on sixty-five. He likes to sit and
boast by the edge of the sea on calm days, like an Ionian Canute.
He is the author of three fine sons, one of whom is young Nicholas
the village schoolmaster. Under his pendulous trumpeter's cheeks,
under the sculptured fall of the great moustache, his mouth is
always smiling. He still wears the blue pantaloons, and curving
Turkish slippers of the older generation, and he is pedantic about
the whiteness of his three heavy silk shirts, two of which are always
out on the line being watched over by his timid, retiring wife.
Father Nicholas sits manfully in the shadow of his own vine, prod-
ding the grapes from time to time with his oak stick—in a faintly
sardonic manner, as if to dare them to ripen. He has the good-
humoured scolding manner—the scornful affection—which is the
mark of the finest Greek temperament. He boasts and boasts. The

story of his sailing voyages have become a sort of saga in his own mind; and when he begins a tale it is always to show how worthless the Ionians have become as sailors since the Diesel engine was imported. As he talks he consumes cup after cup of red wine, which is brought for him from a rapidly emptying keg in the magazine. His long nose ravens over the heavy Kastellani wine—his favourite brew. He illustrates his stories by drawing in the earth with his stick. The lack of variation in them is astonishing. In every one of them he is returning from Goumenitsa with a load of wood when he is overtaken by an immense 'fortuna'; everything goes overboard to lighten the craft; amidst thunder and lightning the ikon of Spiridion is consulted, but on this occasion the Saint is about other business because while they are praying a waterspout stoves in the boat. Father Nicholas at this point leaves the tiller and goes overboard clutching an armful of kindling (it is astonishing how few of these islanders can swim), which bears him up until he is washed ashore next day at Govino. All the crew perish, and the wife of Socrates, the mate, who is a woman of remarkable saintliness, is washed up two days later in Kouloura harbour. Her hands are folded on her breast and her eyes shut—Father Nicholas at this point folds his own hands, closes his eyes, and assumes an expression of saintly resignation. He is extremely affected by his own narrative, and wipes his eye in his sleeve, calling for more wine as he does so.

It goes without saying that Father Nicholas is an extremely cautious sailor; picking his wind, he occasionally makes an autumn trip over the water to Albania to gather a bit of fuel. But the slightest inequality of weather makes him run for harbour with a frantic and undignified haste. At home he is the complete autocrat, and spends all morning on the sunny terrace with a little plate of figs, bread, and olives before him.

He is occasionally guilty of an aphorism which sounds as if it were a proverb adapted by himself to suit his own experience. He enjoys uttering blood-curdling threats against his wife in the hearing of strangers, and she repays these with her quick sad smile and a remark which could only be translated as: 'Get along with you now.'

'Women', he grumbles, 'should be beaten like an olive-tree; but

44

in Corfu neither the women nor the olive-trees are beaten—because
of the terrible laziness of everyone.'

We have given Nicholas a set of chessmen, and Theodore has
managed to teach the game to the old man, who is delighted. Un-
lettered as he is, he plays chess with tremendous imagination and
certainty. When Theodore comes to stay he always strolls across to
the little vine-wreathed balcony and challenges Father Nicholas to a
game. More often than not he loses—and when this happens the old
man becomes flushed with triumph, and begins to boast more than
ever. 'What good are letters,' he rumbles affectionately, 'and learning? Everything you have in your head, doctor, is little use against
the wide-awakeness of the Romeos—the Greek.'

Theodore takes it meekly and in very good part. 'My learning
tells, O Nicholas,' he replies, 'that if you continue to drink wine
like this you will have an affection of the foot—which we have no
name for in Greek. But it will be painful.'

'Bah,' says Father Nicholas equably. 'Since you cannot get the
better of me in this game of bishops and kings, how can I believe
you in other matters?'

In this flow of banter they disguise their affection for each other;
for when Theodore is hunting for malaria specimens Father
Nicholas will walk miles besides him to show him the location of
a particular pond or well. While, whenever illness visits the family,
either the sufferer or a letter is despatched at once by caique to
Theodore in his laboratory. And we, as Theodore's friends, have
become partly involved in these questions of the community's
health. The encyclopaedia, a medicine chest, and a thermometer
enable N. to perform miracles of diagnosis. So far we have successfully diagnosed two cases of whooping cough, one malaria, one
case of rheumatic fever, and a case of incipient rickets due to
malnutrition.

15.11.37

You wake one morning in the late autumn and notice that the
tone of everything has changed; the sky shines more deeply pearl,
and the sun rises like a ball of blood—for the peaks of the Albanian
hills are touched with snow. The sea has become leaden and sluggish and the olives a deep platinum grey. Fires smoke in the

villages, and the breath of Maria as she passes with her sheep to the headland, is faintly white upon the air. All morning she will sit crouched among the bracken and myrtle, singing in her small tired witch's voice, while the sheep-bells clonk dully around her. She is clad in a patchwork of rags, and leather slippers. In her hands she holds the spinning-bobbin upon which she is weaving her coarse woollen thread. Later on the treadle-loom in the magazine Helen will weave the coarse coloured blankets which the shepherd boys take into the hills with them where they mind their sheep in the deeper winter approaching. Maria watches the younger women picking olives through her wrinkled violet eyes and spits contemptuously before taking up her little song—which is about two ravens sitting in an olive-tree. Golden eagles hover in the grey. The cypresses hang above their own reflections like puffs of frozen grey smoke. Far out in the straits the black shape of a boat sits motionless—or dragging slowly and uncouthly with the flash of oars—like an insect upon a leaf. Now is the time to break logs for the great fireplace we have built ourselves, and smell the warm enriching odour of cypress wood, tar, varnish and linseed oil. It is time to prepare for the first gale of tears and sunsets from Albania and the East.

IV

Karaghiosis: The Laic Hero

We tie up at the old port on Tuesday and find little Ivan Zarian dancing down the great staircase under the lion of St. Mark to meet us. He has been waiting to tell us the great news. Karaghiosis has come to town and there is to be a performance this evening. All the children of the town and of course numbers of peasants will be there. We send Spiro to book seats for us all, and spend the afternoon sitting on the esplanade drinking lemonade in the white pure sunshine, and listening to clinking of ice in glasses around us. It is one of the innumerable Saints' days, and as such a whole holiday. The cafés are crowded, and the green grass of the Esplanade studded with the gay clothes of the Corfiot girls. Zarian, aroused from the abstraction into which his weekly Armenian literary article always throws him, discourses amiably about the art of the shadow-play. He has come across Karaghiosis under different guises in Turkey and in the Middle East, where the little black-eyed man wore, instead of his enormous prehensile baboon's arm, a phallus of equal dimensions. Translated into Greek he is no longer a symbol of pornographic buffoonery but something much more subtle—the embodiment of Greek character. It is a fertile theme. National character, says Zarian, is based upon the creations of the theatre. Huxley has remarked somewhere that Englishmen did not know how the Englishman should behave like until Falstaff was created; now the national character is so well established that everyone knows what to expect in the average Englishman. But what about the Greeks? Their national character is based on the idea of the impoverished and downtrodden little man getting the better of the world around him by sheer cunning. Add to this the salt of a self-deprecating humour and you have the immortal Greek. A man of impulse, full of boasts, impatient of slowness, quick of sympathy,

47

and inventive as well as assimilative. A coward and a hero at the same time; a man torn between his natural and heroic genius and his hopeless power of ratiocination.

In the middle of this discourse we are joined by Nimiec and Peltours who take an innocent delight in teasing Zarian; meanwhile the little Ivan is dancing about like a wasp waiting for it to get dark. As we have some shopping to do N. and I move off about our business with a promise to meet at 'The Partridge' for a glass of wine before we all go on to the shadow-play.

The shadows hang deep in the arcades by the little shop of Nomikos the bookbinder. He is binding some sketch-books for us. Farther down in what we call the Street of Smells, the ghosts of various dishes are being conjured up in great copper cauldrons: fish, sweetmeats, bread, onions.

The northerners are down for a dance; I catch a glimpse of Father Nicholas bending over a stall and haggling fearfully about the price of a cantaloupe. Farther on Sandos is walking in his Sunday clothes listening raptly to the cries and shouts of the hawkers, while his little black-eyed daughter walks beside him, sucking sweets. We have just time to do our shopping so that I dare not stop to talk. 'Will you come back with the caique to-night?' bawls Sandos, 'or did you come in the little '*lordiko*'[1] to-day?'

It is towards the hour of seven that, mellowed by the excellent wine of 'The Partridge', we cross the little cobbled square by the Church of the Saint, and seek our way through the alleys and fents of the Venetian town (the women touching hands as they talk on the balconies over our heads) to where the shadow-play is to be shown. In a little sunken garden by the Italian school the lights and the grumble of a crowd had already marked the place. A prodigious trade in ginger-beer and sweets is being carried on with the schoolchildren and the peasants who sit crammed into the small arena before the dazzling white screen upon which our hero is to appear. Two violins and a drum keep up a squalling sort of overture, punctuated by the giggles of the children and the pop

[1] The Van Norden is called 'the little lordcraft' by the peasants because of her upper-class lines.

of ginger beer bottles. (Important note. Ginger beer, first imported by the British during their occupation of the Ionian Islands has never lost its hold over the Corcyrean public. In places such as the Canoni tavern it may even be bought in those small stone bottles which we remember from our childhood, and which are quite as aesthetically beautiful as the ancient Greek lamp-bowls with which the museum is crammed.)

Our seats are right in front, where the orchestra can scrape away under our noses, and the sales of ginger beer increase noticeably owing to Ivan Zarian who persuades his father to buy us a bottle each. N. prefers nougat while Nimiec has found a paper-bag full of pea-nuts. Thus equipped we are prepared for the spectacle of Karaghiosis, whose Greek is sure to baffle us however much his antics amuse.

Presently the acetylene lamps on the hedge are extinguished, and the rows of eager faces are lit only by the light of the brilliant screen with its scarlet dado. The actors are taking up their dispositions, for now and then a shadow crosses the light, and the little peasant children cry out excitedly, hoping that it heralds the appearance of their hero. But the orchestra is still driving on with the awkward monotony of a squeaking shoe. I catch a glimpse of Father Nicholas at the end of a row, and seeing us smiling at him he feels called upon to make some little gesture which will put him, as it were, on the same plane as ourselves. He pushes aside the ginger-beer hawker, blows his nose loudly in a red handkerchief, and bawls to the tavern-keeper across the road in superior accents: 'Hey there, Niko—a submarine for my grandson if you please.' 'A submarine' is a charming fantasy; Nicholas' little grandson would much rather have a ginger beer but he is too experienced and tactful a child to interrupt the old boy. He sits vaguely smiling while the waiter darts across to them from the tavern with the 'submarine'—which consists of a spoonful of white mastic in a glass of water. Nothing more or less. The procedure is simple. You eat the mastic and drink the water to take the sweetness out of your mouth. While the child is doing this, and while Father Nicholas is looking around him, pleased at having caused a little extra trouble, and at having been original, the orchestra gives a final squeal and dies out. Now expectancy reaches its maximum intensity, for the familiar noise of sticks being rattled together sounds from behind the screen. This is a sign for the play to begin.

The crowd draws a sharp breath of familiarity and pleasure as the crapulous figure of Hadjiavatis lurches on to the screen, cocking an enormous eyebrow and muttering a few introductory remarks. 'It is Hadjiavatis,' cry the small children in the front row with piercing excitement, while Father Nicholas remarks audibly to the row behind him: 'It is the rogue Hadjiavatis.' But even his gruffness cannot disguise the affection in his tones, for Hadjiavatis is beloved for his utter imbecility. He is to Karaghiosis what Watson is to Sherlock Holmes—his butt and 'feed' at the same time. At the appearance of Hadjiavatis the orchestra strikes up a little jig—his signature tune—completely drowning his monologue, whereupon he gives an indignant shake of his whole body, commands it to be silent, and recommences his groans and exclamations. Apparently everything is rather gloomy. Nothing is right with him. He is poor, he cannot pay his rent, he has been recently set upon and badly beaten in mistake for someone else—in fact the whole universe is out of key. That is why he wanders erratically down this cardboard street with its fretwork houses searching for a friend—and of course there is only one friend that Hadjiavatis would go to seek in such a case. Karaghiosis. He bangs at the door of a hovel insistently and calls, 'Karaghiosis, are you there?' For a while there is no answer; the tension of the children is agony to watch. 'Are you there?' calls Hadjiavatis more insistently. A rather unsteady-looking coach passes across the stage almost running him over. He curses it, and recovering himself bangs ever more insistently at the door of the hovel. Finally a flap flies open and the head of the hero sticks out. At this a roar goes up from the children and a burst of joyous clapping which is hastily stilled in order not to miss what is being said. Karaghiosis has a great curved nose, a hump on his back, and the phallic arm already mentioned. He also has a wicked lidless eye, as ripe with mischief as a mulberry. 'You wish to speak to Karaghiosis?' he says with becoming caution. 'If it is about the rent then I am afraid Karaghiosis is not at home. As for the money you lent me last week I paid you back, as you no doubt remember.' With that he disappears and Hadjiavatis returns to his hammering once more. This time the head of one of Karaghiosis' innumerable children appears. Father is in bed and not to be disturbed. Hadjiavatis implores in nasal accents for an interview, but apparently Karaghiosis' wife refuses. Finally, in the course of the dialogue the word 'bread' is mentioned, and at this the front door flies open and the hero bounds out of it, asking in accents of hope and hunger: 'Did you say bread, O Hadjiavatis? Did I hear the word bread?'

Hadjiavatis manages to find a crust of bread on his person which he hands over to the famished Karaghiosis who agrees to talk to him at some length. Indeed their conversation lasts a considerable time, and is punctuated by the most endearing asides of the hero: 'A beautiful woman, did you say? Then keep her away from me. You know what it is. My beauty and charm—and, above all my social position—would make her fall in love with me immediately.'

Everyone is delighted by this kind of by-play. Karaghiosis' absurd vanity about himself is one of his strongest characteristics, and one which gets most of the laughs.

But the real problem which besets Hadjiavatis is one of power. Why should other people have carriages and servants and not he? Why indeed? echoes Karaghiosis, absently helping himself to some fruit off a fruit-stall.

'I tell you what,' says the hero at last. 'Would you like to be Prime Minister?' Hadjiavatis, despite his innumerable experiences of Karaghiosis' virtuosity in the matter of getting them both into trouble, eagerly agrees. 'Very well, then,' says Karaghiosis, 'have you any money?' It is apparently necessary to organize votes. Hadjiavatis unfortunately has only two drachmae which he is unwise enough to produce. The mulberry eye of the hero takes on a wicked glitter of cupidity and the children (who know quite well that whatever else happens, Hadjiavatis is sure to lose his money) roar with knowing laughter. Karaghiosis makes quite sure that the money is real and then, by one of those fertile and abrupt transitions for which his Hellenic mind is famous, he decides to make them both rich in a very short time. Hadjiavatis, like Doctor Watson, maintains a troubled faith in him while he shows a certain unwillingness to part with the money itself. 'It is simple,' says Karaghiosis, 'We will buy a bottle of wine for one drachma. We

51

will sell it to the public at a drachma a glass. In that way we shall make considerable profit. With our profit we will buy more bottles of wine and sell them at a drachma a glass. In this way we shall become extremely rich and bribe enough voters to launch a party.' They traverse several celluloid squares, each garish in its many-coloured fretwork frame, and at last the bottle of wine is bought and they take up a station in the street to hawk their wares. Karaghiosis maintains a running fire of mild obscenities to attract the public—raw enough to keep the members of the audience in a roar. Old Father Nicholas is now laughing quite helplessly and unaffectedly, and wiping his eye in his sleeve, while his little grandson is laughing in little suppressed bursts, in order not to miss anything. Meanwhile on the stage things are not going too well. There is an altercation with a policeman; carriages pass; but few customers show any interest in the wine, and at last Kara-ghiosis says: 'Listen, Hadjiavatis. I have one drachma left over. Let me be the first customer. It is rather hot, and—who knows?— if we open the bottle it might stimulate trade. What do you say?' He pays over the drachma and Hadjiavatis carefully opens the wine and measures out a glass which the hero drinks with a rather over-done enjoyment. Meanwhile, Hadjiavatis himself is feeling the pangs of privation, and feels that he himself would like a glass of wine 'just to take the taste of dust out of his mouth'. The drachma changes hands again. Karaghiosis assures him that so long as the glass of wine is being paid for they need not fear for a profit, and this seems to console both of them—for very shortly Karaghiosis again feels rather faint and buys himself another glass, and Hadjiavatis again follows suit. This is agonizingly funny. Everyone is in a roar except one small spectacled child with a pale face, sitting in the front row, who leans forward and shouts: 'Hey, be careful, you are eating your capital.' A remark which is greeted with a further burst of laughter. The father of this budding bank manager (himself a clerk in a counting house) leans forward and pats the child's head approvingly.

And now of course the wine is finished, and the two puppets are busy trying to work out their profits. Karaghiosis' great mulberry eye cannot conceal his satisfaction while a certain thickening of his speech indicates that he is now full of a sense of warmth and well-being.

Karaghiosis: the Laic Hero

From now on the play becomes a surrealist fantasia. Their rise to fame is meteoric and is accomplished by the unblushing cunning of the hero, with Hadjiavatis suffering here and there for his errors of judgement. Almost nothing is too fantastic to present, and I can see from the glowing face of Father Nicholas that what our surrealist friends might call 'the triumph over causality' is considerably older than Breton—and indeed is an integral part of all peasant art. The succession of figures on the dazzling screen glow with a kind of brittle life of their own; the voices (whose volume and pitch betray their human origin) crackle and spark with a kind of suppressed hysteria. All Greece is in this scene; the market-place, the row of Turkish figures, the wonderful power and elasticity of thought and verbal felicity; the tenderness and vulgarity of Karaghiosis; and all indicated with so little of the landscape to which I had hoped to be a guide. Karaghiosis, whose humour is cast in a townsman's mould, is still surrounded by memories of the day when he and his kind were mad, violent clansmen in the hills around Olympus: or scattered colonies across the Black Sea, still tenaciously holding to an optative mood and a pronunciation which Piraeus has forgotten or only remembers as a joke. On this little dazzling screen you have the whole laic mystery of Greece which has been so long dormant in the mountains and islands—in the groves and valleys of the archipelago. You have the spirit and the unconquerable adaptability of the Greek who has penetrated with the leaven of his mercuric irony and humour into every quarter of the globe.

By now we have met a number of characters who are to become familiar in the immortal Karaghiosis cycle of plays. There is Gnio-Gnio, a lunatic figure in a top hat and cutaway coat, whose singing Zante accent is a joy to listen to. There are the Salonika Jews, each tiny and clad in a shapeless sack-like robe, out of which they speak shrill and clever, hands firmly folded in front of them. There is even an unusual figure called 'The Lord' who is dressed in what Father Nicholas must imagine to be the conventional English fashion—in a tail-coat, buttonhole, spats, and a topper. There is also the appalling Stavrakas of Piraeus whose vanity and vulgarity make him justly the object of little children's derision. There is the Grand Vizier, a most sympathetic figure, and of im-

Karaghiosis: the Laic Hero

posing size—not to mention the Cadi, who orders beatings with a cool impersonal air of detachment.

The drama reaches its peak with a faked election, in which Karaghiosis, in order to win, manages to resurrect all the corpses in the local cemeteries, who pass in a grisly single-file across the stage to the polling booth to vote for the hero.

And now, with abrupt suddenness Karaghiosis appears to recite a short epilogue and while the applause is still deafening us, the screen goes out and we are in darkness. The orchestra has long since packed up, and we stumble yawning from the garden in the darkness, pressed all about by the eager bodies of the children. The warm sign of 'The Partridge' welcomes us and the company is enriched to-night by the seldom presence of Nimiec, who has tales to tell about the caves off the north end of the Saint Angelo cape. He has just spent a week with the fishermen there trying to catch a shark. Zarian is in form too. His memory has been strengthened and awakened by Karaghiosis, and he has stories about Georgia and the Caucasus dancers which will last well into the night. Only Theodore, whose constancy in erudition is the marvel and envy of all of us, has succumbed to the lure of documentation and is writing a few notes on the back of the menu, which must be incorporated in the book. There is some fresh squid, smoking hot with green vegetables, and some Spartila wine to whet the appetites of our imaginations; and to round it all off, the three puppet-players drop in to the tavern for a glass of wine. The leader is a sharp-featured young man, whose sallow boredom of expression conceals his gifts of mimicry and satire; his helpers are both small and podgy and nondescript of feature. All three are clad in cheap suits and felt hats. Invited to a glass of wine they sit awkwardly among so many 'foreigners' and answer questions with pleasure; I think they distrust our interest in the shadow-play; there is the faint Greek suspicion at the back of their minds that they are the victims of a misplaced politeness; also why the bearded professorial gentleman should be writing details about Karaghiosis on the back of a menu is rather a mystery. But Theodore's charming mildness and the convivial bacchic warmth of Zarian soon thaws their shyness. Also the blind fiddler's son has begun his acrid tunes on the violin, standing by the chair of his father—and under cover of the music and the clink of glasses confidences are easier. They come from Patras. Every year in the autumn they play up as far as Preveza, and then come across the straits to tour Corcyra, Cephalonia and Zante. One of them has a couple of the Karaghiosis chap-books in his pocket, and, turning from the garish cover (which shows the hero engaged in ferocious argument with the Vizier) I happen upon a list of some hundred titles of plays which deal with the adventures of this latest addition to the Greek Pantheon. 'Karaghiosis the Architect', 'Karaghiosis the Martyr of Virtue', 'Karaghiosis the Archaeologist', 'Karaghiosis in Love', 'Karaghiosis the Financier'.

Meanwhile Theodore has compiled his list of characters with the help of the saturnine young man, while Zarian is well and truly launched upon an anecdote about his early life in Armenia, his mane of silver hair flying and his expressive voice rolling. The copper cauldrons are smoking, while the scavenging cats are feasting piteously all round our feet, and the wooden sign of the 'Partridge' is swinging in a light breeze—a good augury for the night journey home. Calm, upon the dark calmness of the night outside, the tangoid music of the guitar and the fiddle grazes and moves; banal but wonderfully moving, the words are taken up by the diners, until even the cook beats with a ladle on a cooking-pot to mark the time.

The three players take their leave with warmth, promising us to play us any piece of our choice the following day, and Zarian shakes hands warmly with each while continuing his faultless recitation of adventures in French to Nimiec, whose energies are divided between laughing and feeding a tabby cat under the table.

It is after midnight when we separate, N. guarding the precious menu upon which the fruits of Theodore's scholarship are written in his flawless miniscule handwriting. The port is dark, and alive with the lick and slap of dark water; there is a spark of light off Stiletto; wind south-westerly upon a clean tranquil darkness. The little boat rides clear in her white awnings; turns to Albania her sharp cheeks, and slides clear of the fort. And so home to the white house, tired and happy, and with a sense of many blessings.

'Karaghiosis,' writes Theodore, 'and the shadow-play which created him, are both ancient. The tradition of the hero in drama is medieval. His adventures rival those of Tyll Owlglasse in the German—and his place in the popular imagination is one which one could compare with the Elizabethan Tarleton. The disturber of social justice, he never does anything to alienate the audience, and his political licence is almost absolute (for example, despite the Metaxas dictatorship Karaghiosis enjoyed uninterrupted powers of critical comment, at a time when even Plato was banned in the University of Athens—or at least expurgated). He is the spirit of the little man—but the Greek little man; he is splendid at loafing, borrowing, and playing practical jokes on his friends which have a strong profit-motive. He is a current symbol for the whole Middle East under varying forms. The comic phallus, we have already noticed, has been translated into an arm so long and so expressive as almost to satisfy the psychological theory of symbolic substitution. The fun is not by any means clean fun by puritan standards and nothing like it would be allowed on the stage in London; but is essentially pure in that it is broad and unmalicious. The list of characters which appear from time to time in the Karaghiosis mythology is quite considerable; of his own family there is first of all his wife (Karaghiozaina: Καραγχιόζαινα). She is quite conventional, while his numberless children (Kollitiri: Κολλιτίρι) supply unvarying comic relief without becoming distinguishable from the average street urchin. Karaghiosis' uncle (Barba Giorgos: Μπάρμπα Γιῶργος) is made of sterner stuff. A shepherd from the mountains, he wears the fabulous foustanella and speaks with the crackling dialect of Aitolia and Akarnania. His huge moustaches bristle with avarice and friendliness. Gullible at times he is usually honest and bold. His particular opposite number is Dervenagas (Δερβέναγας) who is Albanian and resembles Barba Giorgos in many ways. Their meetings are usually accompanied by tremendous tussles in which Dervenegas is almost always beaten. Karaghiosis dislikes him hotly and takes every opportunity of humiliating him. The Vizier, the Aga, and the Cadi are conventionalized Turkish figures of extraordinary size; the former is the most important and is on the whole sympathetically represented.

Hadjiavatis is the Turkish town crier and is associated with all Karaghiosis' rascalities—in which he usually suffers instead of their author. Next in importance come Sir Gnio-Gnio and Captain Nikolis. Gnio Gnio (Νιόνιο) is an idiotic, lisping imbecile in a top hat and tail-coat with a long pointed beard. He represents Zante, and speaks with the curdling sing-song accents of the island. This of course is from our point of view. It is presumed that when in Zante he represents Corcyra with a changed but still sing-song voice. Captain Nikolis is a makeweight (Καπετὰν Νικολης) whose atmospheric value lies in his baggy breeches and his Aegean fez.

And now we move from character to myth; for Alexander the Great (ὁ Μέγας ᾿Αλέξανδρος) survives still in the Karaghiosis cycle of plays as a huge warrior dressed in full armour. He even kills the dragon (τό θεριὸ) in certain plays, and obviously owes something to St. George. Next comes Morphonios (Μορφωνιός) though exactly what he is one cannot decide. A hideous mommet with a vast lolling cranium, he speaks with a frantic affectation of voice, and dresses in conventional European clothes. He is sometimes played off against Stavrakas (Στάβρακας) an extremely nasty specimen of Piraeus bravo clad in exaggerated modern dress and felt hat—which, in the course of his lengthy conversations, he is in the habit of cocking over one eye. His self-assurance is the comic vein in him, and this Karaghiosis exploits to the full.

To bring up the tail-end of this procession one could list The Lord or The Frank (ὁ Λόρδος, ὁ Φράγγος) tail-coated representatives of European culture, as well as Abraham, Moses, Isaac, etc., an endless series of Salonika Jews, uniform in size, dress and accent. Female figures seem very unimportant in the plays, and besides Karaghiosis' wife they include an occasional Vizier's daughter, a princess, and a wife of Barba Giorgos.

The puppets themselves are the result of curious workmanship; since their dimensions of operation are so limited, and since the light which illuminates them comes from behind the screen, it is necessary to do as much filigree-work as possible to enliven the bare outlines of the figures. Great ingenuity is shown in their manufacture, and the use of a kind of many-coloured gelatine material enables their clothes to be as brightly coloured as those of the island peasants themselves.

Karaghiosis: the Laic Hero

18.10.37

Three days of squall and rain. The wind moans on the promontory, and all day long the threshing of sea sounds on the white rock outside the house. In the interval as the undertow draws back you hear the dull patient throb of the hand-loom in the magazine, and the cough of the old billy-goat. Trees lean and whirl where the wind pours through the vents and boulder-strewn crevices of Pantocrator. The roof has been sprung in several places, but this is the first taste of winter, and it is good that we should be proven wind-and-water-tight before the real thunderstorms of December. Theodore has unearthed another charm against accident; it is for fair-weather sailors on moonlit nights. 'It is widely believed that the figure of a woman rising from the sea beside the boat calls out in wild accents "How is it with Alexander?" (*Τὶ κάνει ὁ Μέγας Ἀλέξανδρος*). The correct answer for those who do not want their craft overturned by her rage and grief is "He lives and reigns still" (*Ζεῖ καί βασιλεύει*). I do not know whether this charm will be of any practical assistance to you, but since you say you always run out to the Bay of Fauns at the full moon, it would be better on the whole to memorize it. One can never tell.'

I ask Anastasius about the belief. He denies it with rather an uncomfortable look. He likes to consider himself superior in intelligence to the ordinary peasants, but I can tell from his manner that he has heard of it. 'Does old Nicholas believe it?' I ask, and he turns his black eyes out of the window for a full minute before shrugging his shoulders and replying 'How can I tell what these old men believe? He cannot read and write.' Father Nicholas is not an heir to our common European culture!

V

History and Conjecture

12.9.37

Confused by our clumsy gestures of interpretation, history is never kind to those who expect anything of her. Under the formal pageant of events which we have dignified by our interest, the land changes very little, and the structure of the basic self of man hardly at all. In this landscape observed objects still retain a kind of mythological form—so that though chronologically we are separated from Ulysses by hundreds of years in time, yet we dwell in his shadow. Like earnest mastodons petrified in the forests of their own apparatus the archeologists come and go, each with his pocket Odyssey and his lack of modern Greek. Diligently working upon the refuse-heaps of some township for a number of years they erect on the basis of a few sherds or a piece of dramatic drainage, a sickly and enfeebled portrait of a way of life. How true it is we cannot say; but if an Eskimo were asked to describe our way of life, deducing all his evidence from a search in a contemporary refuse dump, his picture might lack certain formidable essentials. Thus Ulysses can only be ratified as an historical figure with the help of the fishermen who to-day sit in the smoky tavern of 'The Dragon' playing cards and waiting for the wind to change. The Odyssey is a bore, badly constructed and shapeless, dignified by poetry everywhere degenerating into self-pity and rhetoric; the characters are stylized to the point of irritation, and their conventionalized drama serves simply as a decorative frame for the descriptive gift of the author which is a formidable piece of equipment.

Yet with what delightful and poignant accuracy does the poem describe the modern Greeks; it is a portrait of a nation which rings as clear to-day as when it was written. The loquacity, the shy cunning, the mendacity, the generosity, the cowardice and bravery, the almost comical inability of self-analysis. The unloving humour and the scolding. Nowhere is it possible to find a flaw.

59

History and Conjecture

17.9.37

Three towns contend for Ulysses and Nausicaa; Kassopi in the north, with its gigantic plane-tree and good harbour, its bluff ilex-grown fortress where the goats graze all day, might have well been a site for such a fantasy. Fronting the ragged scarps of Albania, the north wind fetches in the blue sea with a crisp lazy power quite foreign to the gulf. South of Corfu town, the peninsula of Paleopolis is supposed to be the site of the ancient town; but there is nothing left of the arcades and the fountains and columns of the fabulous capital. The shadow of the marshy lake is hardly disturbed by the ripple of water from Cressida's stream. Dried out Venetian salt-pans have eaten away the original form of the lake and here the sea settles in tideless green stagnation, a haunt for pelicans, wild duck and snipe. In the dazzle of the bay stands Mouse Island whose romance of line and form (white monastery, monks, cypresses) defies paint and lens, as well as the feebler word. This petrified rock is the boat, they say, turned to stone as a punishment for taking Ulysses home. It might have been here.

Last and most likely is Paleocastrizza, drenched in the silver of olives on the north-western coast. The little bay lies in a trance, drugged with its own extraordinary perfection—a conspiracy of light, air, blue sea, and cypresses. The rock faces splinter the light and reflect it both upward and downward: so that, staring through the broken dazzle of the Ionian sun, the quiet bather in his boat can at the same time look down into three fathoms of water with neither rock nor weed to interrupt the play of the imagination: so that, diving, he may imagine himself breaching the very floor of space itself, until his fingers touch the heavy lush sand: so that, rising to the surface borne upward by air and muscle he feels that it is not only the blue sky that he breaks open with his arms, but the very ceiling of heaven. Here are the grottoes. Paleocatrizza has two of them, one reachable by boat and beautiful. The walls are twisted painfully out of volcanic muscle, blood-red, purple, green, and nacreous. A place for resolutions and the meetings of those whose love is timid and undeclared.

For the benefit of the more recondite, or for the mere specialist, one must record the existence of a great cave in the point immediately before the beach marked Hermones on the maps. It is

approachable only when there is a calm, and the entrance is im-
posing, being formed in the style of a great gateway. Empty
plaques of metamorphic stone stand above, as if the inscriptions
have been melted from them. The entrance is knee-deep in water
and slimy with rock; but this first cave leads to a second, higher and
drier. The walls of this are palpitant with the bodies of bats, which
hang like a heavy curtain, trembling and squeaking at any intruding noise. This second cave is perhaps ten yards across and as high
—and in one corner, like the secret to one of those puzzles one has
sought for a lifetime, opens a door. There is space enough to pass
if one stoops. Nothing is revealed beyond this barrier. For those
who have the courage and the curiosity to proceed, a torch is
necessary.

At first nothing; a rubbish-heap of broken stones at the beginning of a corridor. But a clearly defined corridor leading, it seems,
into the very heart of the earth. Within twenty paces it branches
into a multiplicity of corridors—like a dream, or a poem too
charged with allusions—and the walls become heavy and damp,
as if with mist. It seems a thousand miles away that the summer,
with its quickened heart-beat of cicadas and wind, livens the
meadows of Corcyra; we are here, deep in the ground, and our
voices are low as if they sensed the dreadful unyielding rock which
surrounds us. The many corridors menace us.

'We will never remember the way back,' says N.

The torchlight is barren and futile with its white beam moving
along the walls. Holding N.'s hand I am aware of the small resist-
ing pulse of the heart-beat like a message to say that we are not
really part of it—the echoing and uncomfortable night of the rocks.

In 1912 a scientist tried to negotiate the corridor, using a light
twine as a guide; but somewhere in the heart of the world the
twine broke, and, it is presumed, his torch gave out, for he never
reappeared in the light of day. This story, which I invent to
frighten N., brings back to us both the seducing sweetness of life
there outside the cave; the fishermen at their lobster-pots, and the
whole endearment of the Valley of Ropa, with its dapple of vines
and figs. The soft throaty call of turtles in the arbours above
Perama. The poison-green line of water perching and falling upon
the shoals off the northern point.

History and Conjecture

The walls of the outer cave tremble in their membrane-like covering of bats; strange shudderings and copulations, strange disturbances and awakenings, strange departures and arrivals—like the unconscious in its outlawed slumber. One's own flesh has become chill and puckered by the cold of the place. Very dimly now the sea can be heard outside, familiar as snoring, rapping and licking its way among the rocks. The pools are empty of fish.

The little white boat rides glib and pert in the shadow of the cliff, with Niko anxious at the tiller; wind has sprung up from the south-west, and the breakers are beginning their clock-like momentum sheer from the shores of Africa. It is time to make the half-hour run for the narrow harbour of Paleocastrizza. Shaken free, the sails immediately draw like a white fire, and crisp at the lips of the *Van Norden*, the sea draws her seething line of white. In the spaces of the wind the ear picks up the dry morse-like communication of the cicadas high above on the cliffs; while higher still in space sounds the sour brassy note of a woman's voice singing. N. caught in one of those fine unconscious attitudes sits at the prow, head thrown back, lips parted, long fair hair blown back over the ears—the doe's pointed ears. Drinking the wind like some imagined figurehead on a prehistoric prow one cannot tell from the sad expression of the clear face whether she hears the singing or not. Or whether indeed the singing is not in one's own mind, riding clear and high above the white sails to where the eagles, broken like morsels of rock, fall and recover and fall again down the invisible stairways of the blue. How little of this can ever be caught in words. The last clear point comes out to meet us with the little rock-chapel and lighthouse standing clear. The *Van Norden* turns, trembles for an instant between opposing intentions, and then dives clear through the towering walls of rock, into the bay where Nausicaa found the timorous Hero, washed up as naked as Adam but twice as intelligent.

20.9.37

It is one of the peculiar sentimentalities of the historian, this perpetual desire to trace places and origins by the shallow facts of romance. Fano, a few hours north of Paleocastrizza, is supposed to be Calypso's island—'the sea-girt isle set with trees'. Corcyra, then,

History and Conjecture

is the home of the oar-loving Phaecians, and the place of Ulysses' meeting with Nausiçaa. It is of course the final unkindness that the few scanty facts in Homer's record of the adventure do not offer the historian any help. For Ulysses on his raft, helped by a fair wind, took eighteen days to cover the few sea-miles separating Fano and Corcyra. At least if one is to be browbeaten by such absurdities. Zarian has effectively disposed of this kind of thing in his essay on *Cowardice Among Historians*, from which Theodore has translated the following passage: 'We refuse to be confounded by facts like these. Firstly it is necessary to this enchanted island that its landscape should be sweetened by such a fantasy, and secondly the Ancient Greeks had no sense either of time or distance. No reliance can be placed on their measurements, just as no reliance can be placed on the modern Greeks when they are dealing with space and time. Among the peasants to-day the duration of a cigarette is used to record distance in space. A peasant, asked how far a village is will reply: 'Two cigarettes.' If you reply that you do not smoke he will, with difficulty, hunt about in his mind for the words 'hours' or 'minutes', but it will be quite obvious from his use of them that he has only a very faint conception of what they mean. I maintain that the same holds true of the Ancient Greeks. Deft at the delineation of a psychology which has remained constant until to-day, Homer was all at sea when it came to accurate fact. Thus we are prepared to convict Homer of normal Greek mendacity rather than admit the suggestion that Ulysses did *not* land in this wave-washed cove, his skin bleached and worn like an old sea-shell from the exposure to the elements.'

To the lovers of Paleocastrizza this passage will make a certain appeal; but perhaps this emphasis on Greek character will seem a little wearisome to those whose only interest in Greece begins and ends among the broken columns of prehistory. After all, one might say, what contact could exist between the refined and isolated life of Ancient Greece, and the haphazard life of the modern Greek living in the shadow of Europe, under the inferiority-complex of the top hat? One incident will provide an answer.

Anastasius knows that I am collecting peasant stories; the lunch hour of the workman is the time for smoking, lounging and story-telling, and from time to time when his work brings him into contact with the masons and plasterers of Vigla up the hill, he occasionally comes home with a story about St. Corcyra, or the tale of a haunted well.

Last week we were aware, during the evening, of an unusual disturbance in the family next door. Instead of retiring early to bed, the little oil lamp was burning until after midnight. We heard voices—the voice of Sky in particular—talking and laughing. There was a note of excitement; and the drone of Helen's voice reading aloud. It was unusual for them to stay up late and waste lamp oil, and it was particularly unusual for the children to be awake late.

Next morning Anastasius, still unshaven, appeared at the breakfast table and said with some enthusiasm that he wished my Greek were good enough for him to relate me an 'extraordinary' story; but it was rather complicated in its details. It was about a man called Odysseus who was washed up on an island. As he spoke I noticed that he was holding a small book crumpled in his hand. He handed it to me. It was a first-form primer as used by the village school; it was an account of the Odyssey written in very simple demotic Greek for schools. Little Sky, he explained, had gone to school for the first time the day before, and had returned home at night with this book. In helping her read the first chapter he had suddenly found himself reading the story of Ulysses for the first time. To be sure, he had heard of Homer, but even now there seemed to be little connection in his mind between this delightful tale which had kept the whole family up until after midnight, and the revered name. 'It is such a pity,' he kept repeating, 'that you will not understand it. It is one of the best things I have ever heard —this fable (παραμῦθι).'

When I told him as well as I could that I had already heard the story he was extremely doubtful.

'But the books,' he said, 'are printed in Athens.'

'Yes, but the story is very old. In schools in England the children are made to read it.'

'About Odysseus?'

'Himself.'

'And Penelope?'

'All the same people.'

History and Conjecture

He looked so doubtful and unconvinced that I took him into the drawing-room and found the big English translation of the Odyssey with the ancient Greek medallions on the cover. He spelt out the name of Homer and shook his head uneasily.

'I don't understand,' he said uneasily. 'Then is the story true?'

'Quite true,' I said. 'When Odysseus reached here from Fano —'

'What is that?' he said eagerly. 'What is that?'

'Don't you know that it was here that Nausicaa lived, that the palace of the King was in Corcyra?'

'Before God?'

'Before God. You know Paleocastrizza?'

'Yes.'

'You know the first of the three bays, before the hotel?'

'Yes.'

'There they met. Odysseus arrived there from Fano where at that time Calypso lived.'

His concern and pleasure were delightful to watch. He stood uncertainly in the doorway holding the primer in his hand, not knowing what to say. 'I do not understand,' he said once more. 'It is very strange.'

Later I saw him walk down the cobbled path to where old Father Nicholas sat on a chair, his blue trousered legs set apart manfully. His stick lay across his right knee. On his left knee he was balancing a plate of bread and onions. I saw Anastasius showing him the little book and repeating what I had told him. Two days later he asked me on the next trip round the island to take him and Sky, because he wanted to see the place where Odysseus had been washed up.

25·9·37

Kassopi, among the other candidates, has a style entirely its own. In spring, meadows back it, starred with the foam of wild flowers. The village finds its axis in a giant tree whose shadow falls equally upon the tavern and the church. A good harbour, Kassopi is the port of call for the carbide fishers, and under the ancient fortress the waves shatter themselves upon ledges of clean granite and arcs of dazzling pebbles. Empty beaches to the north and south stun

65

you by their silence and emptiness, and the egg-like perfection of the pebbles. Here and there, in patches of sand, you may see the weird ideograms left by the feet of herring-gulls, the only visitors. Visitors from Rome came here in the past for summers of indolence and solitude. Tiberius, it is said, had a summer villa here, now swallowed by the sea; and here the mad flabby Nero (who had translated himself from a weak human being into a symbol of kingship and all its evils) sang and danced horribly at the ancient altar to Zeus. Tibullus, Cato and the tedious Cicero passed down this channel on the way to Dyrrachium.

Kassopi must be seen on a festival day, when the great circle of coloured women tread hypnotically in a circle under the branches of the plane-tree, and mingled with the sharp whimpering of the bagpipes and fiddles, the flat stabs of the drum, you can hear the excited shouts of the crowd, and the mad giggling of the donkeys. A row of gay caiques drawn up at the beach; the tavern over-flowing with all manner of visitors; sellers of cakes and ribbons and trifles; the priests sitting gravely in the shadow of the porch drinking a glass of wine. The magpie mountain women, glad to relax after their eternity of olive-gathering. The moustached Albanians with their bandoliers; the blue Dalmatian policemen with their musical comedy frown; and a great pure wind beating the waves of the bay into chaff.

The ramparts of the fortress are deserted. Here, it is said, the inhabitants of the town can hear the chink of armour and the foot-falls of ghostly Roman sentries changing guard; and it was in the little harbour below that we discovered the remains (for so we thought them to be) of Tiberius' summer villa, or else of the for-gotten temple of Zeus. One summer evening we tied up in the harbour and, it then being tea-time, went over the side for a swim, while Niko brought out the food. We had just received a pair of diver's goggles, which transform the under-water world into a miracle of clarity. Idly playing, in about two fathoms, I saw a Greek newspaper lying on the lucent floor of the bay, moved slowly by the current, and decided to see whether I could make out the headlines in the green gloom below. Three feet from the floor I struck an icy vein of water which pushed me back with some force. It was so cold that involuntarily I opened my mouth

and drew in a mouthful. It was fresh water. At the same moment
the current moved the thick green fronds of seaweed aside and I
saw the irregular coping of a well-top, and the faint white marks
which seemed to me to look like an overgrown garden path. This
was so exciting, and the stone-work so obviously man-made, that
N. and L. and myself spent half an hour trying to clear the seaweed which obstructed the view, or to move one of the stones. But
such an attempt would need tackle, good divers, and a calm day
to be successful. Yet the sweet spring plays there, in the middle of
the harbour; in the sunken garden of Tiberius' summer villa. No
one seemed to have noticed it; neither the priest, nor the policeman nor the barber. Nor did they show any interest. Kassopi was
too busy with her great dance to bother with trifles.

28.9.37

I must not forget to mention that Kassopi does not boast a
petrified rock in the shape of a boat; Mouse Island suggests to the
lovers of Paleopolis that it was here that the weary rowers on their
return from Ithaca were swallowed up in the stony wrath of
Poseidon. While off Paleocastrizza there is another and more perfect rock which resembles the fantastic boat much more closely.
Zarian never fails to take his friends up the steep road to Lakones
to gaze out across the dazzle of waters towards this motionless boat.
It is sufficient corroboration for him.

29.9.37

Across the rich screen of this landscape many names, ancient
and modern, offer themselves to the mind like the translation of
flesh into ghostly appearances which still delude the living by their
resemblance to them.

Corcyra's history is a chequer-board; little of it is interesting
because of its variety of detail, and the stubborn sameness of the
general pattern. Spawned by Corinth, she was sensible enough to
assert herself as a maritime force during the Persian War of 475.
Herodotus' scornful account of her treachery has earned him the
withering vituperation of Zarian in more than one Armenian
article. Xenophon, writing of the Spartan invasion under Mnesip-
pus, records a paradise of fertility and cultivation; a paradise so

rich in loot that it unmanned the invaders and glutted them with booty in food and oxen, fruit, sculpture and slant-eyed Corcyrean girls.

In this noble harbour Augustus gathered together his fleet for a battle which gave him a world.

Guiscard conquered her, one of the twelve sons of Tancred, and in aspect as terrible and bold as any Teutonic God. Gibbon's podgy prose commends for 'patient vigour of health and commanding dignity of form' while we are informed that the Apulian poet praised him for excelling the cunning of Ulysses and the eloquence of Cicero. Invested Duke of Calabria, he crossed to Sicily in an open boat, and won the island by incredible endurance in hardship. The saga of his life and adventures still awaits a chronicler apt enough for so great a theme.

Richard the Lion paused here on his way back from the farcical adventure of Cyprus.

Michael the Despot reigned and fell.

Caught for an instant assembled in the great harbour, Villehardouin spent some magical words on the shabby hirelings of the fourth Crusade: 'The wind was favourable, and the sky pure and serene, and a profound calm reigned over the waters. Three hundred vessels of all sizes with their colours afloat from their sterns, covered a vast space. The helmets and cuirasses of the 30,000 warriors reflected back the rays of the sun. And now over the waters came the hymns of priests, invoking heavenly blessings, and the tones of the soldiers, lightening the leisure of the voyage with martial songs, the winding of horns and the neighing of horses all mingled with the splashing of oars.' Impenitent glory of that Whitsun Eve, with the great fleet motionless on the shining mirror of the bay. 'I bear you witness,' he cries, 'that never was so gallant a sight seen.'

And then the sleek Genoese Vetrano, fattened with politics and cruelty, described impartially as pirate or admiral. He is Zarian's favourite character. Never, says Zarian, were the Venetians more at fault than when they did him to death.

Corcyra, like her St. Spiridion, was once a dowry for a beautiful woman, destined for a tragic fate. Helen, daughter of Michael II, died in prison far from the island.

History and Conjecture

The waves of the invading East reached as far as the island; burst into these green valleys and groves. Corcyra stands as a boundary stone in the history of Turkish conquest for it did not reach farther east. Here it broke and fell, and the key to the Adriatic was held firm by the Venetians.

Under Venice she prospered—at least in forests; for the Venetians gave ten gold pieces for every grove of a hundred olive-trees planted, until when they left, it is said, the islanders possessed nearly two million trees.

Lithgow published an account of Corfu in 1632. It is as follows:

'Corfu is an island no less beautiful than invincible: it lieth in the Sea Ionean, the inhabitants are Greeks, and the Governors Venetians; this Ile was much honoured by Homer for the pleasant gardens of Alcino which were in his time. This Alcino was that Corcyrean poet who so benignly received Ulysses after his shipwracke, and of whom Ovid said:

> *Quid bifera Alconoi referam pomaria? Vos que*
> *Qui nunquam vacui prodistis in aethere rami.*

> *Why blaze I forth Alconoe's fertile soil*
> *And trees, from whence, all times they fruit recoyle?*

This Isle was given to the Venetians by the Corsicans [*sic*], Anno 1382, because they were exposed to all injuries in the world: It lieth like to a half moon, or half a circle east and north.

'The City Corfu, from which the Ile hath its name, is situate at the foot of a Mountain whereupon are builded two strong fortresses, and invironed with a rock. The one is called Fortezza Nova and the other Fortezza Vecchia. They are well governed and circumspectly kept, lest by the instigation of the one Captain the other should commit any treasonable effect. And for the same purpose the Governors of both castles, at their election before the senators of Venice are sworn; neither privately nor openly to have mutual conference; nor to write to one another for the space of two years, which is the time of their Government.

'The Castels are inaccesable and unconquerable, if that the keepers be loyal, and provided with natural and martial furniture. They are vulgarly called The Forts of Christendom, by the Greeks;

69

but more justly, The Strength of Venice; for if these forts were taken by the Turks, or by the Spaniard who would gladly have them, the trade of the Venetian merchants would be of none account; yea, the very means to overthrow Venice itself.'

Despite the slight inaccuracies Lithgow's sketch of the island is as charming and as fresh as a water-colour. The Corsicans are, of course, mythological—unless the word is a misprint for 'Corcyreans'; and at no time could the hillock upon which the old fort stands be called a mountain. But in its general particulars the account captures much of the charm of the place.

Earlier than Lithgow by about a decade Fynes Morison dedicated a small place in his *Itinerary* to a description of the island which deserves quotation. The year was 1596.

'On Sunday the 5th of May we did see the Mountain Fanon (and as I remember an Iland), three miles distant from the Iland Corfu, and upon the Greek shore beyond the Iland, we did see the most high mountains called Chimerae, inhabited by the Albanesi, who neither subject to the Turks nor Venetians, nor any other, do upon occasion rob all; and the Venetians, and the Kings of France, and especially of Spain, use to hire them in their wars.

'The Iland Corfu inhabited by Greeks is very fertile, yielding plenty of fruits, corn, wine, currants, and this haven is fortified with two Forts cut out off a Rock, namely, the old and the new Fort (which is more than a mile in circuit), both being very strong and held inexpugnable, so as the island is worthily reputed one of the Chief Keys of Christendom.'

2.10.37

The literati of 'The Partridge' have spent a great deal of time upon the etymological derivation of the word 'Corfu'. The current explanation that the Byzantine use of the word was related in some way to κόρυφαι (meaning twin-peaked) is not entirely acceptable to Zarian though Theodore's more exacting scholarship appears to accept the idea. Any modern Greek dictionary will list κόρφος which means 'a gulf'; while research into the word Corcyra will give you the following: κέρκος (a tail, a handle); κέρκουρος (a fish); and κερκὶς (a weaver's comb, a leg-bone, a fiddle-bow).

Each of us has his preference in this burning matter. Nimiec, who is an unqualified cynic in all things concerning the Greek language and character, chooses the latter as being most likely because least logical. N. thinks that the gulf is the simplest and most prosaic derivation. I prefer the figurative and visual derivation from a tail, because the island does taper away into a handle at the southern end—as anyone can see by glancing at the map. Zarian clings to the simple and fishy derivation, declaring that the island has at all times been famous for its abundance of fish. 'You will notice how carefully the wells are blessed by the priests against the summer drought; have you ever seen them blessing the sea?'

Theodore prefers to remain beyond the range of all this inexact and unfruitful scholarship. He merely shakes his head and sips his yellow wine.

4.10.37

According to Diodorus, the Sicilian, Kerkura, the daughter of Oceanus and Tethys was carried into the island by Neptune. Here she bore the loved Phaex who ruled over it calling it Korkura.

Bochart derives the two names Scheria and Kerkyra from the Phoenecian words 'scara' meaning 'commerce' and 'carcara' meaning 'abundance'.

The island's fertility made it the favourite abode of green Ceres; it was here she concealed the scythe with which the first Titians were taught the art of husbandry. Hence the antique name Drepani, a reaping hook.

It was also called Macria after the fair Macris who took refuge here from the wrath of Juno.

5.10.37

As late as the third century B.C. a cave was shown to the super-stitious where the marriage of Jason and Medea was said to have taken place; as well as an altar to Apollo.

In the Naupactican Verses quoted by Pausanias they were said to have returned here, and it is recorded that their son Mermeras was killed while hunting on the opposite coast.

Short-sighted Procopius in the sixth century A.D. was shown the petrified bark of Ulysses but his incredulity transformed it into a fabric of stones dedicated to Jupiter Cassius by a wandering merchant.

6.10.37

Diodorus says that the island was originally colonized from some very remote part of the world; and indeed during the Trojan wars Corcyra was looked upon as a mysterious, semi-mythical island—a beautiful boundary-stone at the very edges of the known world. Enter Calypso's cave on the island north of Corcyra, and you will hear nothing but the faint bumping of the tides against the headland and the thin, shrill appeals of the gulls.

There are no Cyclopean remains in Corcyra; consequently you are free from the oppressive blood guilt of Tiryns—its blocks of hewn stone drenched with blood: of Mycaenae with its burial grounds choked with bodies, and the obsessive numbing drone of bees in the dark tomb of Agamemnon. You are still in a Latin world.

7.10.37

Temples were once numerous; Thucidides mentions temples to The Dioscori, Juno, and Alcinous; Jupiter Cassius was worshipped with sacrifices at Kassopi on the northern gulf.

9.10.37

The Greek permits himself one cerebral disturbance which from time immemorial has been capable of overturning the whole structure of the state: politics. Not the barren politics of abstractions and principles, but the warm cruel politics of the heart: hero-worship, the advancement of parties and personalities. In this alone we catch a glimpse of his bitter dualism of heart—an interior anarchy, which will not let him rest. I have been dipping into Jervis and wondering at the sameness of the general pattern; both in ancient and modern times it is the same impetus which carries affairs forward: arguments, obsessions, pride, panic, self-advancement.

'Mnasippus, bent on reducing the town by starvation. . . .'

'Being in need of money to pay his men Iphicrates attempted to ransome his numerous prisoners. . . .'

History and Conjecture

'Ctesicles attempted to restore order and unity.'

Yet the anecdotal material in the history of this one small island is all the richer for the variety of its detail.

14.10.37

Periander, tyrant of Corinth, gave it as a present to his brutish son Lycophron who became its ruler. For a long time past bitter quarrels had been breaking out between them; at last a reconciliation took place, and so great was Periander's relief that he wrote suggesting that they should exchange thrones. When the Corcyreans became aware of the intentions of the feared and detested father of Lycophron, they rose up in a panic and slew the son—which was, of course, the worst thing they could have done. In revenge for this Periander seized three hundred Corcyrean nobles who happened to be living in his domains and sent them as slaves to the dreadful Alyattes II. Fortunately, however, the ship bearing these unfortunates was blown into Samos by a north-wester, and the indignant Samiots risked the wrath of Periander by rescuing them.

15.10.37

'. . . Of the affairs of this period,' writes Jervis, 'little more than confused accounts remain. It appears from a fragment of Diodorus the Sicilian that not long subsequent to the battle of Ipsus, Cassander beseiged Corcyra by sea and by land, but he was obliged to raise the seige by Agathocles of Sicily himself who burnt the whole of the Macedonian Fleet and afterwards gave the island as a dowry to his daughter Lanassa, on her marriage with Pyrrhus, King of Epirus.

'Owing, however, to frequent intercourse with the East polygamy had become prevalent with Greek Princes; Pyrrhus was already married to two wives, one a Poeonian and the other an Illyrian Princess; and the attention he paid to them aroused the jealousy of the Syracusan lady. In order to revenge herself Lanassa retired to Corcyra.'

It is a landscape that does not nourish jealousies; certainly Lanassa's broken heart was soon mended; for she sent a proposal of marriage to the great Demetrius Poliorcetes himself. This Prince

73

was so handsome that, it was said, no sculptor could be found whose art could do justice to him. His reaction to this proposal was at once thoughtful and deeply considered as befitted a prince and a political man. As he had recently concluded a non-aggression pact with the terrible Agathocles her father, he thought it would fit in very well, if he sealed the pact by marrying the heart-broken Lanassa. A story for moralists.

In Roman times, Agrippina touched here on her melancholy journey from Asia to Italy with the funeral urn of the noble Germanicus. Those few ashes hid all that was left of a world of ambition and pride and uprightness of character. She made only a short stay here *'to calm the agitation of a mind pierced to the quick'*.

17.10.37

Confused and out of key with their own lives Anthony and Octavia landed here from an imperial galley; he was on his way to Syria, while she had decided to return slowly to Rome—and to a world of favours as empty as his embraces. . . .

'A landscape for resolutions and partings,' says Zarian in an essay on famous visitors to Corcyra. 'A landscape which precipitates the inward crisis of lives as yet not fully worked out.' This is from a passage which describes the meeting of Cicero and Cato in the shadow of the fortress in 48 B.C.. The former was on his way to Italy to throw himself on Caesar's mercy; the latter 'not having yet despaired of the Commonwealth' was to set sail in company with Cneius Pompeius, for Africa.

19.10.37

Winter quarters for Consuls during the wars between Macedonia and Rome. The wind whitening the reedy stretches of Paleopolis and shrieking through the olive-groves of Perama. On the northern escarpment the seas pounding at Peristeri (Island of Turtle-Doves), and running white and yellow with the undertow of silt from the Butrinto estuary. Civil servants yawning away a winter over wood fires making inventories of fodder and shipping. 'In the last campaign between Pompey and Julius Caesar, the former increased his navy by the shipping of the isle; and had it occupied by the main body of the Fleet under M. Bibulus.'

74

History and Conjecture

Here Titus, Vespasian's son, watched with some impatience games given in his honour.

Geneseric, the ally of Attila, says Zarian, was a man who always trusted 'that the winds would bear him to a land the inhabitants of which had provoked the divine vengance'. He frequently visited this indented coastline in person with his pennoned fleet; and after the Vandals came the Goths under the terrible crooked Totila, to pillage and burn.

Having secured Rome, Totila had equipped 300 galleys manned by Goths and sent them down to conquer and ravage Greece. Justinian could only muster 50 sail and 5,000 men to oppose them. It was the Ice Age settling down on the Roman Empire; and for all the valour of Belisarius and Narses it could not be averted or withstood.

Somewhere in the lovely Valley Di Ropa you will come upon a small chapel-covered mound remarkable for the two superb umbrella-pines growing thereon. Above you to the left rises the single crag of Peleka above this expanse of green. To the right, almost hidden by the dense woodland, you will see a long curving drive lined with trees which aims slowly round upon a house with peeling green shutters. The cypresses lining the road are perhaps the most ancient in the island; their plumes are almost black, and near the ground are powdered by the fine golden summer dust. Mournful and unkept to the outward view, the house lies hidden from the main road.

This is the retreat of the Count D., and it is here that Zarian brought me one day to make the acquaintance of this celebrated recluse into whom the philosophic scepticism of a classical education had bitten so deeply. The old Count, a man of about sixty, was stocky and heavily built; he possessed a pair of remarkable eyes set in a head which was a little too big for his body. But the small hands and feet gave a distinctly Byronic cast to one's first impressions. When we first met it was some five or six years since he had first retired from the social life of the town to the calm of

75

his country estate. In an island where loquacity and an over-burdening sense of hospitality are the norm it was natural that he should rank as a recluse and an eccentric. Zarian had made his acquaintance in the course of some negotiations about the rent of a town house he was intending to lease from him, and something in the temper of his mind (Zarian was incapable of conducting business except in terms of Neapolitan opera) must have appealed to the Count, for they became immediate and fast friends. And now we spend the first week-end of every month staying in the old house as guests.

27.10.37

Count D. is interesting. Unlike the majority of recluses he is a hospitable man. Comfortably off, fond of his cellar and his immense library, he is content to spend summer and winter beyond the limited range of town amusements and gossip. He shoots, assists at olive-pickings, and christens children; while the wine-yield of his property is a constant and delightful concern. The house and gardens were built by an Italian architect, so that though the walks are unkept and the trees unpruned the whole place retains some of the formal humanist charm of the Italian country house.

Here we spend our time in endless conversations. And here Zarian makes the effort of rising at dawn in order to verify the appositeness of the adjective 'rosy-fingered', which the Count maintains to be the most exact as well as the most moving adjective in all literature. Despite several dawns Zarian has not yet agreed with his friend upon this subject.

The Count is a philosopher—'a philosopher', he will tell you deprecatingly in his faultless English or lapidary French, 'a philosopher who only sits and listens'. He speaks always with the most casual frankness about his own life and interests, his rather fine dark eyes fixed calmly upon his audience. He is filled with what Zarian (who is a born hero-worshipper and who finds a philosopher under every stone) calls 'a speculative calm'. It is rather the calm of one in whom the romantic is dead; and in whom the harder cutting-edge of experience has reached the inner man. Despite the sweetness and repose he is a prey to metaphysical incertitudes such as the artist only encounters; this you may guess from the fine sets of much-thumbed European philosophers which line his bedroom. 'Philosophy,' he said once, 'is a doubt which lives in one like hookworm, causing pallor and lack of appetite. Suddenly one day you awake and realize with complete certainty that ninety-five per cent of the activities of the human race—to which you supposed you belonged—have no relevance whatsoever for you. What is to become of you?'

On another occasion he said: 'I am popularly supposed to have retired here because of the death of my wife. It is convenient but not true. Two years before she died I woke up one morning, dressed very swiftly, and stood at the window of my room looking down on the harbour. I was visited by an extraordinary idea. I have had, I thought to myself, all the women I could want, and all the amusement I can possibly bear. Something has changed. I could not analyse the change—was it in me, or in the disposition of the world around me? It was a kind of detachment—an idea not born within the *conceptual* apparatus but lodged in the nervous system itself. I had become different as a person. Anyone else would have gone away and written a book about it; but I did not want to bring this personal discovery within the range of the conceptual apparatus, and thereby spoil it by consciousness. I retired, it is true, but you will see from my life as it lies around me, that what I am after is not the *interpretation* of the Principle of *x*, as I call it; but I wish to interpret the ordinary world of prescribed loyalties and little acts like shooting or lying or sleeping through the Principle. It is the oblique method of dealing with the platonic fire, after all, that betrays experience. Therefore if you come to me, like Zarian, and ask me why I am not writing down these discoveries, I can only reply that that is not what I mean by philosophy. I am enduring, and that is enough.'

It is for these remarkable flights that Zarian admires him so; and not the less for his gravity and the charm of his address. 'If only he would write a book,' says Zarian, the thirsty literary man, 'it would be a work of genius.' Then he adds rather more slowly: 'And if he can live without the thought of suicide. . . .'

But the Count has, by an imaginative detour, avoided the impasse in which people too heavily endowed with sensibility or the need for expressing it, find themselves. The old house with its Venetian family portraits and tarnished silver radiates an absolute calm. Greek terra cottas lie piled in dusty cupboards— broken jars and oil-dips, all relics of the plough from this fertile valley.

We dine late by candlelight; light almost as yellow as the moon outside the great windows of the dining-room; portraits of Venetian ancestors stare pallidly at us from the walls in their mouldering frames. The floors are full of dry-rot.

After the dinner the Count takes up a branch of candles and leads the way to the wine-covered terrace by the white southern wall on which the dapple of leaves silhouetted by moonlight stand out unmoving. Here we sit and talk away the greater part of the night. In the silences between our sentences we can hear the oranges dropping from the trees in the orchard—dull single thuds upon the mossy ground. The marble table is wet with dew. An owl cries, and the watchdogs at the lodge grumble and shake their chains.

The Count smokes his home-made cigarettes in a short bone holder, stained with nicotine. Relaxing, and spreading out his hands against the moonlight as if to warm them at its white fire, he begins to talk. I have wasted all these words on describing the Count in the hope of isolating that quality in him which is so admirable and original, and when he begins to talk I grasp at once what it is. He is the possessor of a literary mind completely uncontaminated by the struggle to achieve a technique; he lacks the artifice of presentation, the corrupting demon of *form*. It is a mind with the pollen still fresh upon it.

While we sit here Ourania the heavily made but beautiful peasant girl comes out in her bare feet, the corner of her blue head-dress gripped modestly between her white teeth, and arranges glasses of Visino before us; 'Would'st give me water with berries in't?' says the Count reflectively—'have I never told you that Corcyra is Prospero's island? This', he indicates the glass in which Ourania has placed a spoonful of dark viscous raisin jam, 'is one of the links in my chain of reasoning. I cannot think that the scholars would support me, but you, my friend,' turning to Zarian, 'you would take a little pleasure in the knowledge that Shakespeare was thinking of Corcyra when he wrote *The Tempest*. Who knows? Perhaps he even visited it.'

It is the kind of opening which Zarian loves so much. His silver hair gleams in the moonlight. Taking his spectacles from his pocket, as if the better to follow the Count's reasoning, he places them on his nose and says: 'Now then, Count. Defend this contention.'

The Count has taken a small silver-hilted pencil from the pocket of his cardigan and is busy tracing meaningless little shapes on the marble table. He dusts some specks of cigarette ash from his clothes, and writes the word SYCORAX before Zarian. 'Look,' he says, 'Caliban's mother, the mysterious blue-eyed hag who owned the island upon which Prospero was cast—her name is almost too obvious an anagram for CORCYRA.' He pauses for an instant and raises his eyes to Zarian's eager face. He is unable to resist smiling at his friend. 'Shall I go on?'

'You will remember the Principle of *x* of which I was speaking? It struck me that perhaps in the work of the great artists I might find this outpost of the sensibility charted. In the course of my reading I stumbled upon *The Tempest*. I found what I was looking for in Prospero, but while I was reading the play I was struck by a few elements in it of a peculiarly Ionian nature. If you lose patience with the idea please tell me and I will stop. First of all, the shipwreck. Prospero's Island it is abundantly clear is somewhere off the main route between Tunis and Naples. I propose to disregard the claims for Lampedusa and Malta; and I think that if you observe the colouring of the text you will see that it is peculiarly Greek. Think of Caliban's imprecation "A south-west blow on ye, And blister ye all o'er", and reflect to yourself whether this southwester is not the worst evil that could befall an Ionian—sirocco weather. Then, to go a little further with Caliban; he enumerates the qualities of the isle as "The fresh springs, brine-pits, barren place and fertile". I ask myself here whether the Venetian salt-pans in the south of the island might not have been in his mind.' The Count says this with a singular and deprecating sweetness; I can see that he anticipates Zarian's protest. 'Zante has also a claim under that head. There was a prodigious trade with Zante during Elizabethan times; Lithgow mentions the currants which the Eng-

lish used in their puddings; and even if you read mere teachers of
languages like Hollyband you find an unself-conscious reference
to the island—proving that to the average Elizabethan merchant
Zante was already well known. And of course the salt-pans of
Zante would be better known.'

The Count nods patiently. 'Perhaps too well known, not quite
mysterious enough to furnish the imaginative background for the
desert island of *The Tempest*. We are on delicate ground. Yet you
must agree that the colouring is Mediterranean—"And thy broom
groves, whose shadow the dismissed bachelor loves, being lass-
lorn; thy pole-clipped vineyard and thy sea-marge, sterile and
rocky-hard". What do you say to that, my friend?'

Zarian is too patently seduced by the idea to say anything at all;
in his mind I can see he is planning a whole article on this remarkable idea. He sits impatiently in his chair and waits for the Count
to speak. The latter takes a turn up and down the terrace trying
to remember further quotations to support this delightful fantasy.
At each Zarian's enthusiasm grows.

'I must,' he says at last, 'I must drink to this noble discovery.
Count, this is a memorable addition to our knowledge about
Corcyra.'

'Then,' says the Count, in a voice mellow with pleasure and a
certain triumph, 'let us drink a glass of Visino—which I have
christened Caliban's Wine. "Water with berries in't", is, to my
mind, not coffee, as most of the commentators would have it,
but βύσινο—this unusual Ionian drink. Your health, my dear
Zarian.'

The health is unduly prolonged in a bottle of red Kastellani
wine, while Zarian plunges deeper into the maze of surmise and
conjecture. 'We cannot be certain whether Shakespeare ever came
here,' says the Count, 'but we can ask ourselves two things. First,
who is the "Well-wishing adventurer" who is described as "setting
forth" in the dedication to the sonnets? The second is this: Shakespeare was too well known to be the victim of an open piracy by
1609. But if he were *out of the country* it is possible that Mr. Thorpe
might have had the courage to print the sonnets. *The Tempest* was
written in 1611, they say.'

At this point, Theodore, who always retires formidably to bed at nine-thirty, puts down his massive volume of medical lore, blows out his candle and comes to the window above our heads. He receives Zarian's information about Shakespeare's visit with sceptical good humour, remarks on the clearness of the night. Looking towards the west you can see a strip of glittering sea drawing a line between two black olive-groves. Small breathless eddies of air come to us across the valley. Theodore sniffs appreciatively and says: 'Jasmine,' before bidding us good night and withdrawing his bearded head from the window. The three of us walk down across the lawn and through the orchard towards the little circular Rotonde which houses the battered statue of a Roman nymph. 'I trust', says the Count, 'that your wives are not offended with me for refusing to invite them to these meetings. If you permit me to say so, women tire me. Their presence introduces an atmosphere of politeness and favouritism; they will discuss poetry like angels until they notice a mirror in the corner of the room. They lack the magnanimity of the male mind.'

From this small hillock the prospect stretches away—vineyard, orchard and wood, with its insinuating lines: to the last bluff line of limestone crags beyond which the sea coils and uncoils its silver meshes. From Paleocastrizza the fishermen are setting out with their coracles of straw and wood.

'One sleeps lightly these moonlight nights,' says the Count. We pass an arbour in which, sitting like statues at a deal table, we see a peasant and his wife. Their low voices sound clear and rich upon the breathless night. 'To-morrow we shall ride down to the sea together. I have a horse for you each.'

And so quietly back to the house, and through the great doorway. The candles have burnt down to their guttering ends. The Count distributes them like blessings. We make our way to our several rooms in silence.

Closing the shutters against the staring moon, I pick up a book from the pile lying on top of a cupboard in the corner of a room; it is a commonplace book, full of entries in the fine small hand of the Count. More than half of it is given up to accounts, which are entered in Italian. There is a list of Greek peasant proverbs, a rough drawing of a strip of coastline over the legend 'Dodona's Shrine?', two designs for sailing-boats, and the following quotation:

History and Conjecture

'Lingering perdition, worse than any death
Can be at once, shall step by step attend
You, and your ways, whose wraths to guard you from,
Which here in this most desolate isle, else falls
Upon your heads, is nothing but heart's sorrow,
And a clear life ensuing.'

28.10.37

Goodisson records the existence of a 'fine quarry of marble under the western peak of St. Salvador, of a very fine grain, and well adapted to the use of statuary'. Niko has made us a garden table and seat from this lovely stuff, which is of a deep salmon pink and shot with lines of rust-red.

29.10.37

William Goodisson, A.B., whose 'Historical and Topographical' essay on the island was published in 1822 is sometimes interesting, but often dull and moribund. He charms us most when he is most scientific—and surely no more charming feat than his measurement of the 'Chemical Properties of Sappho's Leap' (in Leukada) could be imagined. 'Chemical Analysis of Sappho's Leap' would make a charming sub-title for the following piece of information: 'External properties: of a clear sugar whiteness, with a few glimmering points in the internal fracture resembling that of fine loaf-sugar. Sp. Gravity. 2·263.'

2.11.37

Cressida has left her name and her legend to grace the reed-fringed edges of the Hyallic Lake; but the force of the stream seems much diminished since 1822, when the speed of the current is said to have turned a mill at 300 metres from the source.

7.11.37

The discovery that Judas Iscariot has a direct connection with Corcyra has provided a great deal more grist to Zarian's mill. Theodore happened to be discussing a first edition of Petrarch which has just been discovered in the uncatalogued jumble of rarer MSS. belonging to the Library with the curator, when the name of Pietro Della Valle was mentioned. The quotation, as it

82

appears in Zarian's essay, is as follows: 'Here also lives a man reputedly of the race of Judas. . . . I remember a servant of ours who resided at Corfu affirming that some of the Apostate's descendants still existed there, and that a house he inhabited was pointed out.' The date was 1614.

Walking through the verminous and crooked streets of the Hebraica with Theodore we discuss the problem from all its angles. The cobbled alleys are slippery with excrement. The little shops, made for the most part of the flimsiest materials, are worm-eaten and decayed. Yet counters groan with cheap dress materials, mounds of sweets, and everywhere the tap of shoemakers' hammers emphasizes the gnome-like quality of the place. It is natural, of course, that until to-day we have never noticed the name of Theodore's shoemaker: ISCARIOTES. It is painted in lopside capitals on a sagging board. The man himself is a deaf mute with some of the lowering gloomy aspect of Dr. Faustus. He works from a skilful and pedantic set of brown-paper patterns which Theodore has cut out for him. The skin of his face and hands is ingrained with dirt and cobbler's wax. He never smiles. The hair on his face grows high up on the cheekbones so that, unshaven, he seems to be suffering from powder-markings—as if from the discharge of the gun. 'His eyebrows', says Zarian with disappointment, 'do not meet in the middle.' (Popular superstition suggests that this is one of the signs of the Evil Eye.)

Nevertheless the occasion is too good a one to miss, and Zarian draws his notebook from his pocket. Just how to interview a deaf mute, however, is a problem which none of us can solve. Iscariotes can only move his pinkish tongue in his mouth with a faint snake-like composure; he can groan through his nose. And to complete the record of our misfortunes he is illiterate. He appears to have no family, and nobody in the surrounding shops knows anything about him except that he has been working at his little skin-covered bench for many years. Voluble and excited, Zarian falls into the Venetian dialect which the Jews in this quarter use among themselves, but without result. Iscariotes shakes his head and attempts a laugh; he does this noiselessly by inflating his throat as a snake its hood—until you can see his pink tongue moving among the yellowed stumps of teeth. It is rather a failure.

History and Conjecture

Yet later in the alcove of 'The Partridge' Zarian recovers his composure as he proceeds to give us an account of the Jewish Colony of Corcyra.

When Benjamin of Tudela visited the island in 1160 he found only one Jew there—a dyer.

In 1571 Venice expelled the Jews from her dominions; yet by some chance the Jews of Corcyra were left undisturbed. In 1760 they were a colony 1,171 strong, while when the first French warships arrived to claim the island fortress for France some 2,000 were recorded in the census figures. By 1860 the colony numbered some 6,000 souls according to British computations.

Yet where does the ceremony of casting out Judas originate? At eleven o'clock on Good Friday every year, the unwary visitor is suddenly terrified out of his wits by the discharge of masses of crockery into the streets, pots, pans, and cauldrons, while the air is made hideous by the banging of pistols. This is supposed to be a ceremony for the casting out of Judas; and the banging and yelling continue (with pauses for refreshment) throughout the day.

The Hebraica still guards its isolation and its language, and its members play little or no part in the life of the island. Yet the age of persecutions is by no means over; Zarian has observed how during Easter Week you will never see a Jew outside the confines of their settlement. But the finest wedding embroideries come from the Hebraica, and the greatest range of pottery and the tinsmith's wares are to be seen there.

'On the 13th February 1386 Corfu was once more a Venetian possession. . . . On the 20th of May the people of Corfu, at a public meeting to appoint five ambassadors to submit to the Venetian senate, for confirmation of the treaty already made, had included a Jew in the Embassy named David Somos. . . .'

Howell in his *Travells* mentions the Venetian dialect which they speak even to-day.

10.11.37

'To Napoleon,' says Zarian, who rejoices in great names, 'Corfu was the keystone to an Empire in the East. If he had been exiled here instead of in St. Helena there is no knowing but that his proud stony heart might have been softened.'

History and Conjecture

In his diary the French conqueror wrote: 'Venice must fall to those to whom we give the Italian continent, but meanwhile we will take its vessels, strip its arsenal, destroy its bank, and keep Corfu and Ancona. . . .' 'With Malta and Corfu we should soon be masters of the Mediterranean.' And later, in a letter to Talleyrand he added: 'I think that henceforth the chief maxim of the French Republic should be never to give up Corfu, Zante, etc.'

In 1815 the Ionian Islands were created a single, free and independent state under the sole protection of Britain; and the era of the larger lunacy began. For the curious, the hyperborean prose of Napier will provide an effective counterblast to any suggestion that British colonies are, in the nature of things, perfectly governed. Yet Adams brought the town water, and the remains of the solid and beautiful roads built by the British still remain. Solomos was accepted and even petted. The Earl of Guilford, surely one of the most remarkable eccentrics of the last century, was persuaded to relinquish Ithaca as a home for his Ionian Academy, and to found the University of Corfu in 1823. The relief of the elegant Jervis White-Jervis is exhaled in every line. 'What would it have been,' he writes, 'if Lord Guilford had succeeded in carrying out his object of establishing the University at Ithaca. Visionary ideas of academical groves and of the birthplace of Ulysses do not form men to be useful citizens; and from one student who would have been sent from there, a hundred men would have been turned out upon the world with their ideas confined to a barren rock and a few goats.'

16.11.37

Sitting in the shade of the olive-trees overlooking the dazzle of Mouse Island set in its burnished emerald sea, the Count discourses amiably upon the British occupation, with that quiet mordant turn of voice, while Zarian and Theodore feast upon green olives and white cheese. It is one of our many afternoons in search of lore; we have been scouring the lovely hill of Analypsis for traces of the Temple to Neptune, supposed to have been noted by British Naval officers towards the end of the last century. Now dropping down through the silver olive-groves we have come to Canoni, where Lord Kitchener complete with side-whiskers and moustache keeps a small tavern; and where Edwardian ginger-beer, made after an Edwardian recipe, is served in little stone bottles with a marble for a cork. This is known to the islanders as 'Tsit-Tsin Beera' and provides a convenient point of departure for the Count, who has been supplementing Zarian's store of anecdotes by an account of how Mr. Gladstone and the Bishop of Paxo, in an access of reciprocal politeness (in an attempt to kiss each others' hands) banged their skulls together during a very solemn ceremony and were only restored by a bottle of ginger-beer such as we are now consuming.

'People in search of the vanished Imperial culture of England would find very little in Corfu: and that little curious. I do not speak about prevailing attitudes of mind; we have, of course, a certain number of Greeks educated abroad, who ape the English. I have inherited, for example, from my family—which once governed here under the British—a strong taste for good manners and fair dealing as a living part of my *amour-propre*, not as independent virtues of character. It is the great difference between French culture and British; the British have no character—they depend upon very highly developed principles. It is convenient because they do not have to think. But apart from this Britain's legacy to Corcyra is an odd one; you have seen, have you not, in the dirty little alleys between the Hebraica and the port, a strange symbol chalked upon the walls? No? Wander into the alleys, and you will be suddenly surprised to see the wickets and bails of the slum cricketer everywhere; you will suddenly think you are in Stepney.' Cricket lives on as independently as the patron saint. It is a mysterious and satisfying ritual which the islanders have refused to relinquish; and every year in August when the British Fleet comes in, cricket enjoys her festival. A ripple of anticipation runs through the groups of dawdlers on the sunny esplanade; and the two cricket clubs of the town can be seen practising ferociously at the nets on the hard red earth, in the shadow of Schulemberg's statue. Groups of peasants, mysteriously drawn by their anticipation, stand in the shadow of the trees talking and observing. Meanwhile the British battleships ride squatly in the harbour and their fussy pinnaces throw up lines of ripples which, hours later, will disturb your Father Nicholas at his lobster-pots off St. Stephano and cause him mightily to curse 'the cuckold British'. When the news comes that the challenge to a cricket match has been received, there is an audible sigh of relief and pleasure which runs the length of the town. At once a profound clamour of activity breaks out; a matting pitch is laid in the centre of the esplanade; a marquee is hastily run up; the Ministry of Supply in Athens receives an incoherent telegram asking it to obtain from the British Legation the recipe for rock cakes, which has somehow been mislaid once again this year. The British Consul is to be seen in morning clothes. All British residents of the town gain face in a remarkable way. Some receive presents of fruit and poultry—for this is after all, not far short of a Saint's Day. And when the teams, eleven aside, and clad in their ceremonial white, meet on the ground for the toss, excitement and admiration reach their height. Peasants come in to town and take the afternoon off to sit under the trees on those uncomfortable café chairs, gravely applauding whenever the specialists (who sit in the marquee among the naval representatives and the consuls, and whose role is that of officiating priests) think fit to give them the cue. The British chaplain, who looks like nothing so much as a half-drowned blackbeetle rescued from a water-butt, sits in the midst of the distinguished guests, confirming by his presence the religious quality of the ritual. Everybody except St. Spiridion himself appears to be present. And in the evening, by time-honoured custom, a British Band in brilliant coats, marches to the bandstand and delights the crowds by its martial flourishes until the last light dies away and the fireflies come flashing out in their thousands. For the benefit of Zarian I must add here that the terminology of cricketers in Corcyra has suffered with the passage of years. In some curious way the cry 'How's that?' has come to mean 'Out' while 'runs' are known as 'ronia'. The bails on the wickets are known as 'rollinia' and the drive is called 'pallia'. A yorker and a leg glide are known respectively as a 'Primo Salto' and a 'Sotto Gamba'; there are a few other small anomalies but I forget them for the moment. But while we are on the question of words I recall two English words which have been baptized into modern Greek. One is the verb 'to cost' which is used with a conventional verb-ending and pronounced very much as it is in English; the other is an English draper's measure 'the peak' which has become 'pika'. When you add to all this the private manufacture of apple chutney you have, I think, exhausted the subject of British cultural traces in the Ionian.

26.11.37

Viscount Kirkwall, who has written what the Count calls 'the most exasperatingly friendly and honest book' about the British occupation, captures the Victorian atmosphere of sidewhiskers and sideboots in a disarming manner. He records the dislike of the Ionians for their bluff rulers—a dislike which has changed since their departure into a nostalgic love and admiration. Set in this *décor* of cypress-grove and lake, his characters move creaking with gentility and imperial self-satisfaction. He records the paper-chases and the tea-parties in this outlandish corner of the world; the splash of red coats moving under the fortress to the sound of bugles—beaten thin as gold by the winds across the straits. He records with complete fidelity the humours and trials of guardianship by an Empire which has never cared to condescend to its subjects by the exercise of understanding; but confirms them in its love through an exasperating solidity and shy humour.

'On the 9th of May there was a sham siege and assault carried on in the island of Vido; where a good luncheon was laid out in the tents for the officers and visitors. The affair, tho' well arranged, was on a small scale; as only part of the garrison of Corfu reinforced for the occasion the troops at Vido. But from the picturesque nature of the ground the attack and defence manœuvres formed a pleasing spectacle which even ladies could appreciate. The interest was increased by the fact that some degree of risk was incurred by the troops; as the scaling-ladders employed in the attack did not quite reach to the top of the ditch. But as regarded this difficulty no accident occurred. An artilleryman, however, was, by the hasty discharge of a gun, accidentally thrown into the ditch of the principal work.'

29.11.37

When the Ionian Islands were ceded to Greece, and the evacuation began, the Ionians were horrified to learn that extensive demolitions were to be carried out on the forts. As they had con-

tributed in taxation about two-thirds of the total cost of building
the fortresses, they were naturally bitter. Kirkwall, who showed
some considerable sympathy for the Greeks, and for the Corcyreans in particular, is indignant too. His detailed description of the
demolition work being carried out during that rainy February of
1864 is a brilliant piece of work.

To the English colony it was as exciting as a prolonged firework
display. 'On the afternoon of Tuesday, 29th March, numbers of
English ladies and gentlemen, in spite of wind, heavy rain, and
rolling seas, crossed over to Vido in order to witness from the keep
the destruction of the strong Lunette battery to the west of the
island.'

To the Ionians, however, all this earnest blowing up of 'notable
ramps, earthworks, embrasures' only underlined the bitterness of
the departure. One disgusted Ionian is recorded to have remarked
to Kirkwall as a puff of smoke and a jet of falling clods marked the
blowing up of another 'notable' rampart: 'I wish Lord Roosel
were on top of it.'

'The earlier mines', writes Kirkwall, 'were fired by long trains
of powder laid on the ground in furrows and slow burning fuses.
But after the arrival of a Voltaic Battery from England the affair
was arranged in the Scientific Manner which suited better to this
Age of Wonders.'

The discreet picnics among the olive-groves, the memoranda,
the protocols, the bustles, sidewhiskers, long top-boots, tea-cosies,
mittens, rock-cakes, chutney, bolus, dignity, incompetence, book-
keeping, virtue, church bazaars; you will find traces of all of them
if you look deeply enough. The flash of red hunting coats through
the olive-groves as the officers galloped over the island on their
dangerous paper-chases; the declarations of love among the cypresses, the red-faced sportsmen setting out for Albania. Big Tom,
Adams, Leech, and 'Fusty' Andrews; Lockler, Jones, and Jervis
White-Jervis. Dr. Anstead fussily visiting these 'embayed seas' to
record the lamentable venality of the islanders. Edward Lear's
gloomy pictures of Perama and the Hyallic Gulf. Caught once and
for all and absorbed into the atmosphere and line of the landscape

with its arbours, mountains, and Byronic moonlight; preserved in a style of moustache among the peasants, or in the top-hatted mommets of the Karaghiozis pantheon, or in the fragmentary touching love of the small urchins who will run crying beside the antiquated horse-carriages which no taxis can ever oust, offering 'flowers for the Englishman's lady' in accents no German or Frenchman has ever heard. Nothing has been lost of England's inner accent; yet the forts lie empty of ordnance and cannon-balls. The battleships come now as visitors. And Turnock's Royal Hotel where Anstead met with 'food, civility, and moderate prices' has left no trace behind it.

1.12.37

The French burned the Golden Book in which the names of the Venetian families were inscribed, and the aristocracy died in the flames to be reborn, phoenix-like, in titles stiff and unreal as old brocade.

The British did their best to reinstate the aristocratic tradition—as the Count would say 'by abstract principles'.

When Britain left the abrupt fierce history of the island seemed to cease, and the gradual decay of communications and facilities made it more than ever remote, mysterious, and hard to reach. The landscape reverted to its own prolix disordered pattern. The stout roads have remained to this day; and the water-supply of the town, despite periodic hitches, still operates as smoothly as when Adams first devised and carried out its building. But there is one English eccentricity remarked by the natives which the Count has missed; the English demand for houses with lavatories. An 'English' house in the island, has come to mean a house with a lavatory; and the landlord of such a house will charge almost double the ordinary rent for so remarkable an innovation. Bathrooms are even rarer and are considered a dangerous and rather satanic contrivance. For the peasants a bath is something you are sometimes forced to take by the doctor as a medicinal measure; the idea of cleanliness does not enter into it. Theodore often quotes the old peasant who reverently crossed himself when shown the fine tiled bathroom at the Count's country house and said: 'Pray God, my Lord, that you will never need it.'

History and Conjecture

Nimiec has an anecdote, unsavoury if illustrative, which should find a place in the appendix to Harington's *Metamorphoses*; he arrived at a fishing village in Merlera on one of his fishing jaunts, and was housed in a small cottage with an earth lavatory, primitive and so full of flies that he drew the attention of his host to its condition. His host said briskly, 'Flies? Of course there are flies. If you could do as we all do and wait until just before the midday meal you would not find a fly in the lavatory. They all come round to the kitchen.'

3.1.38

Jervis states that there are only three considerable historians of the island, but if one must speak the truth, there is only one history of the island written in the true Corcyrean spirit, gay, mendacious, and self-assured. This is by Andrea Di Marmora, who published it in Venice in 1670. His record of Corcyra's history is justly considered a standard work by Zarian. 'I confess', says Jervis, 'to have been rather startled when I read in this author that the Romans conquered Britain and defeated the Parthians owing to the assistance received from the Corcyreans, but there was a certain charm in reading the history of Rome in such a new light.'

4.1.38

The Saint does not seem to have played a great part in the age of British Protection; it is presumed that he was sulking since on one occasion the Governor (a dull and brutish fellow) refused the islanders the use of a military band to celebrate Spiridion's festival.

Yet I am happy to find in Kirkwall that a certain Colonel Wright of the Royal Artillery, set matters right with the old fellow. He obtained leave for the saluting battery in the fort to remain untouched as, says Kirkwall, 'he thought it hard that the Corfiots should be denied the pleasure of saluting St. Spiro'.

There is no statue to Colonel Wright on the esplanade. But it is to be hoped that his name has been passed up by Spiridion for inscription in the Golden Book—not of St. Mark, but of St. Peter.

5.1.38

Shooting rabbits on the island of Vido my brother records the following conversation with a man about to embark in a rowing-boat for the mainland.

'Good morning.'

'Good morning.'

'Where are you from?'

'From the prison.'

'Where are you going?'

'Home. I get every week-end off.'

'What is your sentence?'

'A life sentence. I am a murderer.'

Vido was once nobly wooded; but the French cut down all the trees in order to facilitate military operations. The prison is a pleasant white-washed building standing back from the sea. The prisoners themselves keep up a steady trade in little carved objects of wood and beaten metal; workmanship of a stylized Byzantine kind, but sensitive and pleasant in its crude way.

6.1.38

The flying-boats of Imperial Airways have discovered Govino, where the earthworks and embrasures of the Venetian port sink yearly deeper in the silt. Here in the shadow of Pantocratoras the big-bellied Shorts circle and hover until their keels suddenly rip open the emerald lake surface, and the long shavings of water curl up on each side. Spiro is the favourite taxi-driver of the pilots; they like his Brooklyn drawl, his boasting, his coyness; he combines the air of a chief conspirator with a voice like a bass viol. His devotion to England is so flamboyant that he is known locally as Spiro Americanos. Prodigious drinker of beer, he resembles a cask with legs; coiner of oaths and roaring blasphemies, he adores little children, and never rides out in his battered Dodge without two at least sitting beside him listening to his stories. We never see 'his pilots'—as he calls them—yet one of them lives in our memory as the author of a gesture in keeping with the spirit of the island. One of these English boys on the homeward trip takes back a bunch of Corcyrean flowers for his wife; at four in the morning, an hour before the departure, he and Spiro drive out to Canoni and gather flowers in the light of the headlamps from that dew-drenched sward above Mouse Island. With the first light of dawn he is in the air, heading for England, with his wet bunch of narcissi or grave asphodel. It is the kind of little devotion that touches the raw heart of Spiro as he pants and grunts up the slopes of Canoni, his big fists full of wet flowers, and his sleepy mind thinking of the English girl who to-morrow will touch this lovely evidence of the island's perpetual spring. Spiro is dead.

VI

Landscape with Olive Trees

10.1.38

Dominant in a landscape full of richer greens, the olive is for the peasant both a good servant and a hard master. In the good olive year whose harvest stretches across from January to May, the whole country population is busy attending to the tree which provides the island with its staple diet—olive oil.

Throughout the spring months, through the gales of March and the hard sunspots of April, the tireless women are out with their soft wicker hampers gathering the fruit as it falls. In the other islands the fruit is beaten from the tree and the tree itself pruned; but in Corcyra this has been, for hundreds of years, considered harmful. Prolix in its freedom therefore the olive takes strange shapes; sometimes it will swell and burst open, ramifying its shoots until a whole clump of trees seems to grow out of the breast of the parent; in some places (there is one particular grove between Kouloura and Kassopi) the trees grow tall and slender, with bodies not rough, but of a marvellous platinum-grey, and branches aerial and fine of attitude. In the northern crags again the olive crouches like a boxer; its roots undermine roads; its skin is rough and wormy; and its pitiful exhausted April flowering is like an appeal for mercy against the conspiracy of rock and heat.

There is no estate without its oil magazine—a low building with stamped earthen floor which houses the presses and all the machinery of the trade. It is here that the long lines of coloured women come, bearing their baskets full of the sloe-shaped fruit, now covered in bloom. And here they stand, gorgeous as birds, they shake the rain from their dresses and receive their dole of bread and piercing garlic.

Built up against the wall of the magazine lie the cold stone bunkers which slowly brim with the fruit; while monstrous in the

94

Landscape with Olive Trees

shadows stands the massive and primitive mill. This has a stone bed with a gutter about three feet high. From its centre a beam supports a granite millstone. A smaller beam standing at right angles to this can be harnessed to the neck of a pony which supplies the millstone's power.

On wet days when a big wood fire is built at which the women can dry themselves as they come in from olive-gathering, the shadows leap and flap against the gloom of the archways, throwing into sudden relief the strings of onions and tobacco hanging from the roof, the unruffled chickens lying in the straw, the weaving-loom, and perhaps the sagacious evil face of the billy-goat munching in a corner.

The olive-gathering is an all-weather business; in the blinding February storms you hear the little hard berries dropping to the ground, and, if you happen to be standing on high ground looking southward you can see the visible track of the north wind as it strikes the valley, turning the olive trees inside out—so that they change from green to silver and back to green. Under the shelter of archway and wall the women stoop in circles steadily filling their hampers while the rain rattles like small-shot in the leaves about them and the first thirsty wild flowers stir in the cold ground under their feet.

But the olive-tree has hardly suited its internal economy to its position, for its attenuated white flowering commences in April, just when it is most occupied with the ripening of its fruit: so that if its previous year's blossom has been prolific, it has hardly the strength to blossom again. Its crop is irregular, and the lean years for the harvesters are very lean indeed. Bread and oil as a diet hardly leaves any margin for thrift.

After the first pressing in the mill-bed the men come with their wide-mouthed baskets and gather up the magma, piling its greyish mass into a wooden press; the pony, whose efforts at the millstone are now no longer necessary, is unharnessed and turned loose in the paddock. Taking up the long wooden lever, the men begin to screw at the pulp, helping the oil away if the weather is cold, by pouring boiling water upon it. As the pressure becomes stronger, they fasten a rope to a sort of primitive windlass, and give the creaking structure their whole weight. It is like the birth of something in the gloom of the great magazine; their groans echo through the cypress floors of the house. The windlass creaks. The fowls cluck nervously about the feet of the men. Appreciatively sitting in the great fireplace with the light playing upon his beard, the abbot of the local monastery lends moral support as he sips his glass of wine.

The oil itself spurts dirtily in the stone gutters and slips drop by drop into the underground stone tanks where it will be left to settle itself into purity; while the madder coloured acid refuse is run off into the gutters—where its pungent smell and the scorched herbage of its course are familiar characteristics of the landscape.

After many settlings in the various stone tanks the oil is considered pure enough to send to the town to the bulk dealers, poured into leather skins, which bobble and gulp, it is loaded into carts which rumble slowly off down the circuitous paths to Corfu. Bright and greasy in the sunlight the skins jog hideously together like so many truncated corpses.

The cakes of the refuse, now dried brown and stiff, and empty of juice, are stacked in the dry corners of the magazine, to be used later for fuel. Broken up they burn with a subdued smouldering warmth, and added to wood and coal, give our winter stove fuel enough to carry us through the three worst months.

Though the olive is an undependable friend its role never varies; dipped into it, the coarse peasant bread tastes dense and foul—yet the children of the fishermen have warm brown skins and dazzling white teeth. Everything is cooked in it. And it is only poetic justice to observe that every saint's shrine has lamps which are replenished by the offering of the poor, who have slaved nearly the whole year round in varying weather to gathering the yield of the tree.

The whole Mediterranean—the sculptures, the palms, the gold beads, the bearded heroes, the wine, the ideas, the ships, the moonlight, the winged gorgons, the bronze men, the philosophers —all of it seems to rise in the sour, pungent taste of these black olives between the teeth. A taste older than meat, older than wine. A taste as old as cold water.

The olive in Corcyra is the smallholder's pride, and in the wooded parts of the island land values are usually computed on the basis of the number of olive-trees. It is usual for the larger proprietors to let out the season's oil crop to the peasant living on the property, who works the crop and receives half the oil in return. But in the poorer villages holdings can amount to as little as two or three trees—and prospective property speculators take great care when buying a piece of land, to find out who owns the olive-trees, as their possession confers right of way.

14.1.38

Abstemious in the matter of drinks, the Greeks produce their own light wines and cognacs in abundance. Yet during our whole stay here we have seen a drunk person not more than once; and more endearing still, we have discovered that these people have so delicate a palate as to be connoisseurs of cold water. The glass of water appears everywhere; it is an adjunct to every kind of sweetmeat, and even to alcohol. It has a kind of biblical significance. When a Greek drinks water he *tastes* it, and pressing it against the palate, savours it. The peasants will readily tell you which wells give the sweetest water, while even the townspeople retain a delicate taste in water, and are able to recognize the different sources from which the little white town handcarts (covered in green boughs) are replenished.

Two days before Christmas we climbed the dizzy barren razor-back of Pantocratoras to the monastery from which the whole strait lay bare, lazy and dancing in the cold haze. Lines of dazzling water crept out from Butrinto, and southward, like a beetle on a plate, the Italian steamer jogged its six knots towards Ithaca. Clouds were massing over Albania, but the flat lands of Epirus were frosty bright. In the little cell of the warden monk, whose windows gave directly upon the distant sea, and the vague rulings of waves to the east, we sat at a deal table and accepted the most royal of hospitalities—fresh mountain walnuts and pure water from the highest spring; water that had been carried up on the backs of women in stone jars for several hundred feet.

15.1.38

During the last summer visit to the Count D. we attended a ceremony which furnished the seed for a whole train of arguments about pagan survivals, which have since been incorporated in one

Landscape with Olive Trees

of Theodore's many unpublished monographs. The Count was half-way down the avenue of cypress trees when we came upon him, carrying in his hand a beautiful Venetian dish, full of something which only Theodore recognized as Colyva—the offering to the dead. 'You will perhaps walk with me,' said the Count, turning aside after his usual greetings, 'and assist me. I am making a small reverence to a cousin of mine who died two years ago to-day.' Noticing Zarian's hungry eye upon the dish (for our walk had been a long and dusty one) he smiled and said: 'It is a peasant custom still—and descended from who knows what pagan rite.' He removed the lid for us to look at the contents. 'Pomegranate seeds, wheat, pine-nuts, almonds and raisins, all soaked in honey. Here, it really tastes rather nice. Try some.' Together we walked with him through the wood, following the bridle-paths, until we came to the small chapel, surrounded by tall cypresses. The Count undid the heavy iron padlock which secured the door to what appeared to be the family vault. The gloom was intense, and the shadow thrown by the cypresses gave it a greenish radiance. We entered down three earthen steps leading to the concrete floor upon which the uncouth stone tombs stood, primitive in their lack of ornament. 'There is no need for the unearthly hush,' said the Count quietly. 'For us death is very much a part of everything. I am going to put this down here on Alecco's tomb to sustain his soul. Afterwards I shall offer you some more of it at home, my dear Zarian, to sustain your body. Is that not very Greek? We never move far in our metaphysical distinctions from the body itself. There is no incongruity in the idea that what fortifies our physical bowels, will also comfort Alecco's ghostly ones. Or do you think we are guilty of faulty dissociation?' Zarian and Theodore, more at home in the gloom now, potter the length of the vault. While Theodore characteristically examines the moss upon the walls and attempts to recall its medical name, Zarian concentrates upon a tomb in the corner which appears to be empty; the cracked stone lid lies beside it, as if it had fallen off in the struggles of the body to re-enter life. 'Ugly things, these tombs,' says the Count. 'Like the bunkers of a merchant ship. Ah! you are looking at the empty one. It used to belong to my Uncle John, who caused us a lot of trouble. He became a vampire, and so we had him moved to the church behind the hill, where the ecclesiastical authorities could keep an eye on him. You did not know that the vampire exists?'

Walking back to the house across the green grass of the meadow, Theodore and the Count exchange reminiscences of vampiredom. The vampire is still believed in. It is known as a Vrikolax (βρυκολαξ) and is the reward for an exceptionally evil life. In some cases vampires have been reported to have terrorized villages to such an extent that the Church has had to be called in to use its powers of exorcism. 'Uncle John,' says the Count, 'whom I remember as an old grey-whiskered ruffian in jack-boots, appears to have been an exceptionally wicked man. His reappearance was fully borne out by over two hundred witnesses, some of whose children had actually died. It was unpleasant, but they dug him up and put a stake into his heart in the traditional fashion. I felt that it was more politic to move him off the estate into the precincts of a church in order to avoid gossip.'

This theme, sufficiently exciting to wake Zarian from the abstraction into which his weekly Armenian article always throws him, also wakens Theodore in whom there lives a vague Edwardian desire to square applied science with comparative religion. The Count listens with exquisite politeness to a dissertation upon peasant lore. No one could guess that he has already heard it on several occasions. Throughout lunch, which we eat in the shade of the grape-arbour, Theodore unloads his evidence of pagan survivals in Greece—information which Zarian notes down excitedly on his cuff, on the tablecloth, in the battered notebook. Zarian's inveterate note-taking is a charming trait in his character—especially as he has never yet been known to succeed in reading his own notes afterwards, so cramped and illegible a hand has he. Theodore spends hours helping him to decode his own notes every Tuesday when the massive and erudite Armenian article must be begun.

During the afternoon, while the worthies of my Corcyrean pantheon are sleeping in shuttered rooms, I slip down to the house of the peasant family and borrow the Count's placid little mare, which will take me through the vineyards and woods to what is perhaps the loveliest beach in the world. Its name is Myrtiotissa. Lion-gold sand, of the consistency of tapioca, lies smoothly against the white limestone cliff, thrown up in roundels by the force of the sea, which breaks upon a narrow sand-bank some sixty yards clear of the shore. The rocks here are pitted and perforated into natural cisterns, sluggish with weed, and which the receding tide has left full of sea-water and winking fishes; water which the sun has heated to greater than the temperature of human blood. Lowering myself into these natural baths, holding softly to the ladder of many-coloured seaweed, I feel the play of the Ionian, rising and falling about an inch upon the back of my neck. It is like the heart-beat of the world itself. It is no longer a region or an ambience where the conscious or subconscious mind can play its incessant games with itself; but penetrating to a lower level still, the sun numbs the source of ideas itself, and expands slowly into the physical body, spreading along the nerves and bones a gathering darkness, a weight, a power. So that each individual finger-bone, each individual arm and leg, expand to the full measure of their own animal consciousness in this beneficent and dangerous sun-darkness. The scalp seems to put forth a drenched thatch of sea-weed to mingle with the weeds rising and falling around one's body. One is entangled and suffocated by this sense of physical merging into the elements around one. Blinded by this black sun-light, nothing remains of the known world, save the small sharp toothless kisses of fish on the hanging body—now no longer owned; a providential link with feeling, like the love of women, or the demands of the stomach, which tie one to the world of simple operations. One could die like this and wonder if it was death. The density, the weight and richness of a body without a mind or ghost to trouble it.

Here sometimes I come across Matthew, the lame dynamiter of fish, whose illegal operations in these bays have already cost him the sight of an eye and two fingers of his left hand. I help him to dive for those of his fish which for some mysterious reason sink instead of staying on the surface. On a fire of twigs in the evening we have often watched him grilling his fish with the absorbed air of a specialist, while Zarian stood by with the salt, and the Count with his little bottle of lemon-juice. Matthew chooses the afternoon for his fishing, as the noise of the detonations cannot then dissipate the heavy sleep of the policeman in the little guard house up the

Landscape with Olive Trees

hill. He is an admirable companion because he never speaks. Clad in patched clothes and the conventional woollen vest, he moves slowly along the rocky galleries above the sea, his prehensile black toes (now swollen and bloated with damp) gripping the rocky ledges. In his right hand he holds the home-made depth-charge, which is made from a cigarette tin and short length of fuse wire. I follow him at a safe range, to allow for any mechanical faults in this piece of machinery.

At about three o'clock he will invariably climb the cliff above the bay, to where the monastery stands in its dazzling white sunlight, and fall asleep in the shadow of the main gate with his silver catch lying in his old felt hat upon the grass.

Three hundred feet below, I cross the margin of scalding white sand, to the shadow of the great rock, and lie panting for a moment, too exhausted by running to move. Above me, leaking from the heart of the cliff, runs sweet water, down a shallow lip of maidenhair, into a sand-bowl; further to the left a mysterious spring rises in the very sand itself with little regular gushes, as if from some severed artery in the earth. At each soundless pulse a small cone of sand rises in the hollow and slowly spins back to the bottom. Clear and cold, the water plays with the regularity of a clock. It is the sweetest of the island waters, because it tastes of nothing but the warm afternoon, the breath of the cicadas, the idle winds crisping at little corners of the inert sea, which stretches away towards Africa, death-blue and timeless.

In this little bowl I wash the grapes I have brought with me. They are the little early grapes, delicately freckled green, and of a pouting teat-shape. The sun has penetrated their shallow skins and has confused the sweetness with its own warmth; it is like eating something alive.

Then after a rest another burst of running across the sand to where the cliff-path winds upwards, vertiginous and rocky, among the myrtle-groves. At the top of the cliffs, if you look back, you see the sea has become a deep throbbing emerald; the sand is freckled by long roaming silver lines across which an occasional lazy fish will move, indulgent of still water. In the shadows under the cliff a piercing nitric green. Far out across the water a brig moves southward into the sun; the noise of its engine is carried in the empty spaces of the air—a sound rubbed out as soon as registered, though nothing has breathed or stirred around one. A white butterfly wavers in across the blue spaces.

The mare snorts in the shadow of the peasant's house, glad to return. Half an hour later I am under the terrace upon which Zarian and Theodore sit, drinking tea from heavy Venetian-looking crockery, while the Count, an unfamiliar pipe alight in his mouth, sits and methodically cleans the coat of his favourite gun dog. It is inevitable that the discussion of this morning should be continuing. 'But, my dear Doctor,' the Count is saying placidly, 'I do not know how you can reconcile current religious beliefs without dragging in the ancient Pantheon. Our saints are not canonized and forgotten. They walk. The hagiography of St. Spiridion is still being written in those little two drachma books you buy outside the church. And then, the confusions. You have made a study of the folk-songs; have you found a very clear distinction made between the just and the unjust, or the idea of reward and punishment? No. The dead simply drink the waters of Lethe (της Λυσμονιὰς τα νερὰ) and enter into a sort of mirage life, troubled by vague longings for fleshly joys—everything which we sum up in that most beautiful of Greek words Νοσταλγία. And then, of course, you have the Underworld, the Abode of the Dead. It is also known as Hades and as Tartarus, just to complete our confusion. And Charon, as you know, still exists, though he has altered his habits. Sometimes black snake, sometimes black swallow or eagle, he is also the Black Cavalier of our modern imaginations, dragging the souls of the dead behind him into the netherworld. And even he is credited in modern mythology with a wife. No. The only return for the dead seems to be for the unlucky or the evil; they become vampires and roam for a short while, until the Church catches up with them.'

Zarian is wearing his spectacles which means that he is paying extra close attention. Meanwhile Theodore nods his golden beard and, pouring out his tea into a saucer, blows upon it to cool it. The methodical fingers of the Count move through the shaggy coat of the animal, pulling off the fat white ticks, pursed with blood, one by one. 'And then the naiads', says the Count again, with his peculiar sweetness of voice, 'and the nereids that haunt

our fountains and wells—what would we do without them? The
shadow of the cypress which at noonday can drive a sleeper mad?
The sea-maiden that winds her arms about those poor fishermen
whom the full moon has overtaken on the strands?' Theodore is
giving his famous grunt of disapproval which we have all learned
to imitate. It is a kind of humming behind closed lips. 'You cannot, my dear Doctor,' continues the Count ruthlessly, 'make them
compare with your scientific findings, yet we are glad to own
them, even if they are lapses from the material attitude. They are
part of the fantasy of this remarkable country and island, are they
not?'

The dog whimpers softly as the strong antiseptic is applied to
the little raw wounds left by the ticks; the Count's shapely hands
cherish and soothe it. He looks up smiling, and watches Zarian
disposing of a cake in short order. 'And think of the piercing
lamentations of the professional mourners. I have made a collection of them—all spontaneous poetry, and some of the best known
to the language. But there is no trace of the good-and-evil preoccupation. No, we Greeks are not religious, we are superstitious
and anarchic. Even death is less important than politics. There is
a kind of old Mother Hubbard who lives on the hill there; she is
much in demand at funerals because of her poetic gift. Last year
when Taki the fisherman died you should have heard her singing.
It would have moved a stone.

> "My silver boy,
> My golden one,
> Softer the down on his face
> Than breast of the woodcock;
> Keener his mind than a snake striking.
> The silver person has left us.
> The golden man has gone."

'We carried him in his open box to the cemetery on the hill, and
all the time this poetry was flowing out of Mother Hubbard in a
continuous stream, keeping pace with her tears, for she really loved
Taki.'

'Was the coffin open?' says Zarian.

'Yes. There again a point is proved.'

Landscape with Olive Trees

'Is that a religious custom of the island?'

'No. But under the Turks it was a law to prevent the smuggling of arms in coffins under the pretence of carrying corpses to the grave. In some places it has lingered on among the superstitious. So Taki's pale aquiline features were visible all the way as the ragged little procession wound up the hill. He looked as if he were about to smile. Of course no sooner was he dead and buried than Mother Hubbard, who was some vague relation, took out an injunction against his mother, to prevent her disposing of Taki's twenty olive-trees, which, she said, had been given to her as a gift. You see, there seemed to her no incongruity in making poetry for a dead man whom you love, and whose heirs you are trying to swindle. The case dragged on for months and I believe she lost it.'

As we talk we are watching out of the corner of our eyes the little party of sprayers which moves slowly down the rows of olive-trees. The foremost man holds the long canister with the tapering spout, through which he sprays a jet of arsenic and molasses, in a light cloud over each tree, to preserve the bloom against the ravages of its special pest. . . .

'It is fortunate', says the Count, 'to have a rich language. Look at my olive trees. How immeasurably they are enriched by the poetic symbolism which surrounds them—the platonic idea of the olives. The symbol for everything enriched by the domestic earth and private virtue. Then again, we use the word for those small dark moles which our women sometimes have on their faces or throats. And of course, being Greek, I find myself thinking at one and the same moment of all these facts, as well as the fact that the olive brings me in some eight hundred pounds a year on which to philosophize. Poetry and profit are not separated at all. For the Greek there is only the faintest dividing line.'

The evening light mellows very softly into its range of warm lemon tones, pressing among the close bunches of ripening grapes, and washing the tiles of the peasant houses in the valley. The turtle-doves croon softly in the arbours behind the orchard. The cicadas are dying out—station after station closing down. The two great plane-trees are already silent, and only in the meadow where the sun still plays do they keep up their singing. In the altering values of sound one becomes aware of the chink of teacups as the servant-girl clears away.

'The great god Pan', says the Count, reverting suddenly to his original theme, which has been running as an undercurrent in his thoughts all this time, 'was first announced as dead off Paxo, some miles south of us. This island must have been among the first to get the news. We have no records to tell us how the islanders received it. Yet in our modern pantheon we have a creature whose resemblance to Pan is not, I think, fortuitous. He is, as you know, called the kallikanzaros. He is the house-sprite, a little cloven-hooved satyr with pointed ears, who is responsible for turning milk sour, for leaving doors unlocked, and for causing mischief of every kind. He is sometimes placated by a saucer of milk left upon a window-sill, or a kolouri—one of those quoit-shaped peasant cakes. He also is dying out. But there is one story about him which you, my dear Zarian, will enjoy recording. It is said that on the ten days preceding Good Friday, all the kallikanzaroi in the Under-world are engaged simultaneously upon the task of sawing through the giant plane-tree whose trunk is supposed to hold up the world. Every year they almost succeed, except that the cry "Christ has arisen" saves us all, by restoring the tree and driving them up in a chattering throng into the real world—if I may call our world that. Perhaps you will be able to find classical origins for the story. I give it to you for what it is worth.'

Bats are now beginning their short strutting flights against the sky. In the east the colour is washing out of the world, leaving room for the great copper-coloured moon which will rise soon over Epirus. It is the magic hour between two unrealized states of being —the day-world expiring in its last hot tones of amber and lemon, and the night-world gathering with its ink-blue shadows and silver moonlight.

'Watch for her', says the Count, 'behind that mountain there.' The air tastes faintly of damp. 'She will be rising in a few moments.'

'I am thinking', says Zarian, 'how nothing is ever solved finally. In every age, from every angle, we are facing the same set of natural phenomena, moonlight, death, religion, laughter, fear. We make idolatrous attempts to enclose them in a conceptual frame. And all the time they change under our very noses.'

Landscape with Olive Trees

'To admit that,' says the Count oracularly, 'is to admit happi-ness—or peace of mind, if you like. Never to imagine that any of these generalizations we make about gods or men is valid, but to cherish them because they carry in them the fallibility of our own minds. You doctor, are scandalized when I suggest that *The Tempest* might be as good a guide to Corcyra as the official one. It is because the state of being which is recorded in the character of Prospero is something which the spiritually rich or the sufficiently unhappy can draw for themselves out of this clement land-scape.'

'All this is metaphysics,' says Zarian a trifle unhappily.

'All speculation that goes at all deep becomes metaphysics by its very nature; we knock up against the invisible wall which bounds the prison of our knowledge. It is only when a man has been round that wall on his hands and knees, when he is certain that there is no way out, that he is driven upon himself for a solution.'

'Then for you, Count,' says Theodore, 'the hard and fast struc-ture of the sciences yields nothing more than a set of comparative myths, some with and some without charm?'

'I would like to pose the problem from another angle. There is a morphology of forms in which our conceptual apparatus works, and there is a censor—which is our conditioned attitude. He is the person whom I would reject, because he prevents me choosing and arranging knowledge according to my sensibility. I will give you an example. I was once asked to write a short history of sixth-century Greek sculpture. My publisher refused the work because in it I had pointed out that sixth-century sculpture reaches its peak in Maillol, an artist of whom the man had not then heard. He informed me that I could not treat history in this manner. He informed me of the fact in the exact tone of voice used by my own censor when I first happened upon a Maillol statue, standing weighed down by its connections with the Mediterranean earth. Yet an instant's observation will show one that Maillol does not belong to us in space and time, but to them; I mean to the Greeks of the sixth century.'

At this point, according to time-honoured custom, we chant in unison: 'And if you don't believe me there is a Maillol in the

Landscape with Olive Trees

garden to *prove* it to you', at which the Count smiles his indulgent smile and nods twice. 'There is indeed,' he says.

The first bronze cutting-edge of the moon shows behind the mountain, travelling fast. 'Ah, there she is,' says Zarian.

'And here we are,' says the Count, unwilling to relinquish his subject, 'each of us collecting and arranging our common knowledge according to the form dictated to him by his temperament. In all cases it will not be the whole picture, though it will be the whole picture for you. You, Doctor, will proceed under some title like *The Natural History, Geology, Botany and Comparative Ethnology of the Island of Corfu.* You will be published by a learned society in Vienna. Your work will contain no mention of the first edition of Petrarch in the Library, or of the beautiful mother of Gorgons in the Museum. As for you, Zarian, your articles when they are collected in a book will present a ferocious and lopsided account of an enchanted island which has seduced every historical figure of note from Nero to Napoleon. You will omit the fact that communications are bad and that all Greeks are liars, and that the fleas during the summer are intolerable. It will not be a true picture—but what a picture it will be. Hordes of earnest Armenians from New York will settle here to quote your poetry and prose to each other, and I will be able to charge two drachmae for sitting in the chair which you now occupy and which will certainly outlive you.'

'And I?' I say. 'What sort of picture will I present of Prospero's Island?'

'It is difficult to say,' says the Count. 'A portrait inexact in detail, containing bright splinters of landscape, written out roughly, as if to get rid of something which was troubling the optic nerves. You are the kind of person who would go away and be frightened to return in case you were disappointed; but you would send others and question them eagerly about it. You are to be forgiven really, because you have had the best of your youth in the island. And it is only very much later that one grows the courage to return. I noticed that you did not drink of Kardaki's well the other day. I particularly noticed.'

'I do not like being bound by charms,' I say.

At this point Theodore, who has been listening with some impatience to this dissertation upon character, suggests a stroll, and soon we are walking down the avenue of cypresses together, smelling the strong tobacco from the Count's pipe.

'Ah no, Doctor,' says the old man, as if continuing aloud an argument which has been going on quietly in his mind, 'thought must be free. Let us dispense with the formalist whose only idea is to eliminate the dissonant, the discrepant. Let us marry our ideas and not have them married for us by smaller people. Only in this way will our ideas produce children—for the children of ideas are actions. Dear me,' he adds, 'I am hardly in a position to moralize. I live here quietly without children, on money which my grandfather earned. It would be useless my justifying myself to an economist by explaining that I am exercising my sensibility through loving greatly and suffering greatly in all this quietness. Don't you think?'

Insensibly his footsteps have lead us across the green unkept lawns to where the nymph stands in her rotunda. Her loins fall away in their heavy inevitable lines to her shapely feet. The torso is heavy with its weight of lungs and bone. The breasts ride superbly, held by the invisible thongs of the pectorals.

'An old man's love,' says the Count. 'Look at her. There you have desire which is quite still, retained inside the mind as form and volume—like the grapes for lunch which were still warm and a little drowsy from the sun. It is the speechless potence of the old man, the most terrible kind of desire in stillness which this Mediterranean sculptor has impressed in the rock. Was he happy or unhappy, moral or amoral? He was outside the trap of the opposites. It was a mindless act of coition with the stone that made him describe her. Critics would be interested to know if it was his wife or his eldest daughter. Their speculations would lie right outside the realm in which this sixth-century Pomona stands. It is not desire as we know it—but an act of sex completed by looking at her. The weight of her. Feel how cold the stone arms are.'

The moon is up now among the trees, and the first screech of the owl rings out across the meadow.

'Ah! but I see they have lighted the candles and laid the table,' says the Count, suddenly conscious of the dew as he moves his toes in his battered felt slippers. 'And is it our function simply to stand about here making bad literature? Doctor, we are having brain cutlets in your honour this evening; and, my dear Zarian, a bottle of Mantinea red wine for you.'

Seated at the great table by the sedate light of his own candles, the Count turns to me and says: 'It is the pleasantest form of affection to be able to tease one's friends. You perhaps do not know the history of the Society of Ionian Studies and the brain cutlets?' At this Theodore shows the faintest signs of impatience, and remarking it, the Count pats him laughingly on the arm. 'The Doctor's well-known passion for brain cutlets is something of which you will have undoubtedly heard. Well, some years ago, he was asked to become President of a small informal society of local savants, who were bent on the pursuit of Ionian studies. They were a sombre and bearded collection—for the most part doctors and lawyers of the island: these being the two classes which have the least work to do. At this time our friend was pursuing some studies upon forms of idiocy at the local asylum; and he was particularly interested in the mental condition of an inmate called Giovannides, whose brain he had been coveting off and on for a number of years. In those days he used to speak about Giovannides' brain with ill-concealed cupidity, and explain what a splendid time he would have when the patient died. You see, he had been promised the brain for dissection. Now it so happened that this long-awaited event took place upon the very day when the inaugural lunch of the society was due to take place at the Doctor's house; Theodore was in a state of great excitement. He found himself unable to be patient, and spent the whole morning extracting the brain from its brain-case, remembering all the time that he must get home and prepare his speech for the Society. By midday he had succeeded in removing the brain, and, having wrapped it carefully in greaseproof paper, he had managed to reach home with it held in his arms like a precious treasure. On entering the house he realized that the day was exceptionally warm, so he entered the kitchen, where he popped the lunatic's brain in the ice-box, and retired to his study to prepare his speech. All went well. The guests arrived and were seated at table. The speech was delivered and met with restrained applause. And a steaming dish of the Doctor's favourite brain-cutlets appeared, which was greeted with delighted exclamations. As the guests were helping themselves the telephone in the corner of the room rang. It was Theodore's wife, who had rung up to apologize for having been unable to provide him with his favourite dish for lunch. There was, she said, no brain to be bought anywhere in town. An involuntary cry burst from Theodore's lips. To do him justice, it was not really of his guests that he was thinking so much as of his brain. With a muffled cry of "Giovannides' brain" he sprang to the kitchen and opened the ice-box. The brain had gone. Speechless with anxiety the good doctor returned to the banqueting-room and found that his guests were all looking either uneasy or downright ill. Where a lesser man would have carried it off without telling them anything definite, and where a greater would have wrung his hands for science, Theodore simply stood, trembling from head to foot and pointing at the dish of excellent brain-cutlets and repeating: "I get a brain and *this* is what you do. I get a brain and *this* is what you do." By this time the truth had dawned upon the Ionian Society; their dissolution was so sudden as to be amazing. The maid threw her apron over her head and burst into sobs. The inaugural lunch was a failure. But that was not the unkindest thing of all. The brain of the lunatic was at this moment safely upon Theodore's desk, in the study; the cook, who was devoted to Theodore, had spent the whole morning searching for brain, and had found some in the nick of time. The cutlets served to the Society were perfectly genuine brain cutlets. But do you think he has ever managed to persuade anyone of the truth of this? No. The Society is now referred to as the Brainfever Society, and its members are all supposed to be suffering from aberrations brought on by this meal.'

This anecdote, which we have heard perhaps a dozen times, always sinks Theodore into a profound gloom; for Zarian laughs so immoderately that he spills his wine, and has a fit of coughing until he almost rolls under the table. This is the Count's cue, and turning to him on the backwash of his laughter he says: 'But perhaps Zarian will permit me to tell you the story of his explorations into Greek wines.' At this, it is Zarian's turn to look uncomfortable, while Theodore's face is lit by a shy smile. 'You will have noticed,' says the Count, 'that Zarian champions everything

Landscape with Olive Trees

Greek except the wines. It is true they are not very good, but you would expect a few romantic notes to be blown from time to time on his trumpet. No, I might go so far as to say that he is definitely against Greek wine, and I often wonder whether the little incident of the Mantinea 1936 had anything to do with it. May I repeat the story in my own way?' he asks Zarian with elaborate courtesy. The latter runs his fingers through his mane of silver hair, braces his shoulders as one about to bear a burden, and humbly nods. It is charming to watch him ill-at-ease, picking at the tablecloth, searching for non-existent matches in the pockets of his waistcoat, or shaking his finger in his ear with an expression of simulated pain. The Count sips his wine twice, fills my glass, and continues.

'Late one night last year I received a telephone call. The voice was so full of suppressed excitement that I had difficulty in recognizing it as that of Zarian. He had, he said, something of the utmost importance to tell me. The revelation was too secret to be mentioned on the phone, but I gathered that something very frightful or very wonderful had happened to him. At that time I was in the town house, so I agreed to walk across the Esplanade and see my friend. To be frank, I thought he had simply written a poem. As we all know, when Zarian writes one of his rare poems, he telephones to all his friends and asks them to come round and have it read to them. It was not a poem or an accident. When I climbed those tottering stairs to the top floor of the St. George Hotel I found my friend sitting in a room at a table, staring with considerable rigidity at an open bottle of wine. A single candle guttered beside it on the table. Catching sight of me, he beckoned me speechlessly into the room and into a chair opposite. For a moment he said nothing but continued to stare at the bottle of wine. Then at last he spoke in accents positively strangled by excitement. "My dear Count," he said, "I have at last discovered a Greek wine comparable to anything grown in France." He tiptoed to a cupboard and brought me a glass which he filled very gingerly, holding his breath as he did so. I sipped it. It was a very fine Beaune, ringing on the palate like a note of music. The bottle said MANTINEA 1936, and I knew that Mantinea was an ordinary table wine. I congratulated him and drank some more. Zarian was by this time walking up and down in a state of considerable excitement. "A wine for the Gods," he kept repeating. I noticed that he was in his socks. His feet, he said, hurt him. He had been walking round the town since four in the afternoon buying up all the wine of this name and date he could find. My impulse there and then was to warn him against undue optimism, but his pleasure was so warming a sight that I let him ramble on. Finally he lead the way into his wife's bedroom, holding the candle high, in order to let me see the seventy or eighty bottles of the wine lying snugly upon the bed. I remember that he held his finger over his lips and spoke in whispers, for all the world as if we were in danger of waking the bottles up. It took us an hour to finish the bottle with our conversation growing more and more exalted. Zarian felt that the last link to bind him to Corcyra had been forged; always fussy about wine, he had been unable to get used to the heavy sweet products of Greece. When we had disposed of the first bottle his magnanimity lead him to tiptoe into the bedroom and come back with another. He opened it with a flourish, poured some out, and sipped. An expression of disgust came over his face. He held the wine for a moment only in his mouth before bounding to the window and spitting it out. It was obviously a faulty bottle. With a dawning look of alarm on his face he retired and fetched two more bottles. They were both full of superior vinegar. He opened a dozen. They were all the same. I left him that evening surrounded by opened bottles of Mantinea, which he was pouring away down the kitchen sink. The glorious Beaune was never repeated. And now when I offer him a glass of Mantinea—which is after all not a very bad wine as wines go—you observe the face he makes.'

Zarian, to whom the subject of wine is sacred, does not find the story in very good taste, one can see. Yet he suffers it admirably; and later upon the dazzling white terrace, sipping his cognac, he confesses that he is developing a taste for retzina. 'It is not to be drunk alone, but with meat and vegetables cooked in the peasant manner. Lamb with onions, egg-plant, potatoes, and that red sauce which you all know. Then it tastes like a divine turpentine.'

'But speaking of intoxicating drinks,' says Theodore, 'I wonder, Count, if you have remarked that arbutus berries are among the things which can also intoxicate. During the campaigns of Macedonia during the last war I noticed that on several occasions battalions of our troops became quite drunk through eating the berries of the shrub. In some cases their wits seemed turned by the habit. I often wonder whether in Xenophon the mysterious outbreak of madness among the troops could have come from the same cause.'

It is ten o'clock and the moonlight is dazzling. Across the valley I can see the shallow glare of Spiro's headlamps flash as he brings N. to me. We are off to explore the caves near Paleocastrizza and spend the night in the small hotel there. The demented honking with which Spiro always announces his approach sounds sweet and muffled across the silver trees.

Loath to disrupt the speculative calm of my three philosophers I get up and say good-bye. The Count insists on accompanying me the length of the terrace to send a message to N. Faint interior preoccupations stir behind his composed features. 'And you are coming for the vintage don't forget,' he says. 'Bring her with you. It is a time for women.' Then he adds almost apologetically, 'We do not consider them enough perhaps.' And I know all at once that his thoughts have turned to the Roman nymph standing in the rotunda with the leaves turning over around her feet. I would like to say something that was not redundant or out of place but can find no words. The very fabric of this candid and beautiful landscape forbids it. I shake his hand and walk down the long avenue to the gates where the great car stands panting with Spiro jovial behind the wheel.

The western waters of Paleocastrizza will be icy cold to-night; and under the castle of St. Angelo the silver race will be combing out its long strands. Soon there is to be a war.

7.4.38

Coming over the crest of the hill behind Kastellani we see that a dance is in progress. From the grassy glades below, the shadow of the olive-trees is broken by clouds of dust, and the afternoon silence by the terrific giggling of donkeys—like pantomime comedians. Smoke from the fires, upon which whole kids are turning upon spits, rises lazily. Through the hum of human voices one can hear the scratch and squeak of the violin and guitars, and the hollow beat of the drum, resonant and vulgar as a full stomach struck with the palm of the hand. 'Ah look,' says N. 'Just look at the dancers.'

A multi-coloured circle of flowing head-dresses and skirts moves slowly about the axis of the musicians, reversing and advancing with slow rhythmic measures. In the centre of the circle, moved by the current, but free, the young men dance, each improvising his variations upon the theme, hand on hip, head thrown back, face devout and abstract. In the luminous shadows among the trees the crowds are laughing and chattering, the pedlars of ikons, talismans, or bread and sweets, resting for a while upon the boles of the olives in expressive poses. Whiffs of roasting lamb and wine come across the clearing where the old men and women are sitting in groups upon the grass like birds, eating and drinking. Father Nicholas is there in his blue trousers watching his younger son dancing, all dressed in white, with a fine new straw hat upon his square head. Sandos and his daughter are sitting under an olive-tree. Socrates and Demosthenes are eating themselves silly by the turning lambs. Several of the girls from our northern village are in the outer circle; one recognizes them by the sobriety of their costume—black clothes with white head-dress. Here districts still keep their distinctions of head-dress; and in Corfu the women of Gastouri are justly renowned as the most beautiful and the most colourful. Here in the circle of dancers you can see the famous full pleated skirt of shot silk and the old-fashioned bodice, under a bolero heavy with gold stitching—the crust of embroidery. Gold drops dangle at the ear, while the coiffure is a marvellous erection —built up towards the back of the head in tiers, worked over little cloth pads, and tied with red ribbon. A lace-edged handkerchief turned back from the crown, frames the handsome olive face.

'Ah,' says Theodore with pleasure, 'it is a star-dance, called the Corcyrean Dance. As you may know I have theories about the origin of these dances, some of which are very ancient.'

The multi-coloured wheel spins and reverses, spins and reverses, while the lone-moving satellites plot out their intricate measures. The fiddlers have their heads together in a conspiracy of rhythm. The two violins drizzle steadily. The son of Father Nicholas throws his head back from time to time and gives a short excited cry of pleasure as his deft feet in their heavy boots glide and spin upon the green turf, now being beaten to dust by the moving feet of the women. Strange associations come to mind. The wheel of the heavens. The repeating tread of the women, as if caught in the labyrinth of the rhythm, the measure repeating itself, multiplied only by the free improvisations of the men. The mating dance of birds.

'All the circular ones I call star dances,' says Theodore. 'I read somewhere that dancing originated in a desire to imitate the movement of celestial bodies—the early clock as it were.'

The boy in white is dancing now with the faultless inevitability of someone for whom nothing else exists. His head is thrown back and his sharp nostrils dilated. He has thrown his hat out of the circle, to roll unerringly at Father Nicholas's feet under the olives. His brown hair rises and falls on his head. One hand is at his hip, upon the red sash he is wearing; the other is posed at full length like that of a conductor, expressing every subtlety of gesture and balance. He is dancing before the girl in yellow and blue—a swarthy Gastouri beauty—with heavy limbs. Her face is flushed as he reaches out the handkerchief for her to touch. The women, linked together, struggle and cry like gulls. Nearer he dances and nearer. He does not look at her but you feel at once a correspondence, a power, flowing between them. For a moment her face looks panic-stricken and dazed; and then she reaches out her strong brown paw and takes the hem of the handkerchief between her fingers. The music rolls over them. They rotate, buried in the rhythms, latched together by this fateful contact, revolving together in the communion of sound and action.

Father Nicholas has been watching them with a strange mixture of pride and resentment in his face. Of course as a northerner he should not be making advances to a Gastouri girl. Seeing us, however, his smiles reappear and he hobbles across to greet us as quickly as his rheumatism allows. When he speaks I observe that his breath is heavy with wine. 'The young are only young once,' he tells us several times in a voice deepened an octave by red wine. Kastellani is his favourite brew. 'When they dance all the sins of the world dance with them. When I was young. . . .' But the uproar is too great for him to be allowed to reminisce. We are presented in quick succession to the mayor, two policemen, and three monks (who timidly hide their glasses of wine behind a tree before coming across to shake hands). N. begins making her slow painful notes for paintings—a donkey with panniers, an old woman, a policeman lying asleep under a tree with his tunic unbuttoned, a man making a drunken political speech which is completely inaudible above the music.

Zarian sits down upon the earth ledge outside a cottage to mop his silver head. Through the open door one can see one of those strange interiors: a huge carved bed which takes up nearly the whole room, with the ikons of the saints at its head, and on the nail above it the green marriage wreath. 'The Corfiots expend all their decorative talent upon their beds,' says Zarian cynically; 'shall I tell you why? It is not because the bed is the place where they get most pleasure out of life—but because it is the only article in the house which by law is not seizable for debt.'

The dance has changed now to a slower and more stately tempo. The circle begins to wheel. The circle of chance. The wheel of fate. The boy in white is still dancing before the Gastouri girl. She is smiling in a silly tranced way, like a hypnotized bird, as she clutches the handkerchief.

'Making love, marrying, having children and dying,' says Zarian again, addressing nobody but himself. 'Is there no escape from the circle at all?'

Nicholas is upon us with drinks now as the twilight sets in. A priest is examining my sandals with admiration. A rather good-looking villager is making over-friendly remarks to N. who is replying in her bad Greek as best she can.

Theodore, to everyone's surprise, has taken off his coat, and clad in braces and black boots has entered the circle to dance. A cheer goes up. His blond beard flashes in the waning sunlight. Hand on hip he does a few hesitating measures, and then suddenly transfixed by the rhythm begins to dance very well. The women are enchanted by this blond bearded man. 'An Englishman,' they cry. 'No. No,' yells Father Nicholas hoarsely from under the trees. 'A Greek by God. A Greek from Thessaly.' Subdued applause. Head cocked to the music Theodore dances, looking more than ever like an Ionian faun. 'But he is like an Englishman,' cry the women. The voices of men under the trees chorus back: 'No. He is a Greek

in spite of the beard.' Father Nicholas gives the Abbot of Myrtiotissa a stately dig in the ribs. 'Go on and dance, good father,' he
says, 'you have a beard too. Dance.' The Abbot giggles coyly. He
is rather afraid of the fierce old man. 'Dance,' yells Nicholas with
more abandon. 'All you priests ought to dance.' And he gives him
a resounding smack upon the back and spills his wine. A policeman absently fires his pistol in the air for the sheer fun of it. A
donkey breaks loose and ambles through the crowd with two small
shrieking children in the panniers on its back. One of the monks
mounts it and drives it back to the trees with shrill cries. A fresh
round of wine appears from nowhere and gruff healths ring out,
mingled with belches.

Theodore reappears mildly and says that it is time to start. We
have a long walk to make yet before we reach the town. 'Doctor,
that was well done,' cries Father Nicholas in ringing tones. Theodore smartly sidesteps to avoid the approbation of Father Nicholas's palm which at this stage in the feast falls heavily on friend and
enemy alike. 'With dancing like that you should win many beautiful women.' Saying good-bye, we take the road and climb slowly
to the next hillock, from which the dance seems remote and
mystical—like a coloured heart beating there under the trees. At
this range the violins and guitars are inaudible. Only the little
bump of the drum still sounds on in our ears.

Turning towards the east we walk silently down the scented
road in the deep dust. 'I do not think, Doctor,' says Zarian, 'that
the circular dances have anything to do with the stars. I am sure
this kind of dancing originated out of some purely practical impulse or occupation. Now I suggest that the circular dances are
really symbolic representations of the threshing floor, that they are
grain dances. Again, in the dance known as the Trata you can see
that it is based upon the fishermen pulling at a net.'

Theodore is not disposed to quarrel about this interpretation.
We walk down the long winding road into the valley in silence.
At a corner we come upon a pedlar asleep in the ditch with his hat
over his face. Beside him lies a pack full of trinkets; blue beads
against the evil eye, amulets, and tracts about the works of the
Saint. He snores wonderfully in the deep grass, with one arm
thrown in abandon over his face and the other stretched out to its

full length. 'Ah, sweet content,' says Zarian. 'We always miss you. We think too much. What are the odds on all this speculation we indulge in if for once we cannot go to a dance, drink a glass of wine, and fall asleep in the ditch like a Greek god on holiday?'

'Or wake in the morning with lice in our hair and a hangover,' says Theodore severely.

'It will be wonderful to have a bath,' says N.

'And dinner. And then to walk across to the open-air cinema where we shall see *The Sign of the Cross*—this ancient film about the life of Christ, which has caused such a stir in the island. The ecclesiastical authorities are trying to have it banned.'

'It is not so much the film,' says Theodore, 'as the fact that the Corfu daily newspaper carried on its news-page the headline: CHRIST TO APPEAR IN CORFU. The general public grew quite alarmed by the idea.'

The moon is rising.

8.8.38

Bocklin has walked over the hills from Metsovo, and arrived in the island. In our Paris days he was a seedy blond youth, so that we hardly recognize the tough-looking specimen of the new Germany who stands on our doorstep. He has with him a number of his own photographs and drawings which are full of life and sensibility. We spend the week-end together at the Count's country house, where he gets a chance to unload his treasury of demotic songs and fables. He speaks Greek perfectly. Zarian and Theodore are captivated by his manners and his gaiety, and the way he sings to the guitar.

In the morning while the Count and I are looking for swallows' nests under the eaves we enter his room and see a bundle of accurate architectural drawings of the main harbour and fortress.

9.8.38

Riding south from Paleocastrizza in a fair wind we come to Ermones beach just before dawn; and swimming ashore in the grey half light we build in gleaming sand the figure of a gigantic recumbent Aphrodite. N. and Veronica model the face while Dorothy and I shape the vast thighs. We give her a crown of pebbles for pearls and a belt made from withes of sapling, like snakes. She lies staring at the lightening sky, her mouth open in an agonizing shriek, being born. While the sea creeps up and gnaws her long rigid fingers.

By first sunlight we are away again, wondering what the wide-eyed fisher-boys will make of this great relief in sand. Aphrodite rising from the foam.

15.8.38

Theodore says that in the mountains, where shepherds must pasture their flocks half the year round in the fastnesses far from any village, it is customary to have a ewe instead of a wife. Far from betraying any unusual sensitivity to a practice so well known, each shepherd has his own favourite ewe, which he tricks out with bells and tassels according to his fancy. This ewe is known as the favourite one. The Greek word is Λαγιαρνί.

He records a conversation with one of the shepherds in Epirus which carries the authentic Holborn Empire note of cynicism. 'What point is there', asked Theodore in his academic manner, 'in having this ridiculous practice?' (He was referring to the trinkets which adorned one of the chosen ewes.)

The shepherd thought for a moment and then replied, as one who offers an opinion verified by long personal experience: 'From every point of view they are superior to our wives. But above all they do not talk.'

VII

The Vintage Time

20.9.38

Riding southward in the spluttering bus from Kouloura to Ypso at the end of a bright September you can feel the altered accent in things—for the vintage is beginning. Everywhere the turtle-doves are calling in the arbours and orchards; and washed by the brilliant sunlight the whole coast glitters and expands under the swinging blows of the waves. The bay is alive with sails glowing in their many colours, and the atmosphere is so clear that one can see, miles away, the distinct figures of friends holding sails and tillers; my brother's boat *Dugong* lies just off Agni, heading for the house. I can see his characteristic pose, legs stretched out, head on one side and eyes closed against the smoke of his cigarette. He has stowed his guns in their leather cases under the half-decking where the faithful Spiro sits scanning the horizon for something to shoot at. *Dugong* slaps and yaws as she meets the small race of water thrown back, yellow and curdled, from the Butrinto Estuary. He will be sorry to miss us on his way up to the northern lake Antiniotissa ('Enemy of youth') where he is after quail and woodcock.

As we move slowly down from the dead lands the road becomes more and more precipitous, and the green valley comes up at us in a trembling wave of fronds and branches. We roar through several small hamlets, scattering smoke and stones. A woman stands frowsily at her door and empties coffee grounds upon the stones. Two children sit under a bench playing with a tortoise. A policeman shouts something unintelligible. The bus is crammed with peasants going to market, and the air in it smells almost inflammable with garlic and exhaust fumes. Father Nicholas and his son sit just behind us. He has finally conquered his prejudice against southern women, and they are on their way to try and arrange a match with the Gastouri girl whom we had seen at the Kastellani

The Vintage Time

dance. Father Nicholas is in great voice and keeps the whole bus
in a roar of laughter. Our feet rest upon a fluttering floor of
chickens, all tied by the legs in bunches, like vegetables. His son
looks rather ashamed of himself. It is not altogether restful, this
journey. At each of Father Nicholas's jests the driver lets off a peal
of laughter in a high piping voice and, letting go his hold upon the
wheel, hugs himself with extravagant joy. At these moments the
bus shows signs of wanting to mount the stone parapet of the road
and fly down into the valley. This tendency is corrected at the last
moment, when all except the hardiest travellers have commended
themselves to St. Spiridion and flung one arm across their eyes.
With prodigious roaring and scraping of brakes we rattle down the
mountain like some iron cockroach, and draw up at last in clouds
of dust, before the little tavern at the crossroads where Spiro had
already parked his great Dodge under the olives, and is busy
arguing about the price of wine with the innkeeper.

We sit for a while over a glass of wine with him. He gives us the
gossip of the town in his wonderful Brooklyn argot—strange fragments of words with whole syllables discarded from them when
they are beyond his pronunciation. Spiro's noble stomach reposes
comfortably on his knees. His forearms are covered in a black pelt
of hair. He is sweating easily and comfortably from every pore. In
the dark shadow thrown by the trees, with the red reflections of the
tablecloth playing about his dark, good-natured face, he reminds
me of nothing so much as a great drop of olive oil. He informs us,
with self-importance mixed with a certain shame, that a fire broke
out the previous afternoon at a garage. As one of the firemen he
had had his first practical experience of fire-fighting. On the whole
the affair had been rather a scandal. The brigade had arrived in
good time, clinging importantly to the new fire-engine which the
Government had provided, each in his gleaming helmet. Spiro
himself had arrived, but riding majestically in his own car, with his
helmet on. The garage was well alight. The balconies of the surrounding houses were thronged with sightseers, waiting to see the
recently formed Fire Brigade prove itself in its first baptism of fire.
All went well. While the hose was being uncoiled, the Chief of
Police made a short but incisive speech exhorting everyone to stay
calm and not to give way to panic. The fire hydrant was unlocked

and everything placed in position to extinguish the blaze. At this point, however, a disgraceful argument broke out as to who was going to hold the nozzle of the hose. Words became gestures. Gestures became acts. A push here, a scuffle there, and riot had broken out. A struggling mass of firemen began to fight for possession of the nozzle. At this point the hose bulged and began to emit a creditable jet of water, and what was to be a baptism of fire became a baptism of water for the onlookers. A slowly rotating fountain of water moved across the square. The Minister for the Interior, who had been standing innocently on his balcony in heliotrope pyjamas, was all but swept into the street by the force of the jet. Women screamed. The long-averted panic against which the Chief of Police had warned them broke out. The affair ended with a baton charge and a number of arrests. The garage was left to burn itself out. The engine was driven home in disgrace by a civilian. And Spiro tendered his resignation.

Driving easily across the low hills where the vineyards have already taken on their ochre tones, he seems a little hurt that we find the story funny. 'It's not a good thing', he tells N. repeatedly, 'for the nation when the bastards do that.'

We sweep up the long drive and round to the side of the house. The Count is sitting at the edge of the orchard, under a tree, reading with his dogs beside him. He is clad in pyjamas and a straw hat. He waves his hand and signals us to cross the sunlight-dappled walks.

'Ah! you will forgive my pyjamas,' he says. 'The others have not arrived yet. I am half drunk just reading through Mazziari's description of the grapes. Come, let us take our pick.'

The vineyards are already beginning to look gutted and burnt out with shrivelling leaves. The Count walks ahead with us stopping here and there in all the profusion to clip a bunch of grapes with his scissors, which he carries tied round his waist on a piece of string. 'Ah, my dear, where have you ever seen such plenty?' he says. Indeed the variety is astonishing. 'We will ignore these plump ones with the thick skins. But try these violet coloured ones. You may find them too sweet. We have had three days' torture preparing for the gathering. So many extra mouths to feed. Plasterers, treaders, and whatnot hanging about the house.' The great

The Vintage Time

doors of the magazine are ajar. The huge vats and butts have been dragged out into the meadow for caulking and patching. Under a tree a small army of men is at work upon them. Some have been turned upon logs, and are being filled with gravel and water, before being rolled. Others are being mended and scoured. 'The big one in the corner,' says the Count, 'she is the one you have to thank for the crimson robola wine which you think so good—and which even Zarian likes.'

The shadow of the cottage-pergolas seems rich with the scent of grapes—of blunt sweet muscatel and lisabetta. Ourania cuts down heavy clumps of them for the table, holding them in her brown arms and smiling. They are covered in a rich misty bloom still.

Meanwhile across the orchard the Count is in full voice: 'The little amber ones and those which look ice-green and closely packed—they have done very well this year. Farther on we shall see the *rhoditi*. They run blood-red when the sun shines through them; coral rather, like the lobe of an ear. Dear me, we shall all have indigestion. Ah! Here comes the Doctor and Zarian—beyond the olive-trees there. And his wife. Zarian looks extremely puffed as usual. And Nimiec.'

By lunch-time the rest of the guests have arrived, and are seated at tables laid under the arbour which bounds the last terrace. A tremendous meal has been prepared, and three of the prettiest village girls are there to serve it. Zarian openly bemoans having brought his pleasant American wife with him. 'Where do you keep these beauties?' he asks. 'They are never here when we come alone.'

'They would distract us perhaps,' says the Count seriously. The crimson *robola* is passed round. Each pours a drop upon the ground before drinking—the peasant libation. The grounds are swarming with workmen to prepare for to-morrow's picking.

'This year we are going to begin on the hill there. It should be specially good, this year's *robola*. I feel it in my bones. We shall call it, I think, Prospero's Wine. What do you say?'

The valley curves away below the arbour with its delicately curved panels of landscape. From the orchard a guitar strikes up, and after a few moments' hesitation the sound of voices—the men's deep and rough, the women's high and shrill as herring-gulls'. The gatherers have arrived in the hope of an extra day's work. The faint crack of guns sounds in the valley. A puff of smoke here and there marks a sportsman with a muzzle-loader shooting doves. The conversation wells up in waves—overstepping the boundaries of language. The vintage holiday has begun.

Lunch prolonged unconscionably becomes tea. Some of us wander away to bathe or sleep out the long hot afternoon. By nightfall the gang of workmen have done their job, and the vine-vats are ready. They sit upon doorsteps or on the grass among the olive-trees, eating their frugal meal of bread and fruit. But wine there is in plenty for them.

At the end of the terrace Zarian lies majestically sleeping in a hammock, while his wife pauses from her reading at intervals to brush a fly off his face. Theodore and Nimiec have disappeared on a journey of exploration with N.

The Count is pottering round the magazine in his pyjamas giving orders in a peremptory voice to his overseers. 'To-morrow we shall start on the *robola* vat,' he says, and gives orders for it to be moved out of the shadow into the angle of the wall where the sunlight strikes. 'Niko is going to come and do the treading. I can always trust him.' Niko is a slim young man, dressed in a dark suit, who holds his hat modestly in his hand as he hears the Count speak. 'If we put all the women on to the vineyard at once we should have the first vat gathered by sundown to-morrow. Niko can begin at dusk.' His face is radiant and empty of preoccupation. Meanwhile the cellars must be tidied, the magazines dusted and all vanishable goods removed beyond the reach of the pickers' temptation. Ourania is filling the bowls with flowers—autumn crocus and cyclamen from the walls of the vineyards. Donkeys unload mounds of red tomatoes at the outhouse and everywhere the brisk sound of bargaining goes on. Caroline is playing patience upon the balcony, stopping from time to time to pop a grape into her mouth. 'We cannot complain,' says the Count. 'It will be a lovely vintage. We can start Niko off to-morrow. We might bathe to-night. We can use the car. I see that Spiro has stayed on with us. It's bad for trade but he can't bear to miss a party.'

The sound of singing is beaten out thin upon the late afternoon air. I can hear Spiro's bass notes sounding like the eructations of

The Vintage Time

a giant. The Count sits for a while on the garden wall with one slipper off and lights a cigarette. 'And perhaps we shall have an engagement or something to remind us that we are getting old men.' Caroline pretends she does not hear.

Bocklin has brought his flute. Its quaint twirls and flourishes sound unearthly on the empty lawns where the nymph stands. The Count walks slowly down the garden path. 'There is going to be a war, of course. But on days like this one feels that it will go on for ever—I mean this lovely lambent weather: no sense of time, except that the fruit upon our tables changes. By the way, figs are in. Let us hope they will outlive your foreign policy, my dear boy. I see you have been reading Mackenzie. It will be just the same. The Royalists will let us down all the way along. Don't you see that Nimiec and Caroline are falling in love with each other? There is that subtle unspoken polarity of feeling you can see when they are together. They both know it will happen. They both know that the other knows. They both avoid each other's company. And yet the invisible cobweb is drawing tighter. That is happiness—the certainty and inevitability of an attraction like that. It remains for the lock to turn on the event and already it is spoiled. They have had a hundred opportunities to confess themselves—and there he is walking round with the Doctor, holding his test-tubes, while she sits and plays patience and imagines that she does not want him to come and find her there. You know, there is no philosophic compensation for growing beyond the reach of love—that is the one wall one never breaks through. To think that *that* will never happen again. That *that* moment, the germinating half-second during which you recognize your completement in someone else, will never happen again. . . . Any of the peasant girls would supply the physical simulacrum of the event. Ah, but the thing itself is gone. Let us have a glass of wine, shall we? It's thirsty work talking like a Norman Douglas character. Caroline, have a glass of wine with us and let me tell your fortune.'

Just after dawn the cries of the pickers wake us. The grass is still heavy with dew and the sun not yet above the trees. A long line of coloured women are setting forth for the vineyard with their

The Vintage Time

baskets. Mark and Peter are the overseers, and they follow with lordly strides behind them smoking and talking, proud in their blue smocks and straw hats. Spiro follows with the brindled puppy. As we watch the procession the window below us opens and the Count puts his head out to cheer them with some parting pleasantry. The early breakfast daunts everyone but Zarian, who has eaten himself into a state of feverish indigestion and cannot sleep. Spiro sits on the terrace, cap in hand, and prophesies a sunny day in the voice of such heartiness that Zarian becomes all at once quite peevish. The Count, having reassured himself that the pickers have set out to gather the favourite *robola* vineyard, sleeps on for a couple of hours.

By mid-morning we are all up on the hillock overlooking the vineyard, surrounding our pyjama'd host like staff officers watching a battle. On the brilliant dappled sunlight of the slopes below the women have put on their wimples and are moving with swift grace from shrub to shrub, cutting the long branches with their sickle knives—branches of crimson *robola* which droop in their baskets with the weight of human limbs.

In the shade of an olive cloths have been spread, and here the women converge, each with her blooming basket load. Two donkeys with panniers stand by apathetically, flicking flies with their tails. Everything goes with a terrific pace for this the first day of picking and the Count himself is looking on.

Presently, when the Count has been reassured as to the picking, we retire to the arbours by the house to drink coffee and pass the long morning in idle talk. Bocklin plays his flute. And gradually, by journeys, the donkeys bring in the fruit which is emptied into the great wooden vat under the careful eyes of Niko himself. The Count cannot sit still until he has supervised everything himself, and seen everything with his own eyes. 'Niko is a wonderful boy,' he says. 'Don't think that any oaf can tread wine. No, he is pure as island water. Don't imagine that the wine-treader doesn't transform the wine with his feet—that there isn't a communication I mean between his style and technique and state of soul and the response of the fruit. It's an aesthetic performance. No, Doctor. It is no use you smiling in that ironical scientific manner. We could easily use a machine-treader and you would soon see what sort of wine my *robola* had become. Niko treads a part of himself into the vat. He is an angel on earth. Ah! dear me. How over-exotic one sounds when one translates from Greek to English.'

By four o'clock the vat is heaped full and from the sheer black weight of the fruit the must has begun to force the crude spigot. The Count is extremely excited, for it is the moment to begin the treading. Niko has been standing in the trough by the well, washing himself in the icy water. Now he advances to the vat, clad only in a white shirt which is knotted at the thighs. His pale face looks remote and far-away as he hoists himself up. His white feet dangle for a second in the sunlight and vanish. The Count is hoarse with emotion. 'You remember everything now,' he says nervously. 'The old way—as you have done it always.' Niko does not answer. He smiles, as if at some remembered joke, and nods. Gently moving his feet he begins by treading a small hole to stand in and begins to work into it the grapes piled above the rim.

The spigot is now uncorked and the must begins to come out in an opaque crimson spurt. This beautiful colour stains the trough, lacquers the tin measure, and stabs the shadows of the magazine with splashes of red. Keeping the same tireless pace Niko labours deeper and ever deeper into the great vat until by the latest dusk his white face has quite vanished into the depths and only his two crimson grape-splashed hands can be seen holding the edges of the vat. He perches himself up every now and again and rests, hanging his head like a bird. He has become almost intoxicated himself by the fumes of the must, and by the long six-hour routine of his treading—which ends at ten o'clock. His face looks pale and sleepy in the red light of the lanterns. Mark encourages him with gruff pleasantries as he measures the must back into the vat. Since the wine is red the skins and stalks are left in. Now the huge wooden lid, weighted with stones, is floated upon the top, and by to-morrow morning all the leavings will have risen up under it into a scarlet froth of crust, from under which the liquid will be crackling with fermentation. For ten days now the fermentation will go on, sending its acid smell on the gusts of wind from the meadow, into the bedrooms of the great house.

Now that the *robola* is safely on the way, the Count can turn his attention to the kitchens with their gleaming copper ware and dungeon-like ovens. Here he busies himself with Caroline and Mrs. Zarian in the manufacture of *mustalevria*—that delicious Ionian sweet or jelly which is made by boiling fresh must to half its bulk with semolina and a little spice. The paste is left to cool on plates and stuck with almonds; and the whole either eaten fresh or cut up in slices and put away in the great store cupboard.

Sykopita, Zarian's favourite fig cake, will come later when the autumn figs are literally bursting open with their own ripeness. But for the time being there are conserves of all kinds to be made—orange-flower preserve and morella syrup. While the Count produces for the table a very highly spiced quince cheese, black and sticky, but very good.

The ravished vineyards are a sad sight on the brown earth of the property. The Count pauses from time to time in his passage between the kitchen and the dining-room terrace to contemplate them. He is happy with the full weight of his resignation: because October is coming with its first sweep of rain and mist. The remaining vine-leaves and fig-leaves—strange butterfly-like shapes against the massive platinum-grey trunks—will be gathered for fodder. The earth will die shabbily and dully in russet patches, tessellating the landscape with its red squares and octagons. In November the cleaning of guns, the first wood fires, and the putting away of summer clothes. Then the earth will spin inexorably into winter with its gales and storms—the wild duck screaming from Albania, the seas shrieking and whistling off the barren northern point beyond Turtle-Dove Island.

These few days pass in a calm so absolute, that to regret their passing would be unworthy of them. Zarian is bound for Geneva next week. Nimiec for Poland until next spring.

We picnic for supper on these warm nights by the Myrtiotissa monastery. Spiro lights a fire of pine-branches and twigs, and the three wicker hampers of the Count are brimmed with food and drink. In the immense volume of the sea's breathing our voices are restored to their true proportion—insignificant, small and shrill with a happiness this landscape allows us but does not notice. The firelight etches the faces so clearly. The Count with his bright eyes looking over N.'s shoulder as she draws. Theodore's golden beard lowered over a pool in complete abstraction. Nimiec and Caroline walking with linked fingers into the sea. Zarian's lips shiny with wine, his silver scruff of hair flying like a halo round his head. Spiro's great charred features. Everyone. The night around us edges slowly on towards the morning, silent except for the noise of the sea, and the sleepy chirp of cicadas in the plane-tree who have mistaken our fire for sunlight. 'You have noticed how we talk less and less together as the days go on,' says the Count. 'It is not because we have less to say to each other, it is because language becomes inadequate to our parting. I do not know when we shall meet again. Will you all be back by next spring I wonder?'

It is already very late, and the donkeys have stumbled off home with the hampers. Theodore lies asleep in the firelight. His lips move slowly. Zarian has taken the guitar from Bocklin and has started to play it inexpertly. He is trying to find the key for the little island song which Theodore has taught us.

> 'Sea, you youth-swallower,
> O poison-bearing element, Sea,
> Who make our island folk
> Always be wearing their black clothes.
>
> Have you not had enough of it,
> Sea, in all this long time,
> With the bodies you have swallowed
> Down in your insatiable waves?'

Presently Theodore will wake and ask Caroline to sing 'Greensleeves' and 'Early One Morning'—airs sounding in all that emptiness so Lydian and remote coming from those American lips with their limping southern drawl.

To-morrow we are separating.

1.1.41

A postcard from the Count: 'Christmas Day. I spent it alone in happy memory of the year before when we walked across the northern marshes and you were attacked by a wounded hare—remember? To remind myself (and hence you also) of our perpetual spring I gathered a bunch of flowers from the valley—

flowers from every season. Cyclamen and snowdrop. February's irises and a jonquil, cinquefoil, bugloss, corn marigold, orange blossom, clover, and wild roses. Spiro has asked one of his pilots to fly them to you so you will have them by now. They are my invitation for next year. Don't forget us.'

VIII

Epilogue in Alexandria

The sightless Pharos turns its blind eye upon a coast, featureless, level and sandy. One thinks of Nelson on his column turning a blinded eye across the miles of English mist to where by the deserted gun batteries of Aboukir the sea runs thin and green. In these summer twilights the city lies in its jumble of pastel tones, faintly veined like an exhausted petal. Flocks of pigeons wheel in the last sunlight, turning and falling, like a shower of confetti when the light strikes against their wings. The last landmark on the edge of Africa. The battleships in their arrowed blackness turn slowly in the harbour. The loss of Greece has been an amputation. All Epictetus could not console one against it.

Here we miss Greece as a living body; a landscape lying up close against the sky, suspended on the blue lion-pads of mountains. And above all, we miss the Eye: for the summers of indolence and deduction on the northern beaches of our island—beaches incessantly washed and sponged by the green Ionian—taught us that Greece was not a country but a living eye. 'The Enormous Eye' Zarian used to call it. Walking in those valleys you knew with complete certainty that the traveller in this land could not record. It was rather as if he himself were recorded. The sensation of this immense hairless recording eye was everywhere; in the ringing blue sky, the temples, the supple brushes of cypress, the sun beating in a withering hypnotic dazzle on the statues with curly stone hair and blunt sagacious noses. Everything was the subject of the Eye. It was like a lens fitting into the groove of the horizon. Nowhere else has there ever been a landscape so aware of itself, conforming so marvellously to the dimensions of a human existence. At Epidaurus, for example, it is not the theatre that obsesses one or the temples, but the enfolding circle of small hills, as if the very land had conformed to the architect's plan: all contours, no edges, and only the faintest engraving of ilex and olive along the sky.

Epilogue in Alexandria

Something of all this lives on in the keen Athenian faces of our friends—faces so long turned towards the preoccupation of Greece that you can read everything in them: the dark uncombed blue of the Cyclades slowly uncurling about the flanks of Mykonos and Delos: the dazzling windmills and the grey springs. But they are here now like ghosts of the old lucid past in the aura of that enormous Eye—Stephan sailing his boat like a demon, half seas over in blue and gold; girls like Elie with dark slanting arms and long olive legs; the shaggy islanders in their coloured belts; caves echoing to the suck and swish of the water; the long rows of coloured caiques snubbing at anchor in the oilgrey waters of the port; the church bells ringing. Meeting them in these crooked streets one is struck by the potentiality of the drama which the Greeks this time have offered to the world. Maro, the human and beautiful, in her struggle against apathy; the drawn face of Eleftheria with its haunting eyes reading the last few lines of her great poem; the solemn face of Seferiades with its candour and purity ('we are the dying limb, withering on the body of the tree cut down'); Alecco, Spiro, Paul. In them the thousand and one images of that Greece of ours crystallize into pin-points of light: the book-lined room where the woman of Zante was read: the terrace with the figs and the sound of running water: Tinos where the red sails walk down the main street: Corinth with its vermin: Argos and Thebes with their retzina: Kalamata choked in vines: the warm scent of bruised sage on the Arcadian hills.

I think of them all in Africa, in this unfamiliar element, as subtropical men, defeated by a world where the black compromise is king. I see them daily recovering by their acts, their songs and poems, the whole defeated world of acts and thoughts, into a small private universe: a Greek universe. Inside that world, where the islands lie buried in smoke, where the cypresses spring from the tombs, they know that there is nothing to be said. There is simply patience to be exercised. Patience and endurance and love. Some of us have vanished from the picture; some have had their love converted into black bile by the misery they have witnessed. Nimiec died in an Athens night-club. Spiro died in his own vine-wreathed house. Theodore with British forces in Italy punctuates the silence by characteristic letters beginning 'Do you remember?'

Epilogue in Alexandria

Zarian is in Geneva. His silence is complete. Caroline, Mitsu, Rosemary, are in Cairo. The Count is somewhere in the mountains of Epirus—a philosopher with his pockets full of dynamite. Bocklin is on the Russian front. The white house has been bombed and the boats too. History with her painful and unexpected changes cannot be made to pity or remember; that is *our* function.

The day war was declared we stood on the balcony of the white house in a green rain falling straight down out of heaven on to the glassy floor of the lagoon; we were destroying papers and books, packing clothes, emptying cupboards, both absorbed in the inner heart of the dark crystal, and as yet not conscious of separation.

In April of 1941, as I lay on the pitch-dark deck of a caique nosing past Matapan towards Crete, I found myself thinking back to that green rain upon a white balcony, in the shadow of Albania; thinking of it with a regret so luxurious and so deep that it did not stir the emotions at all. Seen through the transforming lens of memory the past seemed so enchanted that even thought would be unworthy of it. We never speak of it, having escaped: the house in ruins, the little black cutter smashed. I think only that the shrine with the three black cypresses and the tiny rock-pool where we bathed must still be left. Visited by the lowland summer mists the trembling landscape must still lie throughout the long afternoons, glowing and altering like a Chinese water-colour where the light of the sky leaks in. But can all these hastily written pages ever re-create more than a fraction of it?

IX

Appendix for Travellers

KARAGHIOSIS
(see Chapter IV)

'C'est à Karakouche, ministre de Salah Edine, que revient l'honneur d'avoir fait édifier la Citadelle. Il proposa en 1176 la construction d'un château ou le sultan pourrait loger. . . . Karakouche, plus communément connu sous le nom de Karaguez, avait fait détruire les petites pyramides de Gizeh et de Sakkara et employait leurs pierres a bâtir les remparts des édifices. Il s'était rendu très impopulaire par les nombreuses véxations qu'il avait fait subir au peuple pour lui permettre de réaliser les travaux d'utilité publique qu'il avait en vue. C'est pourquoi certains, pour se venger, commencèrent a brandir des fantoches a son image, auxquels ils donnèrent son nom. Ainsi, Karaguez entrait dans le tourbillon d'une brillante carrière de pitre qui jusqu'aujourd'hui amuse les foules sur les place publiques.'—
G. ZANANIRI, *l'Egypte et l'Equilibre du Levant au Moyen Age.*

SOME PEASANT REMEDIES IN COMMON USE AGAINST DISEASE

1. *For all Fevers.* Infusion of the plant called Pharmakouli (a type of Erythrea, perhaps E. Centaurea).
2. *Kidney Troubles.* Infusion of plantain leaves (Plantago coronopus).
3. *Earache.* The brown silk with which the pinna shell fixes itself to the ocean bed, is said by sailors to be excellent in cases of earache. The ear is plugged with the silk.
4. *Stings, Bites.* Garlic or onion applied to the wound.
5. *Scorpion Bite.* A living scorpion dissolved in a bottle of olive oil, provides a remedy against the bites of other scorpions. Lotion applied externally.

6. *Dysentery or Diarrhoea.* A small bottle of beetroot juice (about 50 cc.) is corked and placed in the heart of an uncooked loaf of bread. The bread is baked and the bottle removed. The medicine is drunk in small quantities on successive days until symptoms cease.

7. *Open Wounds.* Infusion of cypress-cones used to dress wounds.

8. *Malaria.* The efficacy of quinine is supposed to be increased if taken with a little urine from an unweaned baby.

9. *Open wounds.* Cobwebs or cigarette-tobacco used to stanch flow of blood.

10. *Coughs, Colds.* Infusion of mallow flower.

11. *Indigestion.* Infusion of mint leaves and flowers used for flatulence, indigestion and all minor stomach disorders; often mixed with infusion of orange blossom.

12. *Piles.* Water from boiled onions applied in the form of hot fomentations.

13. *Seasickness.* Suck a lemon.

14. *The Evil Eye.* Blue stone amulet, price 3 drachmae. Worn by all horses and most motor-cars.

15. *Werwolves.* Garlic fixes both werwolves and witches.

16. *Rats.* An excellent rat poison is made by pounding the centre of asphodel bulbs and mixing with a little ordinary cheese.

17. *Warts.* Rub on juice of milk-wort.

18. *Skin eruptions and sores.* Strong infusion of Sambucco nigra used for skin trouble. Applied as poultices.

19. *Hollow teeth.* Juice of cloves on cotton wool.

Many of these peasant remedies show medical knowledge. No. 18 is particularly effective in the case of autumn sores, which are prevalent in Corfu towards the end of the year.

SYNOPTIC HISTORY OF THE ISLAND OF CORFU

B.C.

734 Island colonized by Corinth. (Town probably at Analypsis, Canoni.)

434 First sea victory in Greek history over Corinth. Took place off Lefkimi.

432 Corinthians repelled once more.

413 Corfu helps Athens in second Sicilian invasion.

373 Corfu helped by Athens beats off the Spartans under Mnasippus, who is killed.

361 Civil wars.

303 Corfu sacked by Spartan Cleonymnus.

301 Corfu sacked by Agathocles, Tyrant of Sicily.

229 Corfu conquered by Demetrius the Pharian with his Illyrian freebooters.

229 Taken by the Romans without resistance. Remains a Roman colony until A.D. 337.

A.D.

445 Raided by Vandals.

562 Raided by Goths.

733 Corfu comes under Byzantine Empire of Leo the Isaurian.

933 Raiding Slav pirates repulsed. Forts built on the hill near the town from which the island is supposed to get its name.

1032 Corfu raided by Barbary pirates who are destroyed by the Byzantines.

1080 Corfu conquered by Robert Guiscard, King of Sicily.

1149 Retaken by Byzantines after long siege.

1185 Retaken by Sicilians.

1191 Retaken by Byzantines.

1199 Corfu raided and taken by Genoese under Vetrano.

1203 Retaken by Byzantines.

1205 Conquered by the Venetians, who are however driven out by Vetrano.

1206 Vetrano defeated by Venetians and hanged.

1214 Corfu seized by Michael Douca, Despot of Epirus, who builds Castle of St. Angelo at Paleocastrizza.

1259 Helen, daughter of Michael II, receives the island as a dowry on her marriage with Manfred of Sicily.

1266 Manfred killed in battle. Island seized by Philip Cinardo for himself.

1266 Cinardo murdered.

1267 Island passes to Charles D'Anjou, King of Sicily and Naples.

1286 Island raided by Villaraut.

1292 Island raided by Roger Doria.

1303 Island raided by Catalans under Roger de Flor.

Appendix for Travellers

1373 Island raided by Jacques de Baux.

1382–6 Island passes to Charles D'Anjou II, on whose death the Anjou dynasty ends. At this time the first Jews came to Corfu.

1386 Corfu asks Venetians to take over the island.

1403 Island raided by the Genoese.

1431 Turks under Ali Bey are repulsed.

1537 First great siege by the Turks; 25,000 land at Gouvia and ravage the island throughout August, failing however to take the town. Abandon island in September carrying off 20,000 hostages into slavery.

1571 Don Juan of Austria wins victory of Lepanto over Turks. 1,500 Corfiot sailors in the battle.

1577–9 Town-walls built.

1716 Second great Turkish siege; 33,000 Turks land at Gouvia and Ypso. Repulsed before the town with great slaughter by John Schulemberg, an Austrian general in Venetian employ.

1797 Corfu with Ionian islands taken by French.

1799 French driven out by mixed Russo-Turkish force.

1807 Corfu returned to French by Treaty of Tilsit.

1814 Ionian Islands taken over by British.

1864 Corfu ce ed to Greece.

1923 Shelled and occupied by Italians for two months.

1940 Italian attack on Greece. Corfu used as target ground for Italian Air Force. Town almost completely destroyed.

1941 April. Entry of Germans into Athens.

1944 Battle between Germans and Italians for possession of island. Latest reports indicate starvation rife; town badly damaged; Jews deported; but Church of St. Spiridion still standing.

'During the worst part of the shelling, when the inhabitants were ordered to take refuge in the stoutly built Italian school, a very large number preferred to trust in the Saint, and his Church was crowded with worshippers, who to-day claim yet another miracle; for while the Italian school and other refuges like it were hit repeatedly and demolished, the Church of St. Spiridion was untouched and those in it emerged unscathed. To-day it is still proudly standing (December 1945).'

Appendix for Travellers

PLACES TO SEE

Canoni, Gastouri, Paleocastrizza, Pantocratoras, Benitza.

THINGS TO VISIT

Churches of St. Spiridion and St. Theodora (the Cathedral).
Monasteries of Myrtiotissa, Paleocastrizza, Pantocratoras.
Byzantine Church of St. Jason and Sosipater.
Library of Venetian MSS. and rare first editions.
Mother of Gorgons—beautiful stone relief in Museum.
Two old forts.

FOR SURREALISTS

The Achilleion. A monstrous building surrounded by gimcrack sculptures and lovely gardens belonging to the late Kaiser.
The Theatre. Shadowing the final end of the Italian operatic sense.

FOR HUNTERS

Two brackish lakes, one in the north of the island and one in the
south, called respectively Antiniotissa and Korissia.

DRINKS TO TRY

Ouzo (Οὔζο). Aniseed drink, taken with water. Resembling Arabic
zibib and French pernod. Fairly strong intoxicant.
Raki (Ῥακί). Distilled from raisins. Alcoholic.
Salepi (Σαλέπι). Tea made from bulbs. Excellent. Swamp orchis
provides the bulbs.
Retsina (Ρετσίνα). Resinated wine. Turpentine flavour. Very good
with meals but not for solitary drinking or parties.
Mastika (Μαστίχα). Mastic liquor.

DISHES TO EXPERIMENT WITH

Whitebait fried with lemon. Ask for 'Marides' (Μαρίδες).
Pipe fish fried with rice. Ask for 'Vellanida' (βελλανίδα).

Cuttle fish with sauce. Ask for 'soupya' (Σουπειά).

Octopus with sauce. Ask for 'Ochtapodi' (Χταπόδι).

Meat or mince cooked in vine leaves. Ask for 'Dolmades' (Ντολμάδες).

Ionian Meat Balls, highly spiced. Ask for 'Kephtaydes' (Κεφτέδες).

Macaroni Pie. Ask for 'Pastischada' (Παστιτσάδα).

Red Mullet grilled. Ask for 'Barbouni' (Μπαρπούνι).

Fried Egg-plant. Ask for 'Melitzanes' (Μελιτσάνες).

Spitted meat. Delicious. Ask for 'Souvlakhia' (Σουβλάκια).

Ionian Welsh Rarebit. Ask for 'Saganaki' (Σαγανάκι).

Roasted Pinna shells.

Sole. Ask for 'Glosa' (Γλῶσσα).

(Crayfish is called Astacos ('Ἀστακὸς').

SWEETS TO TRY

Sesame sweet. White flaky blocks made from sesame, honey, and crushed almonds. Ask for 'Halva' (Χαλβὰ).

Yaourti. A sort of junket of curdled milk sprinkled with cinnamon (Γιαοῦρτι).

Waffles. Ball-shaped waffles of flour with honey. Ask for 'Loukoumades' (Λουκουμάδες).

Zante nougat. Sweetmeat called mandolato.

Pasteli. An ordinary nougat.

Other sweetmeats: Trigono, Kadaïfi, Baklava, Galactobouri.

BEST VILLAGE FESTIVALS

Gastouri; Kastellani; Analypsis; Pantocratoras; Kassopi.

BEST LOCAL WINES ON THE MARKET

Provata red and white; Lavranos red; Theotoki white wine.

Excellent private cellars can be breached at Aphra, Lakones, and Ypso.

Brief Bibliography in English

Henry Jervis White-Jervis, *History of the island of Corfu and of the Republic of the Ionian Islands.*

S. Atkinson, *An Artist in Corfu* (1911).

Viscount Kirkwall, 'Four Years in the Ionian'.

William Goodisson, A.B., *A historical and topographical Essay upon the islands of Corfu, etc.* (1822).

D. T. Anstead, *The Ionian Islands* (1863).

Index

Index

REFLECTIONS
ON A
MARINE VENUS

a companion to
the landscape of Rhodes
by
LAWRENCE DURRELL

Acknowledgements

I should like to express my thanks to the F.E.R.T. Institute of Rhodes where, through the kindness of Professor G. Morriconi, I was able to study the history of the island, and make use of the invaluable library. I am indebted to the same institution for permission to reproduce the illustrations to this book. I am also grateful to my friend Dr. Raymond Mills for permission to quote from an interesting paper on peasant remedies which he wrote during our stay on Rhodes and to Mrs. Anne Ridler for her help in editing an overgrown MS.

Contents

Illustrations

Reflections
on a
Marine Venus

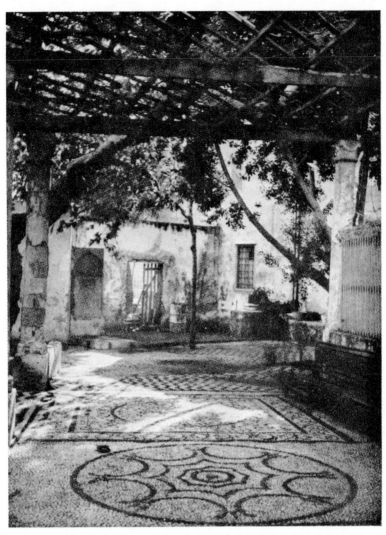

The tomb of Murad Reis and Haçmet; the garden of the Villa Cleobolus

CHAPTER I

Of Paradise Terrestre

Alvarez fled; and after him the doom
Of exile was sent out; he, as report
Was bold to voice, retired himself to Rhodes
         MIDDLETON: *The Spanish Gipsy*

———————— ❦❖❦ ————————

S omewhere among the note-books of Gideon I once found a
list of diseases as yet unclassified by medical science, and among
these there occurred the word *Islomania*, which was described as
a rare but by no means unknown affliction of spirit. There are
people, Gideon used to say, by way of explanation, who find islands
somehow irresistible. The mere knowledge that they are on an
island, a little world surrounded by the sea, fills them with an indescribable intoxication. These born 'islomanes', he used to add, are
the direct descendants of the Atlanteans, and it is towards the lost
Atlantis that their subconscious yearns throughout their island life. . . .
I forget the other details. But like all Gideon's theories it was an
ingenious one. I recall how bitterly it was debated by candle-light
in the Villa Cleobolus until the moon went down on the debate, and
until Gideon's contentions were muffled in his yawns: until Hoyle
began to tap his spectacles upon the thumbnail of his left hand, which
was his way of starting to say goodnight: until Mehmet Bay, in the
house across the oleander-grove, banged his shutters together as a protest against the lateness of the hour. Yet the word stuck; and though
Hoyle refused its application to any but Aegean islands, while Sand
could not bring himself to look a theory so irrational in the eye, we
all of us, by tacit admission, knew ourselves to be 'islomanes'.

This book is by intention a sort of anatomy of islomania, with all its formal defects of inconsequence and shapelessness: of conversations begun and left hanging in the air: of journeys planned and never undertaken: of notes and studies put together against books unwritten.... It is to be dedicated to the resident goddess of a Greek island—Rhodes. I should like, if possible, to recall some part of those golden years, whose ghosts still rise up and afflict me whenever I catch sight of a letter with a Greek stamp on it, or whenever, in some remote port of the world, I happen upon a derelict tanker flying the Aegean blue-and-white.

In Rhodes the days drop as softly as fruit from trees. Some belong to the dazzling ages of Cleobolus and the tyrants, some to the gloomy Tiberius, some to the Crusaders. They follow each other in scales and modes too quickly almost to be captured in the nets of form. Only by a strict submission to the laws of inconsequence can one ever write about an island—as an islomane, that is. And then who could ever hope to pin down, to circumscribe, the charms of a resident Goddess? I have not attempted to cut down below the surface of my subjects' poses. I have attempted to illumine a single man by a single phrase, and to leave him where he sits embedded in the slow flux of Grecian days, undisturbed by literary artifice—as a good host should. ... Gideon with his monocle screwed in sitting soberly before a bottle of *mastika*; Hoyle winding his enormous watch; Mills talking; Sand sucking his pipe; Egon Huber walking the deserted beaches hunting for scraps of wood to carve; and the dark-eyed E, whose shadow is somehow spread over all these—a familiar, a critic, a lover—E putting on a flowered frock in the studio mirror with her black hair ruffled. I have tried not to disturb them in the little eternities of their island life, where somehow their spirits mingle and join that of the Marine Venus standing in her little stone cell at the Museum like a challenge from a life infinitely more remote. If I have sacrificed form it is for something better, sifting into the material now some old notes from a forgotten scrap-book, now a letter: all the quotidian stuff which might give a common reader the feeling of life lived in a historic present.

That spring afternoon of 1945 when the order to embark came through to us in Alexandria, my first glimpse of Gideon, I remember, was not reassuring. We were to be fellow-passengers aboard a military HDML—a vessel whose sleek and powerful lines suggested to my innocent eyes speedy and comfortable travel. We were promised an early morning landfall in Rhodes. In a few hours, then, I should find myself, after some four years of exile, on a Greek island once more.

Gideon stood among a cluster of engineers and seamen, abstractedly reading a book. I recall thinking to myself that he looked the personification of orthodoxy: the monocle, the clipped silver hair, the polished boots. . . . (An Indian Army regular whose knowledge of routine has placed him at the head of a sub-department devoted to sanitation or supply?) If I were to spend twenty-four hours in his company, I thought, I should undoubtedly spend them in politely deferring to judgements based on popular prejudice, or the *naif* self-regard of a regular soldier who has come to regard his regimental mess as the whole wide world. His rather obvious glass eye regarded the world from time to time with what seemed to me to be a somewhat boorish indifference—an impression which was strengthened when I saw him accept without thanks a comfortable chair and a cushion. The rest of us lay about his feet upon cushions improvised out of our kit. He was followed by a little black and white terrier, obviously very well trained.

On one point, however, my mind was soon set at rest. The panting of the great engines as they drove us storming across the oily waters of Alexandria towards the open sea made it quite clear that conversation would be an impossibility. We were each of us to be sealed up in the great throbbing privacy of sound. I cannot say I was unhappy. There was so much to think about, so much to hope for, in the idea of seeing Greece again. I thought of all the letters I had received in recent months—letters with an obituary flavour. 'You will find it completely changed' said one. 'The old life has gone forever' said another. 'Go to America' urged a third. Tomorrow I should see for myself whether the old Greek ambience had survived the war, whether it was still a reality based in the landscape and the people—or whether we had simply invented it for ourselves in the old days, living comfortably on foreign exchange, patronising reality with our fancies and making bad literature from them. Tomorrow I should know whether I must relegate my feelings about Greece to the dusty corners of memory along with so many other mad vagaries of the heart.

As we rounded the old fort I turned back to catch a last glimpse of E standing and waving to me from the corner of the esplanade before the mist began to settle and the whole scimitar-like sweep of minarets and belfries of the upper town dissolved in soft pearl and gold. Egypt and Greece—for a moment the conflicting loyalties of love and habit assailed me. But E was following me to Rhodes after an interval of weeks: and she was my only tie with Egypt. I saw her enter the old office car, and watched it move slowly off in the murk. The journey had begun!

Ten miles off Alexandria we were still carving up a solid brown trench in the waters of the open sea—waters polluted by the dense Nilotic silt—when a solitary dolphin struck surface and galloped alongside us for a moment; my heart rose at the augury, for the fish is a bringer of fair weather and luck. I leaned to follow it with my eye when, with the suddenness of an axe falling, we hit the pure Mediterranean blueness of the true Aegean: a sea with depth and tone, that swallowed and gave back the sky; a sea that belonged to the waterless islands and grey windmills, to the olive-trees and the statues. At long last we had burst through the misty curtain of atmosphere that lies forever over Mareotis.

The sun was slowly setting, lumbering down into the Underworld, My fellow-passengers had, for the greater part, fallen asleep. Gideon alone sat awake over his book, tapping away an occasional yawn with a long index finger and caressing his dog. The crew came up and distributed mugs of service tea. If you leaned to the rail now and stared down into the water you had the impression that we were flying; the flared bows of the HSL were lifted high as she drove her coarse furrow through the still sea. The snarling of the great engines wrapped us all in a deaf silence—a marvellous brutal music of vibrating steel and wood. Behind us we left great stains of oily heat upon the waters and a white cicatrice which slowly healed again. The warmth of the coarse sweet tea was delightful; it reminded one that night was falling, and that the cold was slowly settling in from the west. Presently I too lay down and drifted into a shallow sleep from which all this noise seemed to be like the placid roaring in some coloured sea-shell picked up on the warm beaches of Corfu or Delos in those happy years before the war. It was as if my longing to be back in Greece had all but exhausted itself in fulfilment. I was numbed. Forgotten scenes came into my mind, without form or coherence, yet bathed in the sunny lambency of the Greek past, and even in my sleep I felt something like the absurd disposition to tears with which I last saw the shores of Crete fade into the mists of 1941.

The storm which caught us some eighty miles off Alexandria had been described in the weather report as 'a slight squall'. It seemed nothing so negligible. Indeed the first impact suggested something like the eruption of a volcano. The HDML hit the first wave with a prodigious slap that jolted every bone in our bodies. Such weather would have been bad enough in an island *caieque,* but in a craft which could not throttle down to less than fifteen knots without making leeway, its effect was indescribable. I awoke to see the Aegean heaped up around us in glossy valleys, lit by the yellowish glare of the ship's lamps. The even snarling of the engines was now punctuated by a regular series of sobs and grunts and by the horrible grinding of the screws as they were lifted clear of purchase.

In later days Gideon was used to say (when asked how first we had met) that we had been thrown together. He enjoyed the literal as well as the figurative aspects of the phrase far more, I am sure, than either of us enjoyed the storm which first introduced us to each other. But thrown together we certainly were. At the first impact of wind and water the ship began the butting, goring motion we were to learn so well. The noise of the screws before they buried themselves in the sea once more suggested the noise of a giant grinding his teeth. Hurled into a corner, I found Gideon's head in my lap, and my legs round the neck of a soldier. We lip-read each others' apologies and disengaged as gracefully as we could—only to be flung down once more in a heap. It was impossible to stand upright; it was rather more than difficult to manage to stay in one place. Throttled down as far as she would go the HDML skidded along the surface of the sea with the waves breaking over her in a series of stabbing white concussions. We braced our feet firmly and listened to the dull whacking of the hull against the water, and the dismal sound of crockery being

19

smashed in the galley. From this time forward we lived on all-fours, crouching like apes whenever we wished to move about the ship. Sleep became an impossibility. The terrific slap of every wave was like a punch to the solar plexus. The little dog retreated with a world-weary air to the furthest end of an empty kit-bag where it curled up and slept.

Several people began to be picturesquely sick. Gideon and I retreated in opposite corners like spiders and contemplated this weakness on the part of our fellow-passengers with a disgust so identical that we were forced to smile, catching each other's eye. I saw that he had smashed his monocle. Unbuttoning his jacket he pulled out a cigar-case containing, as far as I could judge, some twenty replacements, and inserted one.

The dawn came up as thick as glue; westward the sky had taken on the colour of oiled steel. The storm had passed over us, leaving behind it only a heavy sea propped up in an endless succession of watery slabs. The prow of the HDML still buried itself in the waves with feverish crunchings and tremblings. Some of us slept, and later by the watery beams of the early sun, were able to extend the limits of our visibility as far as a horizon dipping and swelling—but offering as yet no trace of land.

The passengers lay about upon piles of disordered kit, for all the world like corpses on pyres, waiting for torches to set them alight. As the daylight advanced a few of the hardier souls took courage and stuck out their pallid and unshaven faces to ask questions of the crew. Where were we? When would we arrive? The army showed a disinclination to discuss the question. Indeed it looked as if they knew as little as we did. We had been blown off our course. Speculation which at first seemed academic, began to be ever so slightly tinged with alarm, as we caught sight of the captain poring over a chart of the Eastern Mediterranean. The cook distributed mugs of cocoa over which the problem was discussed from every angle. Gideon, I discovered, was reading an account of Aegean travel published in the eighties of the last century by an eccentric divine, the Rev. Fanshawe Tozer, whose writings were to amuse and delight us so much afterwards. He passed me this work with the opening paragraph heavily scored by his thumbnail, and made a grimace as he did so. I took it and read: '*There is an element of excitement attending a voyage to Rhodes arising from the uncertainty which exists with regard to reaching that island.*' The Rev. Tozer then had shared many of our present misgivings in the early eighties. I hoped sincerely that this passage was not to prove an augury. It seemed a positively ominous quotation to stumble upon at this time and place.

Later we shared some mouldy rounds of sandwich and a bottle of Cyprus cognac which I had had the forethought to bring with me; and finally, inspired by the warmth of the sun and a calmer patch of weather we left the dumb-show in which our politeness had been so far continued (the wind and rain plus the noise of the engines precluding any more civilized exchange) and fell to words: single words carefully shouted across the intervening space to form sentences.

'We'll probably touch Cyprus tonight.'

'Cyprus? Surely not.'

'What will you bet?'

'It's hundreds of miles away.'

'Bah! These Army people never do anything right.'

An officer who happened to be crawling past with that peculiar air of devout forbearance that seamen affect when they are carrying unwelcome passengers, glared at Gideon. He seemed about to say something rather forcible, but my companion had already retreated behind his book. He emerged to wrinkle his nose at the retreating back.

'Mark me,' he said, 'They could land us in Beirut without turning a hair.'

It did not seem wise to continue a conversation any further along these lines. I fell into a doze and the morning passed in a series of watery sunshines punctuated by squalls and the threshings of the sea. In the late afternoon the weather brought us its omens of approaching land—two spring turtle-doves, blown off their course, no doubt. They swerved over us and were gone in the direction of Africa.

The problem of our position had not been clarified by any official pronouncement beyond the bare admission that we were off our course. Speculation still made pretty free with place-names. Dusk closed down in a series of thin, misty rainstorms, which reduced visibility to a few hundred yards; and darkness had barely followed dusk when there was a shout which turned every head in the direction of the lighted cockpit where, above the great illuminated dials of the dashboard the rubber windscreen-wipers bored circles of clarity in the pervading murk of that sottish dusk. Someone had spotted land—the merest etching of darkness upon darkness—and for an hour we thundered along a black and rocky coast, catching fitful glimpses of its capes and cliffs through the shifting packets of mist. To add to the rising emotions of optimism and relief came the pleasant sensation of a calmer sea. We began to reassemble our dispersed possessions and comb our sticky hair. I could taste the sharp brine which had dried on the unshaven stubble of my lips. Gideon traced the parting of his silver hair with something like complacence, and then examined the cavities in his teeth. He seemed to approve of what he saw. Then he offered me his comb. 'You see,' he said, 'it will turn out to be Cyprus.'

It turned out to be Rhodes. We rounded several more headlands before an officer came aft and told us so. As if endowed with powers of human understanding Gideon's little dog (its name turned out to be Homer) emerged from its hideout and began to tidy itself up. 'That's the stuff' said its master.

Vague lights now appeared and the note of the engines mellowed and sank in tone. Dark slabs of harbour masonry wallowed and glittered against the street-lights as we nosed slowly in. All that could be seen of the famous harbour was a small area of some fifty square yards lighted by some makeshift method to guide shipping. The rest was blackness which swallowed up the cracked masonry, the steel pickets and the rusty barbed wire which covered the whole of the waterfront. Absolute blackness otherwise.

The silence that now fell with the extinguishing of the great engines was almost greater in volume than the sound to which we had accustomed ourselves for so long. People still shouted deafly at one another. Space had swollen again to its customary dimensions. We landed in the murk. The yawing and pitching of the ship had given us all a trembling muscular reflex movement of thigh and shoulder—so that we walked like old salts in a musical comedy. Our passes were collected by a tired-looking naval officer who motioned us with a vague gesture of his arm towards the outer darkness. Shouldering our packs we stumbled off towards the transit hotel down a dark street lined with rustling trees, I broke a leaf off and crumpled it in my fingers to inhale the sweet odour of eucalyptus oil. At the end of the long corridor of darkness two tall gates rose up, and behind them the once famous *Albergo della Rosa,* showing here and there a point of light, weak and diffuse. The steps seemed endless—it was like climbing into the sky. . . .

But already as I write the weariness of that late arrival begins to melt the clear outlines of the detail. I vaguely remember the vast entrance hall littered with shed equipment, the buzz of conversation from the dining-hall which served as a mess, the smashed marquetry panels of the lounge, and the timid Italians who serviced the hotel. I remember too the draughts of pure sea air that stole in from the terrace, bearing with them the scent of spring flowers, and the desire for sleep which struggled against the urge to walk into the garden and smell the darkness which stretched away across the straits to Anatolia. But it was no good: the journey had been too much for us.

We lay upon adjacent sofas in the gaunt lounge with its foggy mirrors, waiting for our rooms to be prepared by a sleepy maid with a hare-lip. I remember Gideon lying there, his monocle almost touching the floor—it had rolled out of his eye to the end of its cord: his feet clad in a pair of much-darned socks: his whole body slack and unstrung: snoring.

So we slept.

Much later we were awoken, and blind with sleep followed the clerk to our rooms. The open windows gave directly on to the sea whose melodious sighing was the perfect accompaniment to a landfall as felicitous as a Greek island: to a sleep as blankly anonymous as that which welled up around us.

I speak for myself. Some centuries later (or was it back: had one travelled backwards into sleep like history?) I woke to feel the warm early sun in my eyes, reflecting the running dazzle of water from the white roof of the room. Gideon was already standing on the balcony, clad only in a monocle and a towel, doing his exercises with the rapt devotion of a yogi, watched by his little dog.

Presently we scrambled across the garden, and still half drugged with sleep, burst into the Aegean water, clear and cold as wine.

Before us across the straits the Anatolian mountains glowed, each one a precious stone. Icy though the water was we stayed awhile in it, speechless with gratitude—rubbed by the salt until our skins felt as cold and smooth as the pebbles which tesselated the shining floors of that magnificent beach.

To the memory of that first bathe I should add the memory of that first breakfast (mere bully beef and dry biscuit) eaten in the company of our fellows at the long trestle-tables which filled the once fashionable dining-room. Both were commonplaces no doubt—but translated into miracles by the feeling that, after all, we had arrived. The morning fairly danced and sparkled. Outside the hotel (whose desolate corridors, chipped marquetry, smashed fittings and marble cornices suggested nothing so much as a carnival which had ended in an earthquake)—outside, the blue race of the sea swirled round the stone lighthouse and deployed crisply across what must be one of the finest shingle beaches in the world. The sunlight freckled the foreground of things with blue and gold, while the gaunt backcloth of Caria, only tipped as yet with sunshine, seemed to be softly sifting itself through a spectrum. Utter peace.

'Heavens, I feel well,' said Gideon. We had carried our third cup of tea out on to the terrace, and were full of the warmth and well-being of that spring sunshine.

Idling there upon that terrace we first began our exploration of each other. My own task here was prosaic enough. I had been accredited to the occupying forces as an Information Officer. Gideon's own business was more obscure; he made several mumbling attempts to describe it. Finally he squared his shoulders and produced a crumpled movement order which he handed me to read. I could see nothing very strange about it. It informed me that Captain A. Gideon was proceeding to Palermo via Rhodes on duty. 'You don't see anything odd about it?' he said with a chuckle, and with a touch of fatuous if innocent pride. 'Neither did the provost-marshal.' He beamed at me and explained. He had long ago noticed that the legend 'will proceed from X to Y' on a movement order was sufficiently well-spaced to allow him to insert the word 'via' followed by the name of any little corner of the globe that he might wish to visit. He had spent a good part of the war travelling unwillingly *from X to Y*—but always *via*

24

somewhere or other where he really wanted to go. 'It's my form of revolt' he said coyly. 'For Godsake don't tell a soul.' I promised gravely. 'You've no idea what a difference it makes to go from one hellish place to another when you can go and spend a few days "in transit" in a place you really like.' Rhodes, I gathered from subsequent conversation, was an old love, first visited before 1914 war; more than that, Gideon was hoping to find himself a billet in the administration which would enable him to escape from an O.C. he detested in Palermo. He seemed quite confident that a few days of lobbying in Rhodes would produce something suitable. Behind the idea of a transfer, too, lay another—more deeply cherished: he intended to settle in Rhodes after demobilisation. This was interesting. We were, it seemed, both islomanes.

It was in this context that we began to share reminiscences of the pre-war world and unearth common friends. Gideon too had been a tramp in the Eastern Mediterranean before the war: had lived in Athens and Alexandria.

His figure was undergoing a transformation in my eyes. It was to suffer many others, but none so radical as this first one, from that of the average sightless soldier to the man of culture and comparatively wide reading. One element only was missing from the picture. I supply it from subsequent experiences. I had no idea what an old rogue he was. I was taken in by that air of benevolence, of courtly gentleness. I was tempted to shake my head sadly over the innocence of a man who imagined he could cadge himself a job after a few days in Rhodes. How wrong I was! I realised it a month later when I glanced at a circular which named him the newly-arrived director of —Agriculture, of all things. But none of this could I have foreseen that spring morning as we walked down to the harbour to pay our respects to the military rulers of the twelve islands. I was not to foresee Gideon's numberless state visits in his broken-down old car— visits undertaken with the greatest urgency to consult me upon a Point of Style, or an infinitive that had somehow split like a string-bean in the heat of composition. Nor could I foresee how much pleasure I was to derive 'putting some style' into those fatuous concoctions titled PROGRESS REPORT ON BEET or THE WATERCRESS OUTLOOK FOR NEXT YEAR. We lavished the combined treasure of our not inconsiderable intellects on those reports. To read Gideon on Beet was a new literary experience. Everyone was pleased except the Brigadier, who pronounced Gideon's style abominable and refused to grant him his majority until he had read and studied Swift.

That morning however we made our first sortie into Rhodes town, Gideon 'en pèlerinage', as he expressed it, and I very much on duty—for I had to locate the printing-plant which was to be the greatest part of my inheritance from the Army. Rumour had it that the linotypes were buried somewhere in the castle and accordingly we set off along the sparkling water-front in the direction of the Street of the Knights, Gideon talking discursively on everything under the sun, and exclaiming with pleasure at every new sight and sound.

Taken in by the uncritical eye of a visitor the town looked lovely that morning despite the infernal wreckage of war—and there was plenty of it. Transcribed from a letter which remained unposted in the back of an old writing pad, these few lines give an impressionist view of Rhodes as I found it, 'Absolute chaos still reigns. The esplanade along Mandraccio, the ancient harbour, is studded with pill-boxes and long rows of iron staples from which grave Indian infantrymen are unwinding the barbed wire. Groups of German prisoners, still whey-coloured from starvation, are busy filling in the bomb-craters in the asphalt, dressed for the most part in shorts and forage-caps only. We have thousands of them on our hands. Clouds of violet smoke hang over Monte Smith from some disposal squad's morning offering to the Gods—exploded enemy mines. I have not had time to look at the medieval town as yet, but it looks fearfully disappointing from the harbour with its spattered administrative buildings and truncated statuary: the old walled town looks like a wedding-cake with all the icing chipped and cracked. A deserted market-place. An empty mosque. A very few white-faced civilians picking over garbage-tins for food. Most of the population has fled to the islands of Symi and Casos. The streets are empty of all but troops and forage-gangs of German prisoners.'

Less impressionistic, but as factually relevant to this first view of the island which I was to come to love so much, were extracts from a report which no doubt still lies mouldering somewhere among the archives of a department in Cairo, whose representative I was then. 'The position in the capital is very far from normal. Most of the population has fled leaving behind them shattered buildings and a gutted market. Those who remain have suffered from the prevailing starvation. Malnutrition cases are coming in at the rate of sixty a day. All public services are at a standstill; the buses were put out of order by the Germans, the post-office deserted, and only the little news-sheets issued by the Army Propaganda Executive in two languages maintains a tenuous local distribution. The engineers have nearly completed their work, however, and it is hoped that the electric light plant will be functioning again this week. The island is stiff with mines which await the attention of the Sappers. . . .'

Civic order was indeed to be a long time coming; the restoration of postal services with the outside world, the establishment of news-papers, the patching up of shattered dwellings—upon all these was 'order' in its twentieth-century sense conditional. It is only if one has seen a town reduced by siege that one can get any feeling of how much our sense of community is founded in these small amenities. I was nearer, I realise, to Demetrius Polyorcites that June morning than I shall ever be again; I was near, I mean, to seeing something like the historic Rhodes as it must have been after the great siege, after the attack by Mithridates, after Cassius had gutted it; a Rhodes dispersed into a million fragments, waiting to be built up again.

Mandraccio Harbour ('The Sheepfold' of the Ancient Greeks) presented some odd contrasts; fully half of its surface was covered by wrecked boats and skiffs, huddled together, as if against fear of bombing—or perhaps blown gradually together by the force of frequent bombardments. In a clearer anchorage, under the fort of St Nicholas lay a number of island *caieques* in good repair—visitors no doubt which had been ferrying back refugees. They floated languidly in the sticky mirror of the harbour-water which was now viscid with oil from a German launch which lay on its side, its tanks squashed by a bomb, deep in the sludge. The whole length of the waterfront was picketed and wired with a thoroughness that left one in no doubt as to the original determination of the enemy; stakes driven into the rocky bases of the piers trailed underwater wires, while the shallows bristled with concrete blocks and underwater

defences. Shrapnel had peppered the buildings and snipped off fragments from the maudlin row of bronze Caesars with which the
Italians had thought to dignify the port area.

We sat for a while upon a cracked slab of masonry and contemplated
all this desolation as we listened to the innocent lapping of the water
along the harbour wall. Then we pursued our way across the deserted
market-place and entered the old walled town of the Crusaders,
passing by the lovely and undamaged gothic tower of St Paul. At the
spur of a gentle incline we turned into the famous Street of the
Knights at the top of which lay the Castello—that monument to bad
taste executed by the latest Italian governor. By now the hideous
archness of the restoration work was becoming fully apparent.
Gideon, who had seen the island under a kindlier dispensation, became plaintive and fretful. 'This will never do' he said reproachfully.
But there was worse to come. The Castello, perched on the marvellous spur where once the temple of Helios stood, commanding the
whole shallow spade-like tongue of land below, was in the most tasteless of traditions. Sergeant Croker led us round it, a little puzzled no
doubt by our behaviour. I do not think that the most liberal of conventions would allow me to transcribe half the oaths that Gideon
shed as we walked from room to garish room, from chapel to chapel,
corridor to corridor; wherever you turned you were greeted with
ugly statuary, tasteless hangings and tapestries, and the kind of
marquetry work that suggested the lounges of passenger steamers.
The sweep of Gideon's rage took in the Italian governor, the archi-
tects, the stonemasons, and the decorators who had shared in the
ignoble deed. He spitted them with every thrust of his outraged
forefinger. He had them dragged apart by wild horses. He pursued
their ancestors back as far as the fourth century B.C. and beyond.
Croker, the duty-sergeant, was a trifle annoyed; he had bothered to
memorise a few items about the history of the place and was anxious
to act as guide. But Gideon would not hear a word of his patter.
'My dear man,' he said testily, 'it is no good you rambling on about
it. The thing is horrible. A design for a Neapolitan ice perhaps.'

'Very good, sir.'

'Anyone who thinks it's beautiful is an idiot.'

'Very good, sir.'

'And stop repeating "Very good, sir" like a parrot.'

'Yes, sir.'

Homer followed us everywhere with a sage, judicial and disapproving air. He obviously shared Gideon's views.

Yet the views from the slitted windows, and from the parapet of the roof, were superb. The town lay below us, splashed with sunshine. Swallows and martins dipped and swerved in the warm spaces of the gardens. The tangerine-laden trees of the foreground dappled the landscape with dancing points of fire. The air was charged with all the sulphurous odours of spring. The sea was calm again and blue —bluer than any metaphor could express. 'Well, I don't know,' said Gideon propping his elbows on the warm stones and wrinkling his nose to taste that tangerine-scented wind. 'If you wanted a thesis about totalitarian art, why here it is.' The duty-sergeant looked reproachfully at the back of his head; he was a north countryman with a long sandy lugubrious face and pent-up cheek. His hair grew like a mastiff's and was trained down across a pale forehead into a sort of quiff. He kept his horny thumbs strictly in line with the seams of his trousers, his shoulders square. It was obvious that he thought us a couple of frightful highbrows.

It was in one of the cellars that we at last ran my printing-presses to earth. In an atmosphere whirling with lead fumes and dense with the noise of clacking linotypes the daily news-sheets were being put to bed under the eyes of a watchful young R.A.F. officer. Here I transacted my business as briefly as possible, chatted to the compositors in order to try and assess their professional abilities, and scribbled a few notes. I learned with relief that the presses were to be moved back to their pre-war establishment; their present gloomy location in this crypt had been a measure taken against fear of bombardment. The semi-darkness here made proof-reading and layout as exacting as invisible mending.

Later the three of us walked down the hill into the old town to try and find a glass of wine. Among the loopholes and fents of the medieval town we finally discovered a little tavern called *The Helen of Troy* where we found a glass of inferior Chianti with the distinct flavour of paraffin. As a drink it was disappointing; nevertheless it must have contained some of the right ingredients, for in the corner

of the tavern two Greek soldiers, very drunk, danced quietly together to the monotonous squibbling of a clarinet played by an old
man in a greasy turban who lay, half asleep, upon a bundle of boxes
in the corner of the shop.

We were to separate, if I remember, about our various business,
but it was here, at the Helen of Troy, that we met once more at
sunset—one of those fantastic Rhodian sunsets which have, since
medieval times, made the island so justly famed according to the
accounts of Aegean travellers. The whole *Street of the Knights* was on
fire. The houses had begun to curl up at the edges, like burning
paper, and with each sink of the sun upon the dark hill above us, the
tones of pink and yellow curdled and ran from corner to corner,
from gable to gable, until for a moment the darkening minarets of
the mosques glowed into blue ignition, like the light glancing along
a sheet of carbon paper. No longer susceptible to a beauty become
familiar, the dark shades of the refugees moved among their bombed
houses, their voices clear and shrill as they lit lamps, or disposed
their tattered furniture against the evening, shrilly chaffering. Gideon
was holding a glass of some rosy wine up to the red light of the sky,
as if he were trying to imprison the last rays of the sunset within it.
'Where by association' he said 'would Homer get an adjective like
rosy-fingered from—unless he had experienced a Rhodian sunset?
Look!' And indeed in that weird light his fingers, seen through the
wine, trembled pink as coral against the lambent sky. 'I no longer
doubt that Rhodes was Homer's birthplace,' he added gravely. I
could see that he was a trifle drunk. He motioned me impressively
to sit and imitate him, and for a while we examined our own
fingers through our glasses before solemnly drinking a toast to
Homer. ('Not you, you fool' he said to the dog.) For one moment
now the whole street trembled with the unearthly light of a stage
fiction, and then the darkness slid down from the hill. 'A stained-
glass window shattered by a grenade.'

We walked arm in arm down those narrow unlit streets, losing our
way once or twice, until we stumbled upon the squat gate of St Paul,
and sneaked through its shadow into the twentieth century. A few
sporadic points of light shone in the new town, but the street-lighting
had not yet been restored and we walked in a deep calm darkness as

the first stars began to take shape upon the evening sky. It was now, I remember, that we stumbled upon the little garden which encircles the Mosque of Murad Reis—a garden at whose heart I was later to find the Villa Cleobolus; and here we sat for a while perched upon Turkish tombstones, smoking and enjoying the darkness which had now (spring was advanced) an almost touchable smoothness, the silkiness of old velours. And here, I realise, we were very close to the spirit of old Hoyle—for later it was in this garden that he took the deepest pleasure, lying out on the star-scattered grass to smoke his cigars, or dozing away the long golden afternoons in a deck-chair. Hoyle has not put in an appearance as yet, though it is high time he was introduced, for seen across the false perspectives of memory it seems as if somehow we had already met him. Gideon, it is true, had known him years before; they were of the same generation. But his arrival in Rhodes post-dated this first week of Rhodian exploration by something like a month. He had been British Consul in Rhodes and was coming back. Apart from the printing equipment bequeathed to me by the administration there were a number of other articles which were reputed to belong to the late consul—a series of musty consular tables and code-books, together with some old tin trunks. These we had carefully stacked in the cellar which held our stocks of captured newsprint, where they were a perpetual obstruction to everyone. We were always bruising our shins on them. We had fallen into the habit of kicking the trunks viciously whenever we had any work in this particular cellar, and Hoyle became by extension in our imagination as tedious and obstructive an individual as his personal possessions were to the staff of the newspaper. It was with relief, then, that I heard of his arrival one morning. He was, they told me, even at that moment examining his jettisoned possessions in the cellar. I hastened to present myself to him, and there ensued a meeting for which he, I think, was as little prepared as I. He was standing in the cellar clad in fragments of his consular uniform, an ancient dress hat on his head, gazing with myopic disgust through the wrong end of an ancient telescope. The floor was piled ankle-deep with fantastic objects, both consular and personal. I remember a string of signal-flags, numberless cipher-keys, volumes of birth-certificates, a top-hat, a bird-cage, the remains of a consular uniform, detective stories,

31

a sextant, a film projector, several tennis racquets, and heaven only knows what else. Hoyle looked for all the world like a startled puppy. He dropped the telescope and sheepishly removed the hat. 'Extraordinary', he said, 'the sort of junk a grown man can collect around him'. I agreed. We introduced ourselves with a certain constraint. For my part I was dying to laugh, and Hoyle looked a trifle sheepish. He picked up a fencing foil and fell to making idle passes in the air as we talked.

Hoyle was small and rotund, with a large head and luminous eye. His manner at first suggested affectation because he had a curious slurring way of talking, and a way of varying the register of his voice from treble to bass, which gave one the impression that he was being swung back and forth in a see-saw as he talked. To this he added a mannerism which strengthened the impression—that of sawing the air with the index finger of his right hand, and marking the periods of his sentences with full stops, poked, as it were, in the air. Later I was to discover that his conversation was manufactured for him by a mind which valued exactitude above all things, and a heart which had never outgrown some of the delightful shyness of childhood. But one might easily have been deceived by his slowness of utterance into thinking that it implied slowness of thought. Quite the contrary. Ideas came so fast to Hoyle that his eyes were suddenly irradiated with light; it was the mechanism of exact expression that caused him to halt to grope for the right word, and never to be satisfied with it. Coupled with this slowness of speech was a slowness of gait which also took some time to interpret. Hoyle walked with such exaggerated slowness, with such a sleepy air, that one might have been forgiven the sin of describing him as a slothful man. Here again one would be wrong. A weak heart which needed constant care was the reason for this octogenarian's gait. But what was remarkable was the manner in which his intellect had used this physical defect for its own use. A man who cannot walk fifty yards without a rest might be forgiven if he were fretful of his infirmity. Hoyle was as equable and unruffled as a child; but since he must pause and rest after every little exertion, he had developed an eye for the minutiae of life which all of us lacked. Forced to stand for ten seconds until his heart slowed down, Hoyle would notice a particular flower growing by the road, an inscription

View of the Grand Harbour with the now destroyed Tour de Naillac on the left. Taken from Choiseul-Gouffier (1782)

hidden in some doorway which had escaped us, a slight architectural deviation from accepted style. Life for him was delightful in its anomalies, and no walk was possible with Hoyle without a thousand such observations which none of us could have made for ourselves. Gideon was always fond of explaining that he took a 'bird's-eye' view of life; by the same token one might describe Hoyle's eye as being microscopic in its attention to particularities. 'I wonder,' he would say, 'why the Mufti's shoes are too small? I saw him limping today.' Or 'I wonder why in Rhodes they tie up their cats with string. I saw one attached to a front door-knob this morning'.[1] Gideon used to explode with mock-exasperation at the preposterous frivolity of such observations. 'Really Hoyle,' he would say, 'I don't know where you get it all from.' Hoyle's answer never varied in tone or content. 'I was standing having one of my little rests,' he would say, 'and I distinctly noticed him limping.' Admirable Hoyle!

Among his other qualities was the gift of tongues. In the course of his long consular career he had mastered some nine languages, and the greater part of his life was spent in studying comparative linguistics with the nine fat dictionaries he carried about with him in a tin despatch case. Gideon had an imitation of Hoyle which Hoyle himself very much enjoyed hearing. It turned upon this point, for when a conversation began in Greek or Turkish it was not long before Hoyle's eye lit with professional zeal, and he exclaimed: 'Yes, now that's an odd word, when you think of it. It very much resembles the Turkish "*duff*" the Arabic "*fluff*" and, come to think of it, the Persian "*huff, puff* or *snuff*".' And out would come his pencil and his notebook. Whether the mountain of notes which Hoyle carried about with him all over the world will ever be refined and pruned into a thesis is another question. My own feeling is that it has become too much of a life-passion. What would Hoyle do if he had no great bundle of MSS to play with: to add to, to subtract from, to rearrange, to reconsider, to prune, to shape? He would probably die. Nor, for that matter do I ever hope to see printed his great prose anthology

---

[1] During the siege nearly all the cats of Rhodes were eaten by the starving, and this was later to result in a plague of rats which was only conquered by the import of cat-reinforcements from Cyprus. At this time pets who were valued were carefully tied up.

compiled from the writings of consuls and entitled 'A Home From Home', which contains much good material—the fruit of unhurried choice, of considered opinion ripened in the smoke of many a fine cigar; material from writers so dissimilar as Sir Richard Burton and James Elroy Flecker.

But here I shall permit myself a further digression in time from that hulk of Turkish masonry upon which Gideon and I sat together during that early nightfall: a digression from that garden-graveyard whose guardian, the Mufti, we were soon to meet. I should mention Mills, the young doctor who was later to be placed in charge of the medical service on the island. I do not remember how first we met—it was simply as if he had always been there. I do, however, remember an early occasion in our association when Gideon, for some reason best known to himself, decided that he was developing appendicitis and telephoned for him. (I was later to discover that excessive self-indulgence in food or drink always produced in my friend a form of guilty stomach-ache which lent itself to diagnosis as appendicitis.)

Mills drove about his vast parish in an absurd little Italian sports car with enormous exhaust-pipes and a bonnet held down by straps of prodigious size. He was in build short: in character voluble: in colouring blond as a kingcup. His medical equipment, loosely rolled in a piece of oilcloth that looked as if it had once held wrenches and spanners, bulged in the pocket of the blue seaman's pea-jacket which he wore when he was on duty. It would be difficult to think of any-one who seemed to be such a walking certificate for good health; it simply oozed from him, from his candid face, fresh complexion, sensitive fingers. It took him a very short time to discover little beyond an overworked liver wrong with Gideon. 'Old man,' he said, 'You have been flogging your liver. I shall send you a bottle of castor oil and a lemon.' Gideon's face showed a mixture of feelings; relief that his malaise was not serious combined with annoyance that it did not merit sufficient attention. 'You've hardly examined me yet' he said rather testily. Mills drank a glass of wine and regarded his subject with a steady and equable humour. 'What can I tell you that you don't know?' he said at last. 'Smoking and drinking are your two diseases. Cut them out and you'll live forever.' 'Thank you' said Gideon stiffly, struggling into his bush-jacket. 'No trouble at all,' said

Mills. He rolled his stethoscope up into the oilskin pouch, finished his wine. 'Well,' he said, 'we shall meet again': and he was gone.

Hoyle once said: 'Mills switches himself on and off like a light'— and this was an apt enough description of him, for I have never known him spend more than two minutes in one place, nor five minutes with the same patient. Yet somehow he escaped the charge of carelessness or thoughtlessness, for Mills conveyed a feeling of perception and penetration which remained with his patients long after he himself had vanished down the road in his small car, swerving about like a drunken hornet. His diagnosis of disease seemed somehow to be a criticism, not of the functioning of one specific organ, but of the whole man. Like all born healers he had realised, without formulating the idea, that disease has its roots in a faulty metaphysic, in a way of life. And the patient who took him a cyst to lance or a wheezing lung to think about, was always disturbed by the deliberate careful scrutiny of those clear blue eyes. One felt slightly ashamed of being ill in the presence of Mills. It was as if, staring at you as you stood there, he were waiting for you to justify your illness, to deliver yourself in some way of the hidden causes of it. But over and above his skill, the breadth of his intellectual curiosity and humanity were qualities which added richness and colour to our island society. He was by upbringing a Quaker. He had married a delightful Greek girl who had been his chief nurse in the U.N.R.A. unit to which he had been attached before joining the civil administration. They lived in a small flat upon the seashore, whose rooms were crowded with miscellaneous material for all the studies Mills intended to make of people and things outside the immediate limits of his own skill. Once inside the ever-open front door one stumbled over boxes full of geological specimens, of ancient pottery, of sea-shells. Every time a window opened manuscripts of essays on poetry, on sex, on biochemistry, on Elizabethan music were scattered in the air. His wife found him a delightful trial. I still hear her grumbling musical tones protesting: '*Mais voyons, chéri,*' as he proposed some new field of study—such as the guitar, or the clarinet. '*Ça, alors,*' his wife would groan. '*Soyez raisonnable.*' But Mills did not believe in reducing his enthusiasm to normal proportions; there was so much energy to be got rid of, life was so short. . . . I can hear him protesting in his fluent

French and Greek. And when he had left the room to bring you his microscope slides to see, Chloe would shrug her shoulders and allow herself to smile as she said: '*Comme il est bizarre, lui. Mais dites-moi— est-ce qu'il est un vrai Anglais?*' Like all Mediterraneans she had been brought up to believe that the hall-mark of the true Englishman is an unfathomable reserve. Mills seemed more like an Italian in his bursts of enthusiasm. And listening to him sing his Greek folk-songs to the guitar she would shake her head and sigh—for surely Englishmen didn't sing in foreign languages with so much feeling? And certainly no true Englishman lost his temper, as Mills sometimes did, and threw himself with gusto into a domestic row? This, then, was Mills, and he was part of it all: indeed from points of view this is more his book than mine, since it is he who decreed the shape of it. I remember him sitting in the Villa Cleobolus one dark winter evening, roasting chestnuts before the fire, while Chloe (after her fifth attempt to make him take her home) had kicked off her shoes and gone to sleep on the sofa—I remember him repeating in his clear voice: 'I do so hope you'll write a book about the island sometime when you feel like it. I don't feel Gideon's history will ever get written somehow, nor Hoyle's study of the dialect: but it needs a book. Not history or myth —but landscape and atmosphere somehow. "A companion" is the sort of idea. You ought to try for the landscape—and even these queer months of transition from desolation to normality.' I do not remember what I answered. I realise now that he was pleading for some sort of effective monument to all the charm and grace of our stay there in Rhodes; the golden sun-washed months which only Hoyle has been left there to enjoy while the rest of us have been scattered about the earth by our several professions and that conspicuous ill-luck which, as Gideon used to say, always afflicts islomanes when they have discovered the island of their heart's desire. In the pauses of the conversation the sea roared upon the deserted beach and the wind whistled in the pines and oleanders of the garden. 'Above all,' Mills is saying, as the chestnuts burst in a series of muffled explosions on their bed of soft wood-ash, 'Above all, introduce your main characters right away. Give the reader a chance to see if he likes them. It's only fair. So he can close the book if he doesn't. That's how you should begin.'

36

There is only one portrait I shrink from—that of the Marine Venus. If the reader should ever visit her in her little cell he would know why. The presiding genius of a place or an epoch may be named, but she may not be properly described. Yet the Venus, when she was raised that sunny morning from the damp crypt in which she had lain hidden; when the packing-case which held her had been broken open: when the pulleys finally raised her out of the darkness, slowly twisting on the end of her cable—why, which of us could fail to recognise the presiding genius of the place? ('A statue of a woman: period uncertain: found at the bottom of Rhodes harbour: damaged by sea-water.') I can still see the faces of my friends as they surrounded the dark trap-door out of which she rose so gravely into the sunlight. Hoyle and Gideon sitting astride a plank; Egon Huber, who had helped to bury her, smiling with pleasure to see her undamaged: while Mills and Sergeant Croker and a collection of barefoot urchins grunted and groaned on the ropes which were raising her.

She rose as if foamborn, turning that elegant body slowly from side to side, as if bowing to her audience. The sea-water had sucked at her for centuries till she was like some white stone jujube, with hardly a feature sharp as the burin must originally have left it. Yet such was the grace of her composition—the slender neck and breasts on that richly modelled torso, the supple line of arm and thigh—that the absence of firm outline only lent her a soft and confusing grace. Instead of sharp classical features she had been given something infinitely more adolescent, unformed. The ripeness of her body was offset by the face, not of a Greek matron, but of a young girl. We carried her, swaddled in sacking, down the Museum corridors, up a staircase, to the little room in which you will find her today. It is an ugly enough stone cabin—and chosen for her by a man who had some silly theory that she was too damaged to look beautiful except from certain angles; hence the theatrical north light which plays up the fine modelling of her back and throws those innocent features into dark relief. But in a little while your eyes will have accustomed themselves to the consuming darkness of the room, and you will be able to trace them with your finger, the cold lip and eyebrow, the stone tresses. It is as if she were made of wax: had been passed very rapidly across a flame intense enough to blunt her features, yet not

37

materially to alter them; she has surrendered her original maturity for a rediscovered youth.

The fishermen dragged her up one afternoon in their nets. It seemed to them to be a rich catch; but it was only a heavy marble figure of a Marine Venus, tangled in weeds, and with a few startled fish leaping like silver coins about her placid white countenance with its sightless eyes.

She sits in the Museum of the island now, focused intently upon her own inner life, gravely meditating upon the works of time. So long as we are in this place we shall not be free from her; it is as if our thoughts must be forever stained by some of her own dark illumination—the preoccupation of a stone woman inherited from a past whose greatest hopes and ideals fell to ruins. Behind and through her the whole idea of Greece glows sadly, like some broken capital, like the shattered pieces of a graceful jar, like the torso of a statue to hope.

CHAPTER II

Orientations in Sunlight

From the windows of my office I can overlook some of the twist-ed streets and warrens of the old town. It is an admirable point of vantage from which to look down unobserved upon the conversations and quarrels of the Greeks. At mid-day I caught sight of a small procession consisting of a mother and father followed by two little children and a miscellaneous body of relations. The father walked at the head, carrying an ikon of the Virgin from which hung down a little lighted lamp. They were moving house, it seemed. The man walked with calm circumspection, shielding the flame of the lamp with his right hand lest a gust of wind should put it out and thus prejudice the luck of the new house. Slowly and anxiously the little procession turned a corner and was gone. Watching the serious faces of the children I found myself hoping that the family ikon would arrive safely at the doorway of the new house, and that the happy augury would help them build their luck confidently next year against the bitter trials of the world to come. Surely, I thought, history as chronology is woefully misleading; for the history of a place, dispersed by time, lives on in fable, gesture, intonation, raw habit. No text-book can capture it fully. Here in Rhodes, for ex-ample, one runs across songs left behind by the Crusaders, living on side by side with a belief in a fresh-water Goddess whose antiquity stretches back beyond Plato.

The Aegean is still waiting for its painter—waiting with all the unselfconscious purity of its lights and forms for someone to go really mad over it with a loaded paint-brush. Looking down upon it from the sentinel's tower at Castello, from the ancient temple at

Lindos, you begin to paint it for yourself in words. Cerulean sky touched with white cirrus—such fleece as grows between the horns of nine-day goatlets, or on the cocoons of silkworms; viridian to peacock-tail green where the sea threshes itself out against the cliffs. Prismatic explosion of waves against the blue sky, crushing out their shivering packets of colour, and then the hissing black intake of the water going back. The billiard-green patch edged with violet that splashes the sea below Lindos. The strange nacreous bones of cliff at Castello. But to paint Greece one would have to do more than play with a few colours. Other problems: how to convey the chalky whiteness of the limestone, the chalk-dust that comes off the columns on to one's fingers, the soft pollen-like bloom on the ancient vases which makes so many of them seen like great plums of pure light. And when you had done all this you would still have to master the queer putty-mauve, putty-grey tones of the island rock—rock that seems to be slowly cooling lava. An impossible task when all is said and done. It is pleasanter not to try, but to lie dozing in the shade and watch Gideon working away on squared paper with his little child's paintbox. He stops whistling only to swear and shake his fist at Anatolia which is manifestly eluding him. 'I nearly had it in this one' he says. The paint-box was a present intended for his daughter; but one day, cooped up in a transit-camp he decided to try the colours out. He has graduated via railway-trains and one-dimensional drawings of houses and cows to sedate little water-colours of the landscapes he has visited. Some are quite good; but though I offer to buy them he refuses. 'This is my diary,' he says.

My patrimony has finally been decided upon. I am to inherit three linotypes, a mass of assorted hand-type, and all the greasy junk that goes with a printing house; apart, I mean, from the thirty or so devils who keep the machinery running. Later a Government printer is to be appointed who will take over the staff work and leave me free to be simply and solely an editor. But for the time I am playing the part of peacemaker, lawgiver and minor oracle to this large mixed staff. Italians, Greeks and Turks must be made to work amicably together. Did I say amicably? The rows we have sweep the whole building like thunderstorms. It is, however, the ideal laboratory for a study of national character. The Turk one very soon begins to know; slow,

shy, mole-like and very suspicious he goes about his work with circumspection, doing it grain by grain. In our Italians one sees at once
the large florid feminine sense of decoration, the innate taste, the
desire to please. But the Greek is a terrible fellow. Mercuric, noisy,
voluble and proud—was there ever such a conjunction of qualities
locked in a human breast? Only the Irishman could match him for
intractability, for rowdy feckless generosity.

My terms of reference do not make it any easier. We are to produce
three daily papers: Greek, Italian, and Turkish.[1] The Greek editorial
staff is locked away in a room of its own where its ardours and dis-
agreements cannot be heard. Muffled by the heavy doors I hear them
blasting and bombinating all morning through. One can almost hear
their fingers flying as they argue. And all morning long there comes a
stream of visitors trying to get free advertising or to bribe the editor
to print material full of political bias. It is going to be tiresome work.

By one every day my newspapers are made up, however, and I walk
across the old town to collect Gideon from his office on the water-
front before walking home.

Now at long last E has arrived from Egypt with the rest of the
office staff and enough domestic luggage to enable me to start thinking in terms of a house. It hardly seems fair when she will have to stay
on in the great hotel herself; but the air and the scenery of the island
are enough to compensate her for the prospect of six months in a bed
sitting-room. For years now I have been trying to describe Aegean
scenery to her, but I have always been aware of a suspicious look in
her eye as she listened. It was obvious that she suspected me of poetic
licence. Now she is speechless with it all, and like a woman she says:
'But why didn't you tell me it was so marvellous?' 'I tried to. You
wouldn't believe me.' Sitting under the great plane-tree on the walls
of the fort we dawdle away our afternoons watching the windmills
turning against the blue sky and listening to thin bored cries of the
fruit-vendors in the market stretched out at our feet.

The little Swedish tanker on which she travelled ran into bad
weather and was forced to lie up in Carpathos for a week. She could
not have had a happier introduction to Aegean Greece, for Carpathos
is as pure in contour as a primitive sculpture. The little *pointilliste*

---

[1] *Chronos*, the Greek daily still exists.

harbour with its vivid houses is later work—Seurat plus abandon. After Egypt with its swarming vermin, its population of Apes in nightgowns, its dirt, disease, and truncated beggars on trolleys, Carpathos must have seemed preciously close to Paradise in this spring weather. She spent her days bathing, and lying in an almond-grove near the sea where the village children gathered round her and sang her their songs. Being an Alexandrian she speaks fairly good Greek, and so found herself at home. She has brought with her a couple of Carpathos songs which Mills will soon be singing. One has a delightful chorus:

> 'O sweet lemon tree, with lemons up
> When will you lean and lemon me?'

Lemons are identified with breasts in the popular literature, and this is supposed to be sung by a young girl. By the same token 'olive' in poetry stands as a symbol for the mole upon the dark face or arm of a girl.

This morning the blazing sunlight gives a promise of the coming summer; but a promise which could only take in those to whom the calendar means nothing. E swears that in the plane-tree she heard the first tentative strokes of the cicada; but by lunch-time the sirocco had started up and the clouds were pouring down over the islands and piling up upon the Anatolian hills. Night came tearfully on through a rainbow of watered silk touching Smyrna at the further end. The peasants say of rainbows, that when one crosses over a carob-tree it dries it: and that the wood of the tree becomes deep-scented and pleasant. They put, adds the tale, this wood into their clothes-chests to make them smell nice and to keep the moths away.

I am told by Hoyle that in some parts of the island a rainbow is known as 'Helen's Cord' because, say the peasants, a great queen hung herself with a rainbow from a tree. Is this perhaps one of those curious survivals which delight him so much to unearth? According to one ancient source when Troy fell Helen was driven out by her step-sons and took refuge in Rhodes where Polyxo hanged her from a tree to avenge the death of Tlepolemos in the Trojan War. Torr has already noted the tree-cult of Helen Dendritis in Rhodes during ancient times. The reader must draw his own conclusions. Yet the line of descent seems clear enough. As for Tlepolemos, he enjoyed the posthumous honours of a hero, but there is no record which tells us where his temple stood.

Our circle of acquaintance has widened to include Sand, the newly arrived director of antiquities, and Egon Huber, an Austrian potter who has lived here for some fifteen years and has been responsible for much of the lovely Icarus pottery turned out during the Italian dispensation. Sand is dour and Scotch, with a gibbous face, and the pleasantest turn of humour imaginable. Huber, by contrast, is a born solitary, tall, fair-haired, and living in a state of perpetual and melancholy detachment from this world of wars and conquests. Fourteen years ago he was washed up in Rhodes during a storm. He had been trying to travel from Venice to Alexandria in a canoe. The island pleased him and he stayed, while the Italian governor, who had been appealing to Rome for an expert in pottery for years past, suddenly heard that God had answered his prayers, and had provided him with a penniless and talented Austrian needing some form of subsistence beyond the ikons he was doing for the churches. Huber lives now in a little Martello tower much ruined by damp and neglect. How he avoided having to join the German Army is a miracle—yet he did it, on a series of ridiculous technicalities which only a long Levantine experience could have helped him to think up. He works in desultory fashion at the ruined workshop outside the town where in the past his world-famous pottery brought him tourists in their thousands and where shortage of clay has reduced him to poverty. No word of complaint ever passes his lips, however, for he is one of the aristocrats of the spirit—the poor artist who wishes for nothing but a chance to create.

Gradually the town-characters have begun to assert themselves, to fill out with detail the idiosyncrasies of their various personalities. Emerging to the notice first as people encountered daily in the street, the outlines of character and habit follow. From thence it is only a step to the essential details—for everyone knows them: the subject is married or unmarried, has collaborated or has not, is rich or poor. So, gradually Rhodes becomes people by living people: Mehmet Bey, Manoli the net-maker, Baron Baedeker, and Christ. Characters in the order of their appearance, as they say.

Mehmet is my neighbour. He lives across the oleander grove, beyond the tombs, in a little house of his own. Every morning he salutes the dawn by flinging wide his wooden shutters and expectorating with marvellous precision upon one or other of the white Leghorns which run about the wired enclosure outside the house. Then he creaks down the stairs, growling at his wife for being a slowcoach, and emerges languidly into the sunshine to stretch and light a cigarette. He is a tall, heavily built man with a pale skin and the lazy dark eyes which betray his Turkish ancestry. He wears the blue skirt and high boots of the Cretan mountaineers, but it is as if his courage (or his resources) had failed him at this point, for he tops off the costume with a white shirt and a soiled handkerchief knotted at his throat. His general manner accords with this appearance of lackadaisical piracy. He wanders round the town on a series of small errands, shambling like an unhorsed gaucho, to emerge in the garden towards noon carrying a pair of trussed chickens, a wire box of quail, a handful of parsley, a honeycomb—or some other such item of domestic concern. It is always a bargain, and he gives the impression of having made no effort to achieve his triumph. It is as if, on awakening in the morning, a sixth sense told him immediately into which quarter of the town he must plunge to secure the day's meal. Twice a week he slaughters a chicken with hideous expertness on a block, standing with the bloodstained chopper in his hand, and a cigarette in the corner of his mouth, to watch the headless corpse run bubbling and coughing round the yard until it falls in a heap.

Once a month Mehmet disappears on what is a technically forbidden journey—to Turkey. Nobody knows how he goes or how he returns; but after an absence of some ten days he returns with a cargo of contraband which he distributes to agents in the town at something like the speed of light.

The theory is that he runs his cargo ashore somewhere near Trianda and loads it on to mules. He then joins the dawn caravan of mules which bring the country produce into the markets of the town. I hear him softly crunching along the gravel paths to his house in the early morning; he taps at the door and calls hoarsely. Sometimes he is dragging something heavy along the ground. I shall be sorry if he is caught, as the fines are enormous for smuggling.

But Mehmet is remarkable for other things; in the town he is regarded with reverence as a man who, born very rich, dissipated three fortunes by sheer joyful improvidence. He was also the last Turk on Rhodes to have a harem, says rumour. 'Complètement épuisé, ce type-là,' said the Baron Baedeker the other day, setting down his 'expresso' to jerk a thumb in the direction of Mehmet, who was shambling gravely across the square, led by that unerring sixth sense, towards a sucking-pig or a goose.

Sirocco again—a huge white-capped sea racing away for Anatolia, to dash itself in pieces on the headlands, buried in smoke. 'All poetry,' says V, 'partakes of the epitaph. Even the Epithalamium participates in the death of joy.' It is perhaps a gloomy view. I think of an epitaph scrawled in charcoal above a niche in the catacombs of Rome: a niche containing the bones of a Christian martyr. *Clementia tortured, dead sleeps: will arise.* Ah! Give us the same power of compression, to resume life and death in poems of not more than six words!

The question of origins. . . . Gideon and I have been doing some reading in the little archaeological library which Sand has put at our disposal. I have been ploughing through the lush verbiage of Bileotti and Cottret (to whom Gideon has given the collective name of 'the Abbé Cutlet') while he has been chuckling over the primness of Torr, whose two volume account of Rhodes is perhaps the best history of them all.

Helios was the great God of Rhodes; of all the ancient names for the island, Heliousa, the Sun-friend, is perhaps the one most worth recording, for it is the Sun-God's portrait, more than any other, which emerges from the welter of myth and classical conjecture. The first inhabitants of Rhodes were his children, the Heliades. To his favourite, the nymph Rhodon, was the island bequeathed as a place to live in. The festival of Helios was yearly in September. His priest gave the name to the year. The Colossos was built in his likeness, and the coinage of the realm bore his image, while in the great yearly festival which honoured his name white or tawny lambs, white rams, white horses and red honey were offered as a sacrifice; and the wrestlers, boxers and charioteers contended for a wreath of white poplar. So famous were the festivals of Helios that neighbouring States sent both their best athletes as competitors and their diplomatic envoys. A team of four horses was sacrificed to him by casting them into the sea. This celebrated in symbolic form his daily journey across the sky, from the great submarine palace where he lived to the western darkness of Oceanus. His temple stood where now De Vecci's[1] cardboard fortress stands, and within its precincts was the famous statue of the Sun-God standing up in a chariot drawn by four steeds. Before the town of Rhodes was founded in 408 B.C. the Rhodians, who claimed Argos for their parent state, lived for the most part in the three glittering cities, named after the heroes Lindos, Ialysos, and Camiros, grandsons of Helios. There were other great towns on the island—and every year fresh evidence of forgotten sites comes to light—but these three cities alone governed the island and its colonies. With Cos and Cnidos they formed a religious league and shared a common temple on the Triopian Cape. What induced them to band together and found a fourth town more beautiful than any of the others, to which they surrendered the government of the island? Some suggest an earthquake which shattered the three cities. Was there some feeling perhaps that the site of the new town, on the spatulate north-eastern tip of the island, would offer them both the strategic use of three admirably situated harbours and an immunity against the volcanic disturbances which from ancient time have been the curse of the Sporades? We shall never know. The modern peasant version of the foundation of Rhodes is worth translating from one of the pamphlets of Vronty. 'After the great plague of horse-flies which bit everyone and died there came a great earthquake on the feast-day of St Demetrius. In the earthquake the three cities fell down so they built the new city in a better place where it would not be affected by such things.'

White bread is the great novelty of the day. The Rhodians have become positively snobbish about it, and the meanest beggar would refuse a piece of brown if it were offered to him. 'English bread' they call it. Today I saw a small gesture which pleased me and reminded me once more how deeply significant, almost biblical, is the Greek

[1] The latest Fascist governor of the island whose florid and tasteless rebuilding of monuments has all but ruined the splendid thoughtful work of Mario Largo who devoted half a lifetime to governing and beautifying Rhodes.

attitude to bread. A family party under a tree in some forlorn, bombed back-yard in the city. Grandfather, grandmother and three small noisy children were eating bread and garlic. As I passed them a piece of bread fell to the ground. The old man picked it up, saying in the kind of voice one would use to a child: 'Come up with you, little English breadlet, then,' and kissed it before he put it back into the grubby hand of his grandson. The staff of life!

It is inevitable that we should, in the course of our reading and arguing, rub up against the question of the rose of Rhodes. Is it a rose? Egon Huber has taken some clay squeezes of the device with which the Rhodian manufacturer, in ancient times, sealed and guaranteed his little flasks of oil, wine or scent. In many cases the flower is a pomegranate-blossom. Huber himself is of the opinion that the true 'rose' of Rhodes is a hibiscus. A German archaeologist who visited him during the war told him so. Certainly the hibiscus is everywhere: the three prevailing notes are the reds of the oleander and hibiscus, and the raw massive purple of the bougainvillaea with which the Italians have drenched the modern part of the town. Nearly all the cottage gardens of the peasants, however, are picked out with the scarlet stabs of the hibiscus. Yet Cottret and Biliotti have decided upon the wild rose—somehow too modest a flower I think to symbolise an island as powerful as Rhodes was in ancient times.

In summer, says the naval handbook which Gideon has stolen from somewhere, the Etesian wind springs up to cool the edge of the heat. It hardly marks the sea, yet one will feel it, cool on the forehead and breast, dispersing the afternoon *accidie* which sets in with the noise of the cicadas. This will be called the *meltemi,* unless I am mistaken— Graeco-Turkish hybrid which chimes with 'mellow' 'melon' 'melting' and the Greek for honey, which is *meli.* That should give you a taste of its quality, for it is one of the treasures of the Aegean. In Rhodes, adds Tozer, its younger sister is a shore-wind, eagerly waited for by those who wish to cross the straits. This blows inshore till noon and then offshore until dusk. This is called the *imbat.* 'The whole region from Rhodes and Eastern Crete to Samos and Ikaria' adds the book 'continues the geological structure and configurations of South-West Anatolia'. The poetry of precise observation! We are, then, only part of the rim of a volcano, the Aegean. 'Much of the foothills have been submerged, leaving only the mountains above water. Great heights and depths are thus produced. The sea is 10,600 feet deep east of Rhodes, with Mount Atabyron rising 4,069 feet in height above sea level.' The naval geographer who produced the handbook was no doubt unconscious of any lyrical impulse. 'The old crystalline rocks, schists and marbles, are converted by exposure into a light sandy soil.... The massive limestones are very pure in quality.... Volcanic soils are represented by the craters of Nisiros and Patmos and the pumice gravels of Kalymnos. These usually break up easily into rich red and black soils.'

Writing poetry educates one into the nature of the game—which is humanity's profoundest activity. In their star-dances the savages try to unite their lives to those of the heavenly bodies—to mix their quotidian rhythms into those great currents which keep the wheels of the universe turning. Poetry attempts to provide much the same sort of link between the muddled inner man with his temporal pre-occupations and the uniform flow of the universe outside. Of course everyone is conscious of these impulses; but poets are the only people who do not drive them off.

Poems, like water-colours, should be left to dry properly before you alter them—six months or six hours according to the paints you use.

These reflections are the fruit of an afternoon spent alone, reading under a cypress tree on Mount Phileremo. The valley of Maritsa lay below, its soft creamy limestone carved in a million places by the winter torrents, and overgrown with shrubs until each fissure looked like a mouth half covered in a golden beard. The gaunt burnt-out skeleton of the airdrome beneath with its charred aircraft was a reminder that one was, after all, in the world; for the air of Phileremo is so rare that one might be forgiven for imagining oneself in some more successful dimension where the hero had finally mastered himself, and where the act had somehow become connected once more with the concept of love. The Hellenic fountain breathed quietly, half asleep.

Manoli sits on the sunny wharf all morning working at the tattered seines upon which he depends for a livelihood. His hands are like battered horns, blunt and dirty, yet the evolutions they perform

RHODVS.

The Fortress of Rhodes: an engraving from an unknown hand printed in a volume of 1580, some of whose pages are in Rhodes Museum

among the heavy swathes of net are as finished and delicate as those
of a lace-maker. He sings as he works, in a voice of gravel, his lips
pursed about the sail-maker's needle. He is clad in sailcloth breeches
and a coarse woollen shirt. His tangle of silver hair has been pushed
under a dirty cloth cap to which his daughter has fastened a rose with
a pin. No morning would be complete without a chat with this
fragrant old ruffian who carries in his voice, gesture, intonation, the
whole flavour of the Aegean. Manoli's feet are swollen by salt-
water, and have obviously never been cramped by shoes. He holds
his spare needles and wax between his toes. His finger-joints, too,
have been stretched and blown-up by rheumatism until they look
like sausages.

His sixty-year old body reminds me of some ancient boat, cankered
and swollen at the seams from years of sea-work; yet his heart is in
repair still, and with it that marvellous natural intelligence which
is only to be found among the semi-literate. His daughter reads the
newspaper to him. His interest in world-politics is a consuming
passion and it is wonderful how clearly he reads between the lines of
a conference or a speech to deduce at once its failure or success, its
truth or intrinsic falsity. He is a much keener judge of affairs than
his counterpart in England would be; yet a poorer judge of Greek
matter than any child—domestic Rhodian affairs, that is.

'Finland is waking up,' he says oracularly.

'Do you think they will give in to Russia?'

'Naturally.'

'I don't.'

'You are English. They never see things before they happen. The
English are very slow.'

'And what about the Greeks?'

'The Greeks are fast . . . piff . . . paff. . . . They decide.'

'But each one decides differently.'

'That is individualism.'

'But it leads to chaos.'

'We like chaos.'

'Manoli, what do you most like doing?'

'Sitting about, drinking.'

'What would you do if you became dictator of the world?'

'I should say to everybody: "*Stop. At once. We will change every-thing.*" '

'And if they did not stop?'

'Then I should cause a revolution.'

He laughs harshly at the hopelessness of the situation—the human no less than his own personal situation as a dictator. And, since he is Greek, his immediate reaction is typical. 'If I thought it hopeless I should take all the money I could steal from the Government and retire into private life.'

'And then?'

'And then the world would be exactly where it is now. At least I would not have made it any worse.'

His laughter has no cynicism in it. But he has seen enough not to nourish delusive hopes. He is not at odds with his experience; he has been forced, so to speak, to swallow it, this great weight of bitterness, to accommodate and digest it; and the process of acceptance has given him a kind of joy—a water-tight happiness which plays about his face and gestures, investing them with a strange kinetic beauty. Speaking of the E.A.M., for example, he said yesterday: 'They come to deliver us from poverty. God knows, we need that. But they will end in enslaving us with other evils. God knows, we do not want that.' His style of expression is always gravitating towards the proverb—the only literary form with which he is familiar. 'Take away my poverty but can you give me the happiness which I have in here?' touching that shaggy chest with his fist.

No. His happiness is his own work, cultivated like the tiny pot of basil in the window of his house, by patience and the bitter harmony of experience. 'But to remove poverty is something,' I say. He nods. 'It is very much. But there are many selfish people in the world. Whichever donkey it is, they will always reach the saddle.' 'But you could reach the saddle with better education, book-learning.' Manoli lights a cigarette and exhales a long voluptuous streamer into the blue. He hops about like a crow among the nets for a moment. Then he takes off his cap, sniffs the rose, and replaces it. 'Who can say what I should gain—and what I should lose?'

Who indeed?

How often have I not been into the little churchyard behind the

Mosque of Murad Reis? Then how is it that only today I saw the house which I would like to live in? It is buried in overhanging trees, and hidden in a triple circle of oleanders and rhododendrons: it consists of a tiny studio, bedroom and bathroom. That is all. A coloured table built round the trunk of a baobab-tree makes a shady dining-room. Outside the shrubbery the Turkish tomb-stones lie with the yellowish sickle-shaped eucalyptus leaves drifting over them. I stand listening to my own breathing in all that silence. The green foliage seems to blot out all the sound of passers-by upon the main-road which is quite near. It is simply a match-box of a house, but its situation is more beautiful than anything I could have imagined possible so near to the ugly hotel. It is untenanted too, for its owner has been repatriated to Italy.

'Rising Jupiter means luck in Springtime' says the horoscope which the great astrologer Moricand once cast for me in Paris. I know this is true now, for Martin, the lively and goodnatured South African major who is responsible for Rhodes, has told me that I can have the house provided the Mufti does not object to a Christian living on the edge of the Turkish churchyard. I call upon the dignitary one morn-ing on my way to work, and find him in his little courtyard paved with white and grey sea-pebbles, sipping coffee and—miracle of miracles—talking to Hoyle in Turkish. 'I did not know you knew each other' I say. Hoyle introduces me. The Mufti is a meek-mannered man dressed in elastic-sided boots, who smokes his cigarette in an ebony cigarette-holder. Typically enough he speaks not a word of Greek. I say 'typically enough' because it seems to be a characteristic of Turkish communities outside Turkey. As a nation they are the most withdrawn and the most secretive of any I have met. This does not imply either lack of spontaneity or of goodwill—they have a great measure of both. But the centuries of religious difference have given each Moslem Turk the look of a walled city. In Rhodes they live like moles behind barred windows, inside walled gardens, full of orange trees; as a community they are not divided internally as the Greeks are by petty jealousies and schisms, nor externally by a multiplicity of political interests. If you wish to know what the Turkish community thinks on any given subject you have only to ask the Mufti—for it is he who thinks for them. Yet to judge by his face as he sits now, listening to Hoyle pleading for me in his best K.C.'s manner, you would think he had the greatest difficulty in holding an idea in his head for two consecutive minutes. He wrinkles his face and pushes back his turban with the index finger of his right hand as the argument proceeds with its succession of single syllable puffs and grunts. As far as I can see Hoyle's oratorical methods are flawless. At any rate the Mufti cannot think of a single objection to his new tenant. We shake hands warmly and I make him a little speech in Greek to which he replies in Turkish. Neither of us understands the other, but we are both prompted by a sense of social propriety in the matter of compliments. Our agreement is cemented by a visit to the grave of Hascmet, the Turkish satirical poet, who lies buried in a small walled enclosure in one corner of the courtyard. The tomb is chipped and stained by rain. A goat munches and scratches round it, tethered to a dwarf eucalyptus by the wall. I put my hand to the gravestone and feel the warmth of the sun upon it. Who was Hascmet,[1] and how did he come to be exiled here, to this forgotten graveyard full of the sedate tombs of Turkish civil servants? It is an after dinner problem for Gideon to solve. But meanwhile the house is mine.

We walk back now, the three of us, across the melancholy but beautiful churchyard, pausing from time to time in the shade of the tall flowing trees as Hoyle deciphers the lettering on a tomb, or offers the Mufti a chocolate from the little silver box he always carries about with him in his pocket. Our feet crunch the crisp sickles of eucalyptus-leaf underfoot as we walk. The graveyard is in a sad state of disrepair. Many of the tombs have fallen to pieces, and in places the loose drift of leaves has half obscured others. The majority of those who lie buried here are Turkish civil servants. A few are political exiles. The gravestone records the sex of its tenant: with a heavy marble turban surmounting it, in the case of a man, and with a sort of marble pine-apple in the case of a woman. The greater dignitaries have a small vault to themselves—a sort of stone sentry-box with a domed roof and barred windows. But now with wind and weather many of the stone turbans have been blown off and lie about in the pathways like heads blown from statues. We skirt the final row of

1 He was banished for a satirical poem.

tombs and plunge into the dense thicket of oleander which hides the house. A path suddenly appears, and following it we come upon the Villa Cleobolus with its beds of tiger-lilies and the great baobab-tree which rubs its outer wall. Hoyle too has noticed the peculiar density of the silence here for he says: 'Listen', and raises his hand. We stand and listen to our own breathing. Remote, beyond the curtain of silence, the noise of quotidian traffic sounds from the road beyond. But so dense is the green that it is as if the house and garden were under a glass bell. The Mufti nods his head, as if in agreement, and blows the smoking dottle from his cigarette-holder on to the path. 'He says you will be happy here' says Hoyle.

St Constantine's Day is a day of coronation for the fig and the pomegranate; the owner of the trees pays them a special visit and crowns them with wreaths of oleander and wild marjoram. The peasants call this 'getting engaged', and the object of the ceremony is to make the trees bear. If, adds the story, the owner omits this cere-mony and does not visit his trees, they imagine him to have died and from sadness do not bear. Contemporary beliefs suggest that aspho-dels should not be picked, as this hinders the orchards from bearing.

Four little Turkish children walking hand-in-hand. The eldest, a fat-faced boy of perhaps nine, is smoking a cigarette and laying down the law. They do not see us in the shade of the olive-tree until we are practically face to face. Then they halt in confusion and turn tail. We greet them in Greek but they do not reply. We are infidels. The smallest turns her head and spits as she runs. In a moment all the horrors of Egypt rise to mind: the suffocating beastliness of Islam and all it stands for, bigotry, cruelty and ignorance. Yet here all the jagged edges of the faith have been filed away; the minarets rise above the market-place with slender grace, the call of the muezzin sounds soft and musical in the dawn-light. The patriarchal face of the Mufti in his scarlet fez and elastic-sided boots, moodily smoking a cigarette in the courtyard of the mosque and greeting the faithful. Rhodes has converted Islam and made it part of the island's green and gentle self.

Whitewash, some coloured pottery, and a few pieces of bright curtain-material have transformed the little Villa Cleobolus into as delightful a studio as one could wish for. For the last week E has been busy, diving into the Turkish quarter to buy these commodities as cheaply as possible. Now the work is done and I am at last allowed to see it. Bed, table and bookcase have been borrowed from the Custodian of Enemy Property. The pottery is a laral gift from Egon Huber. The curtains, the bright peasant rug, and the Turkish bedspread which depicts a billowy princess with eyebrows like watercolour brushes playing a lute under a pee-pul tree cost us in all ten pounds. I am absolutely speechless with happiness. So much so indeed that E thinks for a moment that I do not like it. 'Is there something wrong?' she asks. No, there is nothing wrong. But the feeling of privacy and space round one after so many years of living from suitcases and sharing flats is something one will have to get used to again; we stretch out our arms in that tiny room—as if they were antennae, exploring the free space around ourselves, turning about: sitting now in this chair, now in that. Space, light and solitude will have to be rediscovered again here, in all their ramifications. The silence seems saturated with a thousand forgotten essences: contained and held, somehow, in the bright peasant carpet, the crude warm pottery of Rhodes on which Huber has traced so lovingly these dancing figures, this silver-green olive tree, this donkey trotting along a dusty road. It is much the same feeling as comes over one when a poem forms in the mind, its outlines misty, inchoate: until the white paper on which you have scribbled a dozen words and crossed them out, blazes in your face like a searchlight and paralyses you by the multiplicity of possibilities it presents, by the silence it opposes to your inner tension.

While we are still walking about the little room the door bursts open to admit Gideon and Hoyle and a cask of red wine with which, they say, they propose to 'inaugurate' the house. It is a happy thought. We retire to the little clearing which is to be our dining-room, and set ourselves down at the coloured table which has been built around the baobab-tree. This is to be the first of many such evenings I hope—evenings spent in idle gossip and content, until the night falls and the candles are lit, and in the rosy pool they have scooped from the darkness I can see the faces of my friends: Gideon protesting so violently that his monocle falls out, Hoyle smiling his preoccupied little smiles, Mills managing to talk and laugh all in the same breath, and E with her splendid dark head propped on her arm listening to them and smiling.

Later, when they have gone, I walk about the churchyard for a while, listening to rustle of falling leaves among the tombs, and watching the moon rise slowly from the sea.

'I should have knocked perhaps; but coming silently into the darkened room of the Villa Cleobolus (the room you had taken so much trouble to furnish) I found you sleeping on the divan, one arm behind your head, your warm cheek pressed to the painted face of the Turkish lovers on the counterpane. You had been crying in your sleep, for I saw a tear on your dark lashes. It could only have been with happiness to have escaped to this island. Beside you on the bed-side table lay the unfinished letter to your parents. A sad childhood is a poor preparation for unexpected happiness. Cheer up, you have escaped. By the time you wake and read this I shall be swimming. Come and bathe before tea.'

Among the more singular inhabitants of the town is the man whom Hoyle has christened 'The Baron Baedeker'. He is to be seen wherever there is a function, a display, a procession of any kind, darting in and out of the crowd, his coat-tails flying. Over his shoulder he carries the kind of short step-ladder that shoe-salesmen use to reach their more inaccessible wares. From time to time he pauses, grounds his ladder, and climbing to the top of it leans over with a camera between his hands to take a photograph.

The Baron is a tall and finely built man, whose silver hair is cut strictly *en brosse* over his large and sheep-like head. He wears clothes reminiscent of a German diplomat of the old school—a faded frock coat, dark trousers, and a black tie knotted round a celluloid collar. His glasses are very powerful and his grey eyes swim in the pear-shaped lenses with a sweet and reproachful mildness. Whatever the crowd and whatever its size, the Baron's figure may be seen emerging from various parts of it like some strange flower, to hang for a moment by his elbows as he takes a photograph. He is festooned with cameras of different sizes. He palpitates with earnestness.

During the first few weeks of the occupation the Baron succeeded in utterly demoralising the Brigadier who was a bad public speaker. 'Every time I make a speech,' he told Gideon, 'I have only to look up and I see that obscene tulip of a man leering at me off a ladder and aiming something at me. Find out who he is and why he looks so like an U.F.A. spy, will you?'

The bulge in the Baron's hip-pocket is not, as the Brigadier surmised, caused by a gun but by a Bible. So much I discovered when he came to visit me yesterday in order to persuade me to buy some prints from him for use in the newspaper.

He is Greek, born in Asia Minor, and his real name is Panagiotis Kalopodas. He is so devout as almost to be angelic. He has practised photography for fifteen years in Rhodes and for the last ten has been the representative of the Foreign Bible Society—which perhaps accounts for the sobriety of his dress. 'I am known in Rhodes as an honourable man,' he observed once during the course of our talk, with a simplicity that was most disarming. 'Even the Germans, sir, treated me with respect.' In those clothes who could help it?

His photograph albums constitute a unique history of the island which he guards most jealously. 'One evening I shall show you them all,' he says. 'I have recorded everything—even the visit of Goebbels.'

As for the Nereids—they are the presiding spirits of these islands; almost every spring is haunted by them, and everywhere in the long verdant valleys beyond Monte Smith you will find dells and glades where the circles of daisies mark their dancing floors. They are benign spirits, fond of running water and shade; though not all their manifestations are harmless, and the superstitious fear them. All the half-witted children are supposed to have been bewitched by Nereids and woe to the man who unwittingly intrudes upon one of their dances, for they will force him to join in and dance till he drop. Once upon a time near Aphando, where the dates were supposed once to grow, and where now the fig-trees stand in their solid lowering stances, like crocodiles, heavy with fruit; in Aphando there was a shepherdess who had lately borne a child. She was on her way up the hill to her sheepfold when she came upon a group of Nereids dancing. She began to run, but they overtook her; but on her back, in her little bag, she carried the swaddling-clothes of the child, and when the Nereids touched her they recoiled, crying: 'It burns. It burns.' A Nereid could only bear a changeling.

Rodd has a chapter on Nereids which is worth reading. I understand now why the whole countryside folds up like a flower during the midday hours; why the self-respecting husbandman and townee alike prefers a carefully shuttered room to the intensity, the silence and brilliance of the southern afternoons. It is a weird time of day when everything seems to succumb to the silence—everything except the tireless cicada. It is the hour, says Rodd, when Pan takes his rest and he quotes the swain in Theocritus:

> O Shepherd, not at noon, we may not pipe at noon,
> For Pan we dread, who then comes from the chase
> Weary and takes his rest . . .

Hence the haunting fear of the tree's shade; no labourer will sleep under the shade of an old tree, or one that is supposed to have grown a spirit. For it is here in the shadows of trees, at cross-roads, by running water, that Pan's assistants, the contemporary Nereids, lie in waiting. Flash of naked bodies between the trees of Siana and the noise of the spring interrupted by the sound of drinking! Sweep of skirts as the dancers line out on the daisy-clad slopes by St Nicholas!

Christ is one of the bears. There are only six all told who merit this wonderful old printer's appellation—I suppose because the ceaseless walking back and forth, picking up and examining type, which are part and parcel of the handsetter's work, are reminiscent of a bear's movements in a cage. He is the youngest of them, but by far the quickest. A pale youth of some twenty odd years, he is dying of phthisis which has given his eyes a preternatural brilliance. He has long periods of illness, but such is his grace and charm that none of his fellows complains at the extra work his absence involves. This year he has by far exceeded the sick-leave allowance stipulated by his contract, and I have been forced to turn a blind eye to it, because Christ is supporting his mother and two younger children by his work.

But the most interesting thing about the boy is that last week he discovered himself to be a writer. The air-bag was delayed and we were short of material. I do not know how it happened, but some say the ebullient Manoli suggested scornfully that the paper would be better if the printers wrote it and the editorial staff printed it. Christ pulled out a sheef of loose galley and in ten minutes had written a column on this theme which reduced his fellow type-setters to tears. Enquiring what all the noise was about, Kostas, my Greek editor emerged from the printing-house with Christ's work which he read to me with delighted giggles. 'Good,' I said, 'Set it up.' Kostas was aghast. 'Print it?'

'We've always needed a live columnist on this moribund sheet,' I said. 'Open up a column on the left hand side of the second page. Call it 'Ο κοσμακις (a delightful expression which may be translated 'The little Man's World') Tell Christ he must fill it four times a week on any topic he likes except politics. We will pay him thirty drachmae a line.'

Kostas took this news down to the typesetting room. A pregnant hush fell. Earnest debate took place in low voices throughout the morning. It was as if the news had shocked everyone.

That afternoon work took me back to the office in time to see the first pulls come off the machine. It was a feast day, and according to custom CHRONOS was made up with a coloured head. It looked very handsome. In a dark corner by the machine stood Christ with a copy of the paper held in his trembling hands. He was speechless with pleasure. He hung his head with shame when he caught sight of me. Kostas was proof-reading the final page before roaring 'Fire' through the hatch into the machine-room.

Below us in the darkness Christ was waiting at his station (it was his duty-afternoon) to throw the switch and set the great machine in action. 'That boy has been in a dream all morning,' said Kostas. He finished vetting the last page and threw back the hatch into the printing room. 'Okay,' he said, and gave my arm a sympathetic squeeze before shouting 'Fire'.

The great grunting and swishing began below. Christ unbolted the outer door and let in the horde of urchins who were to collect and distribute the paper for us. The newborn writer stood with hanging head beside the machine, smiling to himself. He still looked dazed.

By next morning his fame had spread throughout the poor quarter in which he lived. On his way to work, Kostas told me, at least a dozen people came up to congratulate him on his article. His fellow printers receive him with the same jokes and jibes now, but there is a touch of apprehension, of respect in their attitude. There is nothing like cold print for commanding the respect of the ordinary. Christ has entered the most impoverished aristocracy in the world.

CHAPTER III

The Little Summer of Saint Demetrius

Tomorrow I am to visit my parish for the first time. On the great ordnance map which hangs above my desk I have traced and retraced the outlines of my islands until I know the distinctive shape of each of them. Rhodes might be a flint arrowhead: Cos a sperm whale: Leros an octopus: Patmos a seahorse: Symi an expended meteor rubbed smooth with air: Kalymnos a mussel.

Of their products, their climates and their inhabitants I already know a good deal, thanks to a brief but intensive period of study with the Army in Cairo. Even the tables of industrial statistics which fill the little army source-books seem to hold some undertones of magic for me with their cold hints of sponge, emery, currants and white cherries. Now I am to marry my theoretical knowledge to that of an eye-witness.

I have chosen the Little Summer of St Demetrius for the journey, counting upon its last fine days to enable me to travel as far as Leros and back on equable seas.

Symi

Moving northwards through this marvellous Aegean landscape lit by the intense white light of the sun, I feel the kick and plunge of the little island caique as she aims for Cos. The mountains sweep down into the sea, planted here like the feet of petrified elephants, to revolve slowly as we pass them, as if on some great hairy turntable. On the way to Cos you come across whole hillsides littered with debris from Maillol's studio—half-finished ankles and heads, breasts and toes. Dawn had not broken when we entered the great cobweb of stone which is Symi, so I have no clear picture of it—only a series of impressions. It lies there like a black rusk upon the water—but rock so pitted and perforated by the tongues of sea thrown out by Anatolia that you would think of it as most like some black stone lung. Everywhere the sighing and blubbering of blowholes, the sound of water breathing and snuffling in that black honeycomb. On this unpromising foundation a town was built, by an idle youngster in coloured bricks. It started up the mountain but soon tired of the gradient and dissolved into a scrabble of ruined plaster and heaps of stone which nobody will use now. A human voice launched across the noise of the water and the wind from the open sea sounds small, ant-like—as if you were to scratch upon a rubber bladder with the point of a pin. '*Kalo Taxidi*—a good journey to you. . . .'

Kalymnos

In Kalymnos the infant's paint-box has been at work again on the milky slopes of the mountain. Carefully, laboriously it has squared in a churchyard, a monastery, and lower down repeated the motif: a church, a monastery, a town; then, simply for the sake of appropriateness, a harbour with a shelf of bright craft at anchor, and the most brilliant, the most devastatingly brilliant houses. Never has one seen anything like it—the harbour revolving slowly round one as one comes in. Plane after stiff cubistic plane of pure colour. The mind runs up and down the web of vocabulary looking for a word which will do justice to it. In vain. Under the church the half-finished caieques stand upon a slip—huge coops of raw wood looking for all the world like the skeletons of dismembered whales.

Three little girls in crimson dresses stand arm in arm and watch us. The harbour liquefies under the keel as we throttle down and move towards the port, our engines now puffy and subdued, yet quickened like our heartbeats as we sit and watch the island. The echo of our passage—the hard *plam-plam-plam* of the exhaust—bounces gravely off the rusted iron hull of a steamer which lies on its side in the shallows, its funnels sticking up like nostrils, but all the rest of it submerged in water as clear as the purest white gin. This is Kalymnos.

High up, under the walls of the Church of the Golden Hand a woman is singing, slowly, emphatically, while from the wharves across the way a man in a blue overall is hammering at a coffin. Uncanny isolation of sound and object, each dissimilar, each entire to itself. Detached from the temporal frame. A song and a hammering which exist together but never mix or muddle the hard outlines of each other.

Cos

Cos is the spoiled child of the group. You know it at once, without even going ashore. It is green, luxuriant and a little dishevelled. An island that does not bother to comb its hair. Hard by the port the famous tree of Hippocrates (to which Mills has promised himself a sentimental pilgrimage) stands, in a little arbour of greenery, like some Nubian women stricken with elephantiasis. Whole trees have burst out of it in all directions, and with no reference whatsoever to gravity or proportion. The kindly worshippers have propped, here an arm, there a thigh, with votive pillars of bricks or stone. Somehow the whole improbable structure still stands—indeed its luxuriant foliage covers a whole courtyard like a tent. The children play wonderful games among the branches. 'A stranger,' they cry, 'a stranger.' I must be the first foreign civilian they have seen for some time We exchange oranges against sweets and discuss life in Cos. Everywhere it is the same—conversation revolves about food. They look ragged and thin but not actually starving. We climb the Frankish castle with its mounds of rubble and shattered ravelins. Once more one comes upon mounds of twisted and rusting steel— machine-gun ammunition and shells and empty petrol tins. There is no time to see the Aesculapium on this visit, as it lies some way outside the town, and the captain of the caieque is anxious to make Leros while the good weather holds. Our journeys must still be made in swept channels, as the whole sea hereabouts is mined, and I think he fears that bad weather might push us into one of these fields. . . .

Leros

In Leros one always seems to be weather-bound, according to the captain. It is a beastly island without any character, despite its rather noble Frankish castle and picturesque village. There is, however, no pastoral or agricultural land worth the name. Simply gigantic port installations now crumpled with bombing, and rotting away in the damp—prodigious jumbles of copper, steel and brass. The harbour is choked with sunk craft, and the little town has been very badly bombed. A miasmic gloom hangs over everything. God help those born here, one mutters, those who live here, and those who come here to die. The water is brackish—like the wits of its inhabitants. As far as I am concerned I am wholeheartedly on the side of the poet Phoclydes who used the name of Leros to throw mud at an enemy of his unlucky enough to be born here. An early example of literary mud-slinging! And 'Leros' still means dirt today. Yet weather-bound or not, there has been time to think, time to jot down some notes about poetry in the little black note-book E bought me, which is now stained with salt water and brandy. Major France, who presides over the officers' mess, is a delightful eccentric, an ex-commando who has spent many years of his life, in peace and war, travelling among these islands; in pre-war years he carried cargo in a small tramp-steamer belonging to himself, while during the war he exchanged his role for that of secret agent. Clad in rubber boots with soles a span thick, and armed with the most fearful assortment of cutlery the mind of man can devise, he travelled about cutting throats, piloting one of the tiny caieques belonging to the Sea Raiding Forces. Now he sits at the head of a hospitable table, covered in campaign medals as thick as confetti, and pines for the rigours of the Burma campaign.

In the smoky tavern whose frail walls quiver at each blast of rain and wind I spend half a day transacting business with the agent who is to handle distribution for me in Patmos and the other small islands. He is a little man whose appearance is one of extreme indigence, and of a cast of feature so terribly pessimistic that it is obvious one can hope for nothing in the way of efficient island distribution. While the Greeks have kept their language, only a very few can write it, and fewer still read it, he tells me. But that is not to say that they will not subscribe to a paper. No. He swigs tot after tot of burning mastika, settling his neck more deeply after each emergence into the collar of his ragged overcoat. People will buy the newspaper all right, but he cannot guarantee readers. Owing to the great shortage of wrapping paper, he says, almost *any* paper is welcome to the inhabitants of the island. They need it for wrapping fish in, or eggs. They need it for parcels and packages. So that my sales will be safe-guarded by this great shortage in a way that even full literacy and the keenest interest in the affairs of the world could not achieve for me. It is one of the anomalies of war that the daily newspaper which we issue at a penny is worth twopence as wrapping paper, and already in Rhodes our receipts for scrapped issues are greater than our receipts on current sales. It puts journalism in its right perspective somehow. Meanwhile I am delighted to think of the inhabitants of these atolls subscribing faithfully to my newspaper simply in order to wrap fish in it. The agent does not smile. He is beyond that. As we part he depresses his cheeks into a sort of deathmask of a smile and says: 'At any rate you know the truth now.'

The evening comes down, smudged with rain, from a sky of dirty wool. We stand at the great bay window and watch the skirls and eddies roar into the landlocked harbour and dance like maniacs in the riggings of the caieques. A loose foresail cracks and cracks like pistol shots. Above us the shattered Frankish castle stands its ground as it has done for centuries; but each year a few more bricks are pried loose and come rumbling down the hill into the main street, a few more shreds are blown off the towers. As it gets darker the sheet-lightning starts and France tries to take a photograph of us all sitting round the table playing pontoon by its blank staring stabs. By dawn, he says, it will have blown itself out and we shall be able to start for Patmos, the last island on my visiting list, and the one I most want to see.

Patmos

Just before dawn there were one or two flashes of lightning and I woke to see the hunchback standing in the dark hall, with a telephone in one hand and a lighted candle in the other. 'Hullo', he was calling in his cracked voice across the miles of water, 'Hullo there Patmos!' A thin crackling came back across the German field-telephone from the island, like the leaky discharge of a low electric current. The lightning flashed twice again—milky throbs of whiteness behind the dense clouds that covered Leros. 'The storm has lifted a little,' shouted the hunchback, grimacing with the effort of maintaining that tenuous contact. 'We are sending them over.'

Outside, I thought I could still hear the roaring of the sea and the whack-whack of the wind in the palm tree up the hill. The hunchback entered the room and placed the lighted candle beside me with the cup of tea. 'The sea is calm,' he said, and as if in sympathy with it, his own voice lost its harshness and became calm too. 'They will be here in a little while to take you.' For four days we had been marooned in Leros by the weather. I said nothing, drinking my tea and exploring the warm corners of the bed with my feet. He stood looking down at me for a moment, and then taking his squat pipe from his pocket, lighted it at the candle. 'Get up,' he said, and marched off in his creaking black boots to the kitchen.

I lay and watched the whiteness of the daylight slowly leak into the sky, outlining the black paw of cloud that lay across the town and shrouded the top of the castle. The air in the room smelt stale and used up. The high cracked ceiling, the odd-shaped windows above which hung the pelmets of mouldering brocade disturbed one by their associations: a Venetian etching. Lying here I felt that I was breathing in the desiccated air of another century; and the candle with its rosy pool of light added to the illusion. A room, you would say, in the house of an exiled Prime Minister in the reign of King Otto. The assassins entered by the window. In the far corner, where the wallpaper has faded, stood the sofa on which they laid him. . . .

The faithful E was awake, combing her dark head by the light of a candle and yawning. I sat and watched her dress eating some bread and butter, talking in whispers so as not to wake the others, who lay in odd corners of the old house, peacefully snoring. 'Do you think we can make it?' she asked from time to time, dreading heavy sea as much as I did. 'It's only three hours,' I said. 'It will be rough of course.'

I was wrong as it turned out. We heard the rapid imperative note of voices in the hall, and tip-toed down the cracking staircase, packs on our shoulders, to where they stood waiting for us. We left the house like thieves.

Beneath the darkness of the cloud the immediate foreground was wrapped in a dense ground-mist, raw and chilling. It was not raining, however, and the boatman grunted his satisfaction at the fact. 'The sea is calm,' he said, 'too calm.' We walked down the avenue of chestnuts together towards the town, listening to the chilling noise of torrents which had swollen with the rains. A flash of lightning showed us the main street which the storm had turned into a swirling black stream; then the darkness came down, ominous and complete —the darkness that comes with the closing of a camera's shutter. It is difficult to explain: for behind it, at the edges of the sky, the light advanced in degrees of dirty white. It was as if all one saw was the silhouette of the darkness itself.

We splashed through the narrow warrens of the port and emerged at last on the quay-side where the caieque lay, its crew stuck fast, it seemed, in attitude of complete apathy, awaiting us. The captain hung from a rope, leaning his body out at an angle, staring down at the water. The boy and the man sat, submerged in themselves at the tiller, their splayed bare feet among the twists of rope. They shook themselves as we whistled.

She was called 'Forgetfulness': a powerful little caieque built to the shallow-bosomed shape which the fisherfolk call 'Racers' because they are judged speedier than the normal deep-hulled models. The sea-raiding people had put a tank-engine in her which gave her about twelve knots. You felt the power at once as she fanned away from the stone-quay and out into the harbour, edging towards the black buoys which, the captain said, marked mine-fields. Huddled in our coats we watched the black, uninviting headland of rock paying out past us like a rapidly diminishing rope, drawing us nearer to the proper sea. Across the waters, from the direction of Turkey, the light had broken through in one place; a drop of red had leaked between the interstices of sea and sky, and was running round the rim of the horizon like the knife that slips along the rim of the oyster to let the light in with it. The red mingled with the black and turned it purple; the meniscus of the sea copied the tone: strengthened it: turned it green, and an edge of the sun shone for a second across the waste of waters and islands, hideous, like a head with one eye. Then the darkness again and the steady throb of the engines. The boy was posted at the prow. He strained through the mist and guided the helmsman with shouts and gestures.

65

'So we'll get to Patmos after all,' said E, unpacking the sandwiches and the little bottle of cognac.

Patmos, I thought, was more an idea than a place, more a symbol than an Island.

Yet to the boy crouching at the prow, his eyes fixed upon the mist-darkened territory ahead, it had no doubt become a name like any other, marking only a brief stony point in an oft-repeated routine, distinguished at the most by a special tavern where the wine was resinous or a house where the conversation seemed the better for a beautiful elder daughter. From time to time as he peered, he saw the shapes of islands come up on us like battleships, and with a brief wild cry—as of some trapped seabird—shook his arm to right or left, guiding us to the safety of the deeper channel. A few yards away the wet fangs of rock would emerge and slide back into their unearthly vagueness, and the note of the propeller deepen in the deeper sounding as the vellum of a drum when the player alters its tensity. Once the mist drew back for an instant and we saw, tinkling upon a scrubby headland, a swarm of sheep like gold bugs, loitering among arbutus, while on a rock commanding the prospect stood a motionless hooded figure like a janitor. Their bells were softly dumbed out in the mist, losing volume but not their richness.

The sun had somehow swindled us and climbed into heaven without once shining directly upon the water. Through a cloud-surface with a thick yellow nap like a carpet it allowed its beams to diffuse themselves over everything with a dense coppery hue, turning the water to lead beneath us. It increased our range of sight, however, and with it our speed. From where he sat at the tiller the captain made a chopping motion with his hand to indicate, in Greek fashion, the fact that we were making better time. The boy came aft and sat for a while to make conversation. Points of water glistened in his beard and hair. 'Patmos', he said, 'you will like it. All foreigners like it. They have good fruit and water.' Then raising himself the better to cup his hands about a box of English matches as he lit a cigarette he added, with a touch of medieval wonder: 'And there is a telephone. The Abbot speaks to it every day.'

'Have you ever used it?' I asked him.

'I? What for?'

The sense of blindness had now given place to a sense of headache. The atmosphere had become warmer, but the clouds still lay between us and the sun, which burned with a bilious humid intensity upon the sea. The last of the islands that lined the corridor between Leros and Patmos like ancestral totems, was kicking in our wake. Presently we should see our objective through the trembling curtain of the mist.

The captain handed over the tiller and came forward to the prow; hanging outwards he stared long and intently towards the vapourized horizon, and then came aft to consult a watch—not without a touch of pride, for it looked like German booty. We had been going two hours.

'In the channel it is often rough', said the old man. 'Praise God, it is all right. But tonight there will be more storm.'

We informed him that we had determined to return to Leros that night, and he nodded once or twice in a protective manner as he puffed his cigarette. 'And if you can't,' he said, 'there is no need to worry. There is the telephone.'

Our attention was caught by a cry from the boy who had returned to the prow. Away to the northward the mist had shifted and beyond it, gleaming in a single pencil of sunlight was a white cape—lifted like the wing of an albatross upon the very place where sky and sea met. For an instant this snowy apparition paused, and then the beam moved slowly along the mass to pick out a turret, a battlement, the cupola of a chapel. 'The monastery,' said the captain. 'Patmos.'

W stood for a long time now watching the lights playing upon the island, now touching up a dazzling pane of glass in the monastery, now extinguishing the whole seascape to the tones of a black and white drawing. The sun was trying to find a way through the clouds.

'In another half hour,' said the old captain, as if he were trying to instil patience into himself. 'In another half hour we shall be there.'

'Come,' said E, 'we should eat now.'

We had neither of us had much appetite before, but now with the still straits before us and the island in sight, we turned with real hunger to the cognac and the sandwiches. The boy boiled a kettle of water and I saw with some surprise that the whole crew had developed the habit of drinking British Army Tea, brewed sweet and strong—surely the most disgusting drink ever invented. This was a legacy of the sea-raiding days no doubt, as was the expertness of wrist with which the captain opened a tin of bully beef.

We finished eating just as the caieque fanned into the little harbour of Patmos, free from cloud at that moment, and blazing like a diamond among the hillocks.

'Welcome,' cried the figures on the quay as we tied up, and at once we felt grateful to be back in the traditional type of Greek island after the rather spurious Italianate atmosphere of Rhodes. They were all there in that little whitewashed port; you could see at a glance the representatives of the six or seven types which have furnished Greek islands since the beginning of history. The old sea-captain with his knotted hands and shaggy whiskers, the village schoolmaster in his dignity and European clothes, the mad boy who plays the violin outside the tavern door—the island poet whose wits, says tradition, have been turned by the Nereids. Their clear eyes and lovely brown skins proclaimed them islanders, born in this clear blue air; and the pleasure and warmth with which they cried 'Welcome'—and uttered among themselves the sacred word 'Strangers'—proved them as Greek as one could wish. We declined in rapid succession, a donkey, a bunch of flowers, and a conversation about how old we were, where we had come from, and what our business was. The tavern-keeper swept us a disappointed bow from the door of the tavern in the shadowy interior of which the familiar Homeric group sat round a table playing cards. We walked through the narrow main street between the smiling faces of the women, past the old date palm tree—last of many palms which earned for Patmos the name of Palmosa among the Venetians—and addressed ourselves to the bare hill whose brown rocks were still wet with the rain and noisy with overflowing torrents.

Before us, balanced against a cloud, stood the monastery, its odd arrangement of machicolated turrets and belfries reminding one of a medieval castle—such as one only sees in Russian films. The great gate stood open. One expected to see a troop of Tartar horsemen swing out of it suddenly, waving their lances and hide bucklers, uttering shrill cries; but nothing passed through the door save some small children singing an island song in tiny cracked voices, perfectly reproduced by the blue atmosphere despite the distance.

Halfway up we met a shepherd, sitting on the stone parapet crook in hand, talking to his daughter, and occasionally uttering barbaric whoops at his flock. We sat down and rested beside him, for the going was steep and hard. In exchange for the piece of bread he shyly offered us we took his photograph, while he showed a hospitable annoyance with the Patmos weather for not favouring our visit more conclusively. The ominous wrack of cloud still stretched away to the east and west of the island; while everything lay, enchanted by sunlight, in an oasis of midsummer. Even the bees in the little white hives by the monastery were duped by it.

'Are they expecting you?' asked the shepherd.

'We telephoned to the Abbot.'

'Then you will eat well,' he said comfortingly; the monastery lay about a quarter of an hour off, along the great sill of red-brown stone. The smaller monastery of St John, where the Apocalypse was written, lay beneath us with its cave of the illumination and musty banners. The three ruined windmills glimmered on the ultimate crags.

'We'll be going', I said.

'God be with you,' he responded, reluctantly, for conversation with strangers is a rare pleasure among islanders who have known each other from childhood. 'God be with you,' repeated his daughter, enchanted by her own grownupness.

We entered the great gate and found ourselves immediately in a warren of cobbled streets, each just wide enough for the passage of a loaded mule, and thrown down upon each other in a sort of labyrinth. We followed them up stairways, down alleys, round corners, doubling back upon ourselves at different levels until we found the great door of the monastery. It also stood ajar. From every nook now the prospect began to shine out, the brilliant bay and the further seas, set in the green and grey.

In the courtyard the hush was intense. The faces on the painted wooden screens glowed softly. Then from the gloom of the chapel came the thin scribbling noise of Byzantine Greek, lifted in prayer. Another voice began a humming twanging response. 'There's a service going on,' said E. Several voices now attacked the silence as if heard through a comb and paper. The faint chink of censers, the faintest whiff of incense leaked out of the darkness. I eased the heavy pack off my back and coughed twice. Immediately a servant came out of the recess under the staircase and told me my name, showing no surprise when I did not disagree. 'At once,' he said in a low, urgent voice, 'at once.' He sprang into the dark chapel like a diver into a pool and re-emerged holding the Abbot by the hand. We began our greetings, seasoning them with apologies for the interruption. The Abbot smiled in his beard and waved the latter away. 'Come,' he cried with a spontaneous good-nature, 'we have nearly finished. Come with us.' And led us by the hand into the little darkness where by now the very anna livia plurabelle of a service was going on.

They looked for all the world like benign tree-bears which had burrowed into the trunk of an old tree for honey. The deacon was humming and yawing from a muscle-bound byzantine evangel which he held against his chest. The Abbot subsided into his place, and we each fitted ourselves into those uncomfortable pews where you hang by the elbows like a bat. It was an admirable introduction, for while the utterances and responses rose and fell in the darkness, I was able to rest and let my eyes wander over the rich altar-screen with its ornaments and paintings. The only light came in through a foggy piece of glass in the dome. The darkness was restful, and I found myself inclined to doze, as the monks trotted backwards and forwards to various points of the darkness, shouting and twanging out of various books, or swinging the censers and spinning round upon themselves with predetermined smartness. One had a sense of infinite remoteness—these voices rising, it seemed, from the bottom of the sea, muffled by the mushroom-shaped dome of the monastery, muffled by the darkness, by the dense gloom.

Presently the service came to an end; facing the altar one of the deacons lifted his mouth and blew out a candle; and at once we were among friends. Six large priests, with luxurious curling beards and expressive hands. 'Praise be to God,' the Abbot said, 'at last some English we can talk to.' Later he doubtless revised his opinion of my lame Greek. But E chimed in, and under her interest and delight everybody came alight, falling naturally into that generous full-bodied loquacious amiability which is so truly Greek, as we streamed out once more into the courtyard to have the painted wood screens explained to us, and the intricacies of the corridors exhibited. In a little dark magazine behind the altar we were shown the treasures of the monastery—richly embroidered copes and stoles, a dozen different kinds of pyx, diamond-studded bindings for books.

By now the weariness of our journey was upon us, and we asked leave to rest; but this was not to be. There was the whole rambling architecture of the place to see; and then there was the fatal bait of the camera which I carried slung from my shoulder. I could see several pairs of dark eyes fixed meditatively upon it, and several pairs of dark hands beginning with an anticipatory combing-out of beards, the adjustment of black stove-pipe hats. Presently we should have to take everyone's picture.

The monastery of St John was itself as much a treasure as any of its heavily priced treasures in silk or ivory or vellum; it was a wilderness of chimneys, cupolas, belfries, turrets and dazzling white walks. Connecting battlements complement each other so you can walk from the eastern side where the island lies and study the shapes of other islands, faint as a wash drawing on the smooth surface of the sky. Leros, Icaria, Amorgos, Samos. The clouds had turned them down like wicks, but there they lay stubbornly insisting on their identity against the darkness of the horizon. 'Bad weather,' said the Abbot, learning that we intended to start back that afternoon. 'You should have stayed for a month with us.' This gave him a chance to show us the commodious quarters for guests, eight lovely whitewashed rooms, with angle-windows looking out on to the sea. I would have liked to stay for the rest of my life, but did not wish to seem fulsome in expressing so a thought which must have sprung to so many minds. 'Are you not lonely?' said E to the Abbot. The old man repeated the word once or twice, looking from one to the other of us, holding it, as it were, so far away from himself as possible, the better to see the concept which it represented. He did not answer directly. A few drops of rain fell loudly on the terrace. The rent in the cloud-scape was rapidly closing once more. Below us the harbour with its viridian borders and the pearly tones of the hill beyond, began to dissolve and fade, as the thunder opened up in the west. He led us into the library and showed us the famous manuscripts, writhing painted bestiaries and ancient scripts, pressing our shrinking fingers to the thick vellum to feel its weight and quality. When we had exhausted these treasures he allowed us to photograph him leaning in the narrow window-sill, conscious of the elegance of his beard and beautiful hands. Outside a rain of thistles had begun to descend blotting out all perspectives, and turning the whole monastery in a moment from dazzling white to soaking neutral grey. The rain stood for a moment in great drops on the lips of the bell and then ran down to the courtyard, seeking the already swollen gutters. 'We shall never get away tonight,' I muttered.

In the refectory, whose windows were lit by yellow stabs of lightning, we watched the storm slowly wheeling the clouds into formation. The islands had vanished. Strange manoeuvres were going on in the dark sky beyond which the sun still shone. We ran from window to window calling to each other to look. Through holes in the cloud long shafts of yellow light played down on the leaden sea like searchlights, circling slowly, or running the whole length of the horizon before going out. Such tense needles of light as one saw piercing the gloom of those old oil-engravings to the shilling Bible, on which the dove descended as upon a scaling ladder.

An old woman had laid out supper for three, and presently the Abbot joined us to pour out the heavy red wine into the glasses and serve us portions of the delicious chicken with lemon-rice. He seemed obscurely troubled and looked up nervously as each heartbeat of lightning lit up his bearded face. For a while we attempted a desultory conversation which could compete with the storm. Drops of water climbed down the windows. Somewhere a shutter banged again.

'It was you who telephoned?', asked the old man.

'Yes, from Leros. Major F's servant spoke to you.'

He nodded twice with something like impatience and ate another mouthful of chicken. 'So many people ring up and say they are coming,' he said. 'Some do. Others never seem to arrive.' He issued some impatient orders over his shoulder to the aged woman and began to tell us of the war. The monastery was forced to play the role of philanthropic neutral to three nations. A smile lit up his face as he told us how three separate units, Italian, German and English, had been sheltering in the monastery at the same time. 'Two of the three might have shot us,' he said. 'What could we do? An Italian signal section on the top floor, a wounded German officer whose life I saved in the granary, and six British commandos in the cellar which was their H.Q.'

It had been as difficult and dangerous a time as any he cared to remember. Naturally they were pro-British—but a monastery is a monastery. 'We could not leave the German to die outside on the hill. As for the Italians. . . .' He shrugged his shoulders.

Suddenly he turned round and said: 'And this man Anthony— why did he not come with you from Leros?' We looked at each other. 'An English Major who also rang up.' To the best of our knowledge there had been no one else in Leros intending to make the crossing; had there been he would certainly have had to ask the permission of Major F, our host. We should certainly have known. 'That's what I mean,' said the Abbot in a distressed tone. 'People are always ringing up.'

The storm had travelled over the peak and was now thrashing the palm tree in the valley. We finished the excellent chicken, and the Abbot led us slowly from room to room of the monastery, down winding corridors, up and down stairs. This was where the brothers lived. This was a reception room. This was where the conclave met to discuss ecclesiastical problems, or those connected with the admin-istration of the monastery. In one of these large echoing rooms stood the German field-telephone, a replica of the one at the mess in Leros—an ugly bakelite box with a handle and a small receiver. As the Abbot looked at it I saw an expression of disgust and anger cross his face. 'This is the telephone,' he said. The rain was pouring in at an open window, stirring the dust on the floor, and shaking the heavy red hangings by the dias. I closed the window, and we went down the corridors in single file. As we emerged upon the penultimate balcony overlooking the courtyard we heard the sound of voices. Looking over, I could see the soaked figure of our captain standing in the great door with a piece of sacking over his head. In half an hour, he shouted up at us, there would be a lull in the storm. If we chose to take advantage of it we could be back in Leros by dinner time. If not. . . .

'We have not spoken of St John,' said the Abbot. 'Of his wonderful book. You must see his church. Stay with us.' His tone changed to one of hospitable coaxing. It was very difficult to explain that, if we missed the motor-launch which was due to start for Rhodes at dawn the next day we should be stranded for a week over schedule—delightful as the idea seemed. He was sad. He had intended an exposition of the Apocalypse.

However, he helped us pack our belongings, and one by one the brothers came out of the various rooms to shake our hands and bid us goodbye. 'Come again,' they cried, 'come and stay with us. We are on the telephone, you know. You can always ring up and say you are coming. Just come any time, and stay with us as long as you like.'

We passed out through the great doorway into a blinding drizzle that thinned off as we neared the harbour; the little caieque was standing off with her engine going. It had all been timed to a second. With hardly a moment to say a breathless goodbye to the friendly loafers in the tavern we were aboard, and drawing free of the harbour towards a sea that looked foully disturbed, with whitecaps flicking the horizon.

Darkness fell before we had cleared the rough straits but we were making good time. The caieque rode superbly, her round canoe-shaped nose chopping down the head-sea. By seven, the black shapes of rocks gleamed wetly at us from either bow, and we slackened speed. Leros hung against the sky, a part of the darkness and yet separable from it if one looked carefully enough; but the middle distance was blotted out by skirls of rain. One could taste the dry salt on one's lips, feel its powdery dryness upon the throat and ear. Soon we crossed the bar and the few dim lights of the harbour bulged greasily at us. It was still raining as we disembarked and crossed the wet deserted streets towards the mess. The rain rattled like shot among the chestnuts.

In the dark hall we stood for a moment, peeling off our clothes and shouting for the hunchback, who came from the kitchen at last, bringing with him a great bar of light and the gleam of an oven.

Upstairs, the two officers were finishing dinner. It was good to sink into one of the luxurious armchairs with which the German commander of Leros had furnished his mess and sip a drink while our baths were heated up. We gave an account of our trip to our host and thanked him suitably for the use of his caieque. As we were talking the telephone in the hall began to ring. 'The damned thing,' said the young officer running downstairs to answer it. 'It's been out of order all day.' In a moment he returned and said: 'It's the Abbot. Wants to know if you are safe. Would you like to go down and do your stuff?' I picked my way down to the dark hall and picked up the ugly little receiver. Damp crepitations echoed inside the ear-piece. 'Hullo,' I called, and for a moment I heard, as if in a sea-shell, nothing but the sibilance of sea-water lashing those stony promon-tories, boiling among the shapes of volcanic stones, among the deserted quays of Patmos harbour.

'Hullo'. The Abbot's voice emerged from a criss-cross of scratch-ings and whirrings, as if from some old prewar gramophone disc. 'Your Beatitude,' I said, giving him, for good measure, what was really a patriarch's due. 'We arrived safely, thank you.' And I added compliments suitable for the occasion. The young officer came down-stairs and stood beside me as I spoke, putting a cigarette between my lips and lighting it. 'After you,' he said. The Abbot sounded squeaky and alarmed. No doubt he was unused to telephones. 'This man, Major Anthony,' I said, 'who is he? The old boy wants to know whether to prepare food for him or what.' The officer took the phone from me and began a bantering conversation with the island. 'No such person, Abbot,' he said. 'Your imagination again. No. You won't be disturbed for some time now.'

Together we walked upstairs to the lighted room where the cards had been laid out upon the table and where a sleepy E was already beginning to put her things in order against packing. Tomorrow, at dawn, the naval launch would take us back to Rhodes. Much later, when I was already in bed, listening to the whacking of the palm tree up the hill, the young officer came to say goodnight standing at the open door with a candle in his hand. We should not see him before we left. 'Is the Abbot often mistaken about visitors who ring up?' I asked on a sudden impulse.

'It's just one of those things,' he answered indifferently. 'Beastly things, these German phones.' Then he added: 'It's curious. The

Abbot always seems to be getting phone calls from this Anthony chap. I wonder who he could have been—if at all, I mean. . . . Well, goodnight.' I wondered, too. Lying in bed, tasting the luxury of the sleep which was moving toward me across the noises of the house, and the deep hushing of the wind and the rain, I suddenly thought to myself that perhaps this was a ghost which for some reason or other was destined forever to long for Patmos (which is after all a symbol of something for which we all keep a place in our hearts).

On the way home, another storm is brewing. Heading for the harbour we pass a poor wretch in a leaky boat, half-naked, setting out lobster pots. He does not even turn to watch us as our wash sets him bouncing. Through those patched rags I see the lean muscles of his arm tighten as he struggles for purchase in that crazy cockle-shell. Yet he does not even turn to curse us—and in a flash I see the Greece I love again: the naked poverty that brings joy without humiliation, the chastity and fine manners of the islanders, the schisms and treacheries of the townsmen, the thrift and jealousy of the small-holders. I see the taverns with their laurel wreaths, the lambs turning on the spit at Easter, the bearded heroes, the shattered marble statues. Eastward now lies Anatolia, its sunburnt mountains brooding under the eagles where the shepherd treads all day among myrtle and arbutus stabbed scarlet with berries. Some day I shall find the right way of dealing with it in words. . . .

The run is perfectly timed; behind us, the wrack of the coming storm, before us a dead calm bathed in afternoon sunlight. From this angle Rhodes looks unbelievably romantic. It is this entry into the harbour which I thought of when I wrote:

'If you should have the luck to approach it, as perhaps one should, through the soft yellowish tones of a June nightfall, you would undoubtedly imagine it to be some great sea-animal asleep in the water. The eastern spit of sand upon which both ancient and modern town were built shelves slowly down into the channel from the slopes of Monte Smith, so called because Sir Sidney Smith once set up his battle headquarters there. This would constitute the hump of your whale. Eastward loom the weather-worn Carian Mountains, casting shadows so dense that the sea is stained saffron by the last rays of the sun. Nestling in the natural amphitheatre where once stood the white buildings and temples of the ancient town, the Crusader fortress with its encircling walls and crumbling turrets looks for all the world like a town in pen and ink, situated upon the margins of some illuminated manuscript: the medieval dream of a fortress called Rhodes which the mist has invented for you, and which will dissolve again as you enter the little harbour of Mandraccio to anchor under the fort of St Nicholas where once, it is suggested, the Colossus stood.'

This is the entry that Gideon and I should have chosen for ourselves when we set out for Alexandria.

In Rhodes things are moving. The portentous soldiery has entrenched itself securely in the rococo building which once housed De Vecci's staff. A martial hauteur may be remarked upon many faces. Gideon has been making a few friends and many enemies—the usual proportion, as he says. 'I never could get on with haberdashers in pips and crowns,' he adds sourly. However, there are compensations. The lighting-unit for the town has been fixed, and the whole harbour cleared of enemy equipment in record time. The post office has started to work, and has been inundated with remittances from Dodecanesians all over the world. One street lamp in ten has been persuaded to light after dark. These are not small things—they are part of that unknown quantity, civilization—for the street lamp brings order, and the post office confidence. Nevertheless, Gideon says that he smells the odour of garrison life creeping over the town. This is because he hates the British Officers' Club and yet the cheapness of whisky there forces him to have his evening drink there. He is making a list of conversational gambits overheard within those august precincts. Some of them, I fear, have the air of being manufactured. We amuse ourselves in trying to guess the speaker in the cases of phrases like: 'O Fuzzy-wuzzy is a jolly decent chap when you get to know him,' and 'I found the Swahili a perfect gentleman', and 'The Greeks are perfectly bloody don't you think?'

A passage from a letter which reached Gideon yesterday from G:

'So you are in Rhodes? We landed there briefly among the first few units. I was shocked. It was simply a shell of what it had once been. Walking on the shattered sea-front in the dark I tried to reconstruct a pre-war incident whose flavour has never quite left me.

I was walking here in 1939 at that indeterminate twilight hour, after dark but before the lamps had been lit. I collided in the darkness with the soft figure of a woman. She stood before me without speaking. 'Who is it?' I said. She did not answer but softly placed a hand upon my arm, and I understood. We stood thus for a moment by the harbour wall.

'I fumbled for a box of matches and struck one, saying as I did so: "All right, if you are beautiful." The match-flame copied itself into two dark eyes: a face much older than itself—serious, beguiling, and most world-weary. We climbed the slopes of Monte Smith and lay down together in one of those rock-tombs, still warm.

'She was lean and half-starved and her clothes tasted of sea-salt. Her poverty was poignant in a way that no one who has not experienced the Mediterranean can understand. In her I tasted the whole of Greece, its sunburnt airs, dazzling bony islands, and the chaste and honourable poverty which the people has converted into a golden generosity. Her name was Aphrodite—I know! I know! She walked all day by the sea gathering firewood and sea-coal. Her husband had been a prosperous fisherman but he was now in the last stages of consumption. She made a little money as a casual. Everything that might have seemed ugly or dirty was transformed somehow by the human experience which underlay her actions; she knew the full measure of them, so to speak. It would have been unworthy of me to regret or criticise either of us. Life had been too big for her; by accepting she was conquering it. It may sound silly to philosophise over a casual encounter with a prostitute but there are lessons to be learnt from her. She had a rock-rose fastened to her shawl with a pin. When we parted she detached it and handed it to me with a magnificent friendliness. I had an inkling then that the Greeks were still the natural poets of the Levant. They understand, you know, that hunger is not proud and that the Tenth Muse is really Poverty.'

'Poverty,' mused Gideon. 'Well, I wonder.' He added that what he respected in G was his readiness to *make a place* for new experiences. 'Most of us simply cannot squeeze in a new sensation which does not conform to the established prejudices with which we have been paced. I should have been horrified—or should I?'

Hoyle lit a cigar. 'You know,' he said, 'on such a high literary level the whole incident was probably invented. Though of course that would not invalidate its essential truth.'

'Nevertheless,' said Gideon, 'I think it is true. This last passage convinces me, where he says: "Here I am, a writer, thirty-one, who cannot bring his equipment to bear upon material of this sort without running the risk of sentimentalising something which was as clear as a glass of water. If I touch it I damage it. What a dilemma." '

CHAPTER IV

The Sunny Colossus

I have profited by the absence of Hoyle and Gideon in another island of the group to assemble a few hasty notes upon the Colossus—in the manner of a man talking to himself. Mills is away also in the south of the island upon some errand of mercy. And while I miss my companions I have taken the precaution of borrowing their works of reference on Rhodes. Thus I have time at last to tackle history—that vast complex of analogies—without getting lost among the shoals and quicksands of argument and polemic. For no companion to Rhodes would be complete without a reference to the island Colossus; and yet the subject cannot be touched upon without some reference to the siege out of which it was born, and to commemorate which it was designed.

The siege itself was a colossus in kind—so that to write of the statue of the Sun-God is to write of a colossus born of a colossus: of a peace born of a war.

Demetrius (surnamed Polyorcites or 'Besieger' after this epic attempt) was the direct author of the battles and the indirect author of the statue which commemorated them. The coins, Gideon tells me, show a fleshy face and a long sensitive nose, expressing clearly the mixture of coarseness and sensibility which one reads into his character as Diodorus described it. If the motto of Cleobolus was 'nothing in excess' that of Demetrius must certainly have been 'excess in everything'; as a general he was considered a candidate for the honours of a second Alexander. He excelled in two qualities: science and lubricity. The inventive side of his genius came to full

80

flower in the giant Helepolis—a third colossus—which so nearly overpowered the defences of the Rhodians. By the time he arrived off Rhodes in 305 B.C. he was already at the height of his powers as a soldier. He had thrashed Ptolemy and Cassander in summary fashion, and was a claimant for the empire which Alexander had left to fall to pieces after his death—an empire disintegrating under the attacks of many claimants like a jelly-fish stranded on the beaches of Time.

The causes of the war were as follows: Antigonus, the father of Demetrius, had solicited an alliance with Rhodes against the Egyptian Ptolemy; this had been refused by the Rhodians on perfectly logical grounds. Their trade with Alexandria played too large a part in the economy of the island to be surrendered at the whim of a predatory old tyrant.

Rhodes, at this time, could afford to decide for herself. Her history, like that of England, might have been summed up in the words sea-power, gold and neutrality. Both by geography and temperament Rhodes lay just ouside the storm-centres of trouble, and at every turn in her ancient history she took advantage of the fact. Where possible she reserved judgment and trusted in a fleet so powerful and skilful that it was famous in ancient times as the mythical colossus is in modern. The Rhodian sailor was famous for his courage and daring. Ἡμεῖς δεκα ῾Ρόδιοι δέκα νῆες they said of themselves— 'Ten Rhodians, ten ships'. For a great trading-station lying upon the main routes of the Aegean there was no other course. But here and there this enviable neutrality was broken. A choice was forced upon the peaceable Rhodians. Always they chose with an eye to the main chance: their one objective was to retain their independence. They did not always manage to do so: Artemisia, Cassius, are fateful names among those who broke the spell, and there were others. . . . So that the news of Demetrius' arrival off the coast of Rhodes must have been received with mixed feelings. The Rhodians had sought no quarrel with him; indeed they continued to treat for peace right up to the moment of embarkation, and even voted a public statue to Antigonus in the hope that flattery would do what policy had failed to do; but it was in vain. Demetrius had been sent to teach them a lesson, and there is nothing to show that he was loth to add yet another victory to those already to his credit.

The general was a thorough man; whether it was a question of debauchery or of scientific invention he gave himself wholly to it with admirable singleness of mind. His preparations for the siege left nothing to chance. Transported laboriously across those miles of sea his infantry numbered some 40,000 men. This figure excludes cavalry, sailors and engineers. The 170 troopships were convoyed by some 200 men-of-war of different sizes—some perhaps the fifteen-bench galleys designed by Demetrius himself which struck such terror into the defenders of the coastal forts who watched them advance to the attack. This great fleet, as it rolled across the blue carpet of the straits, under the Carian mountains, was followed, say the chroniclers, by countless ships of provision, and a horde of smaller vessels—vulture-boats—manned by itinerant adventurers who had followed the conqueror in the hope of chance spoil. Standing on the flat roof-top of his house, with the whole dazzling panorama of the town glittering in its marble amphitheatre below him, the Rhodian sentry who first caught a glimpse of this armada might be forgiven a momentary pang of fear as he watched it, contrasting the peaceful temples and colonnades of his capital below with that minatory horde of vessels forming up for an attack on the harbours. Across the still waters of the gulf he must have heard the creaking of tackle, the neighing of horses, and the hoarse voice commanding; the shrill squeaking of bosuns' pipes and the crunch of oars as the galleys moved up the channel.

Yet to do the Rhodians justice their preparations were complete, and if their military leaders awaited the onslaught with comparative calm it was because they knew how powerful the defences of the town were. Six thousand citizens and a thousand aliens within the city had been marshalled and armed; all who refused to bear arms had been expelled. The very slaves had been armed for the siege. Torr suggests that they alone must have added some 16,000 men to the standing garrison. Later there came reinforcements from Crete and from Egypt, for throughout the siege the superior naval skill of the Rhodians enabled them to keep the sea-routes open to the south and west. A sympathetic Crete pushed a reinforcement of 150 men into the town, while Egypt sent 2,000 to help her ally. It was a case of some twenty-five thousand men besieged by roughly twice that number. If Demetrius was a thorough man the Rhodians showed themselves no less so; their defences were strengthened as much as possible, the armed slaves were promised citizenship if they fought well, and the fleet was ordered to stand by for action. Meanwhile such citizens as were not standing to arms were busied in the construction of catapults and balistas to mount along the parapets of the town-wall. While Demetrius' scouts worked their way slowly round the walls, cutting down trees to make palisades and destroying any suburban houses they came across, the Rhodian fleet made a sudden sortie against some provision-ships which had arrived for Demetrius. These they captured and brought into harbour together with a number of captives from them. This was a rich gain in ransoms.

Demetrius, however, was taking his time. He had decided upon an assault to be launched against the main harbour—indeed there were no other anchorages of any use to him along the shovel-shaped end of the island; and if he failed to take the port he would be unable to refit and refuel his forces. He had built two great tortoises—floating pent-houses strong enough to carry assault-crews, archers, and a great armament of catapults—and these he proposed to float into the mouth of the harbour. He had also constructed two great towers of wood which would enable him to overshoot and enfilade the towers guarding the moles. These were also contrived upon a float. The whole of this uncouth equipment was assembled and the signal to engage had been given when a storm sprang up, and the whole battle-order was disturbed. During the day the sea lashed the siege-craft of Demetrius until it seemed that he would lose everything; but as night fell a calm came over everything. It was an opportune moment for an attack, and he took advantage of it, with qualified success. Four hundred men got ashore and captured a small eminence about 500 paces from the wall, where they dug themselves in. Early next morning the rams were brought up and the signal for the general attack was given to the sound of trumpets. A series of violent exchanges began which were to last the whole of that day. Several breaches were opened in the wall which guarded the mole, but the Rhodians resisted with tenacity and held the enemy off. At nightfall Demetrius withdrew his main forces for refitting, and while he was doing so the Rhodian fleet, under cover of darkness, tried to float fire-ships amongst the enemy units. At first they were unsuccessful, but later they did him considerable damage with their sudden sallies from the port. But the major action of the siege was yet to be fought. Demetrius tried several times to force the harbour; a series of skilful and exhausting actions were fought in the breaches of the mole. Giant catapults mounted on the hillock he had captured pounded the city-wall until it rocked under the great bullets of stone. It should be remembered that the missile engines of these early times had been developed into formidable instruments of offence and defence. They could throw from seventy pounds up to six hundred pounds of stones; or launch darts from six to twelve feet long. Archimedes at the siege of Syracuse constructed some which could lift and throw no less than eighteen hundred pounds of stone. The ranges offered considerable variation according to the size of the machine, but for the larger ones six hundred yards was the average for direct fire and a thousand yards for curving fire.

But to return to Demetrius, his picked infantry tried escalade after escalade only to be forced back from the parapet by the defenders. It became obvious that an attack on the harbour would fail; it became obvious moreover that a blockade was impossible in view of the Rhodian naval superiority. Demetrius withdrew temporarily and refitted his fleet for yet another attempt on the harbour; he wanted to be quite sure that it was impregnable before adopting other methods or objectives. His second assault met with the same fate—due once more to weather and to the Rhodian navy, which made a sally when it was least expected and damaged many of his ships. There seemed to be nothing for it but to construct a Helepolis and let it loose upon the Rhodians. Once more the forces of Demetrius were stood easy while the general indulged his scientific turn in supervising this colossus among siege-engines. Meanwhile the Rhodians had recovered some of their usual fire; their nimble fleet harassed his communications, and in one sortie carried off a number of rich presents, pictures, and a letter from Demetrius' wife Phila— the whole of which, including the letter, they sent to Ptolemy of Egypt: an act which infuriated Demetrius beyond endurance. To add to his troubles Rhodian infantry made sorties during the night and set fire to some of his batteries. Meanwhile, however, the giant Helepolis was well under way. Diodorus describes it lovingly—almost rubbing his hands along its massive sides. It must have been an awe-inspiring machine to look at.

The Helepolis was a moving tower on wheels of oak. The base of it was square and the sides sloped inwards. There has been some argument about the original size of it. Diodorus says it was 150 feet high by 75 feet broad. Much later Vitruvius calculated its weight at 125 tons but this may have been an academic exercise in mathematics only. Nine stories high, it towered above the Rhodian walls. It was replete with catapults, grappling irons, and drawbridges which could disgorge its infantry upon the parapets they had not succeeded in scaling. It groaned and creaked as it moved, but it worked—and what is more astonishing, it took an operational crew of three thousand four hundred men to propel it. In common with most of the siege-weapons of the day it was given a tough outer skin of plaited osiers or hides. The top floor was a nest for archers, but the floor beneath carried tanks of water serviced by force pumps with hoses made from the intestines of cattle. On either side of the Helepolis were built supporting tortoises with rams, and covered gallery for the sappers to work in. It is not hard to imagine what the Rhodians felt as they saw this great siege-piece assembled and dragged within assault-distance from their walls. They must have seen the engineers testing the monster, testing its great battering rams and drawbridges before it was dragged towards the walls of the city. Indeed they had made frantic attempts to impede the work of construction, but in vain. Desultory sorties had not been undertaken in sufficient force; burning arrows had been quenched by the sappers; while industrious mine-works had been met with counter-mines which advanced the ends of neither party. Hopes had been raised by the arrival of a Cnidian embassy to Demetrius which had been sent to offer mediation. Demetrius however refused to countenance any further talk. The Helepolis was his answer. He had it moved into position for the assault, noting with his professional eye how little effect the hail of stone-shot had upon it. Certainly the Rhodians showed no weakening of resolve. Their morale was high. Abundant food supplies had reached them from their allies. The first victory had been theirs—a good augury; while Demetrius had failed by sea twice, and had recently failed to buy his victory with a bribe. His agents had approached Athenagoras, the captain of the Rhodian guard, with the offer of a vast sum of money in exchange for his complicity; the offer was promptly announced to the Rhodians, who voted Athenagoras a gold chaplet and five talents for his honesty. Since he himself was not a Rhodian but of Miletos, and in command of Egyptian mercenaries, the augury was a good one. To bind the resolve of the besieged still more firmly the Rhodians announced that those citizens who fell in action would be buried at public cost, their parents and dependents maintained out of treasury funds, and their daughters dowered by the state when they married. Their sons, added the decree, would be crowned in full armour in the Theatre at the Festival of Dionysos, when they had reached manhood. It was a sound stroke of policy. Emboldend by these announcements no less than by the sudden arrival of supplies, the Rhodians manned their walls and prepared to defend them or die.

It was perhaps during this part of the siege that the attacking forces broke through a part of the wall and took back with them the news that there, in a walled garden, they had seen the painter Protogenes painting away with perfect calm in all the din of assault and counter-assault. His famous painting of Ialyssos as a hunter was occupying his mind to the exclusion of anything else. A deputation of Rhodian citizens had already pleaded with Demetrius to respect this work and guarantee its safety. According to Pliny's anecdote, Demetrius asked Protogenes to present himself at his headquarters, and when he did so he asked him how he could work away at his painting while the fate of the town hung in the balance. The painter replied: 'I am aware that you are making war upon people and not upon the arts.' There is just the faintest flavour of flattery about it; enough at any rate to win over Demetrius, who assigned the painter a special body-guard and ordered that he was not to be molested.

At the first rush the great Helepolis knocked down a tower and carried away a vital section of wall. Troops poured into the breach like ants and a ferocious mêlée took place across the gap. For a time the pendulum seemed to swing towards the attackers, but the Rhodian line held, though it was strained to cracking point. The battle lasted

86

all day, and when night fell Demetrius saw that his troops had not managed to force an entry into the town. Worse still, the Helepolis was damaged, and would need to be repaired. Once more he was obliged to call a halt. Diodorus does not record the language the general used as he surveyed the stricken engine, mounted upon the rubble of the blood-stained wall it had breached, choked with dead bodies and ammunition. Whatever he had to say must have been sultry in the extreme. Meanwhile the Rhodians were hard at work, taking advantage of the lull to dig in behind the great half-moon of the fallen wall. Siege-pieces were renewed and refitted. A scratch crew went up and towed back the Helepolis to a place of safety where the engineers could work on it untroubled by the whistle of arrows and pointed shot from the walls which still swarmed with defenders. It was beginning to develop into an ugly stalemate. No doubt the Athenian embassy which arrived at this juncture took occasion to point this out; yet even their offers of mediation fell upon deaf ears. Both parties stood firm. The Helepolis was repaired and moved slowly back into position opposite that tantalising breach in the city-wall. Demetrius was like some great cat hypnotised by a mouse-hole too small to admit more than a single paw. The faded arguments of the ambassadors hardly grazed his intolerable restless resolve to attack and conquer the city.

Now for a delightful piece of Greek jobbery. Some time before the siege a certain Callias of Arados had arrived in Rhodes and set himself up as an engineer specialising in siege-pieces. One of his designs captured the popular imagination. He proposed to mount a crane on the walls which, he said, would be strong enough to pick up a common Helepolis in its grab and lift it over into the city at one blow. The idea was charming though mechanically unsound. Yet one can see why it should have made him so popular. . . . A Helepolis suddenly lifted into the air, with its infantry tossed out like weevils from a broken biscuit, its drawbridges flapping loose, its water-tanks pouring. . . . Such a crane as Callias could design would be an even more remarkable machine than the Helepolis itself: so at least they told one another. Callias was delighted at the warm reception the Rhodians gave his idea. He accepted without hesitation the the post of state architect to Rhodes, a post then held by one

Diognetus. The crane was built according to specifications and mounted. But alas, it was quite incapable of fulfilling the demands Callias made upon it; not only did it not drag the Helepolis over the wall. It failed even to lift it. The crash of the falling wall, and the cloud of dust which hung in the air where once the tower stood as a strong-point must have brought the truth of the matter home rather forcibly to all concerned. The Rhodian fathers went hotfoot to the house of Diognetus. They wanted him back as state architect. But Diognetus was in a huff—one of those unfathomable Greek huffs which have been handed down unchanged into modern times, and which every traveller must learn, sooner or later, to deal with. Deeply wounded in his pride, burning with that all-suffusing resentment which today lights up his descendants whenever their slightest whim is not gratified, he refused to consider the requests of his fellow-citizens. He shrugged away the tears and entreaties of the greybeards. He ate fruit and raised his eyebrows to indicate with absolute finality that he had long ago washed his hands of the whole business. People foolish enough to trust charlatans, etc. . . . The pattern of the conversation is perfectly clear. It is a conversation which takes place daily in Greece today. Nothing less than a full-scale procession of ingenuous youths and maidens, bearing branches, would soothe an amour-propre so deeply wounded. *Diognetus wanted the Rhodians to ask nicely.* Thus in the midst of the siege a procession was organised, led by moaning priests from the temples, and followed up by wailing choirs of maidens and youths bearing branches of laurel. 'Help us' they cried; and Diognetus watching the extent of the procession and hearing the heart-felt wails of the suppliants, condescended to accept his former post once more. A wave of relief swept over everyone. Diognetus was back at work. The procession had finally won him over. The vindicated state-architect made his way back to the walls and gazed out across the shattered suburbs of the city to where the great machine stood, waiting for the signal to be given before it advanced toward the breach. Rhodian infantry were still busy digging in around the half-moon of fallen masonry. A sickening suspense—thick as the white clouds of dust from broken statuary and crumbling walls that eddied in the still summer air—hung over everything. The enemy had re-formed. Fifteen hundred picked men were to force the breach by night and effect an entry; while the signal for the general assault was given they were to establish themselves inside the city, based upon the theatre, and there to hold out until the Helepolis widened the breach, and the rest of the infantry could be pushed in to reinforce them. The plan appeared to work. The entry was made, the theatre taken, and for a while the garrison was thrown into a panic by the knowledge that the enemy had gained a foothold inside the walls. But the Rhodians recovered their resolution far more quickly than Demetrius had imagined possible; the area round the theatre was sealed off by the best of the Rhodian infantry and the Egyptian mercenaries were thrown into the battle against the enemy. Fires raged all night long, and fierce hand to hand combats took place. Meanwhile the lumbering Helepolis had met with a second and final disaster, thanks to the intelligence of Diognetus. There are two versions of the story, of which the latter is by far the prettier. The first states that a long mine-shaft was opened along the projected line of advance of the Helepolis; the second states that Diognetus skilfully diverted the sewage of the town into the path of the monster, and that it stuck, ankle-deep, in the quag and could not be budged. This was most disheartening. It ruined Demetrius' chances of pushing his infantry into the town to support the shock-troops. The latter by this time were much reduced by the Rhodian attack, and by the middle of next day, were forced to surrender. It was the end of the attack.

But while the battle was at its height Demetrius had received the most urgent message from his father ordering him to conclude a truce with the Rhodians as soon as possible and to return. Antigonus had other problems on his mind. At the same moment—most opportunely this time, for their arrival enabled Demetrius to save his face—came a deputation from the Aetolians, asking permission to mediate. Demetrius accepted the offer on condition that the terms were acceptable—and ambassadors were despatched to the city to arrange them. The Rhodians, too, by this time were disposed to treat; the latest battle had been for them an extremely narrow escape from defeat—and it had brought home most forcibly the penalties of war which a truce might prevent them from suffering. They were anxious to accept the terms of the treaty—and indeed its articles were not politically unfavourable to the future of Rhodes. In exchange for an alliance with Antigonus against any enemy save Ptolemy they were allowed to keep their freedom. A hundred hostages were to be held by Demetrius against this assurance. Once the articles were accepted the besiegers would decamp and not trouble the island more. It was an honourable enough compromise, and the Rhodians rejoiced in it; Diognetus enjoyed his share of the honours, while the Helepolis was dragged into the city and dedicated to the people.

Walking over the ruined suburbs of the great city with the little knot of treaty-makers Demetrius found himself wondering what he could do with all the useless, half-smashed equipment which littered the ground. Magnanimity was not entirely foreign to his nature. He admired the stubborn way the Rhodians had defended themselves against him. Was there nothing he could do to set a seal upon this contagious goodwill which, now the siege was ended, infected everyone, friend and enemy alike? On an impulse he handed over all the equipment he had brought with him to the Rhodian people; he asked that they should sell it, and from the proceeds of the sale erect a statue to commemorate a siege so notable in the history of their times. It was a gesture quite in keeping with his character, and was accepted in that spirit. So it was that the statue of the Sun God was born. Only a colossus could adequately bear witness to the greatness of the siege, the size of the engines used, the heroism of both sides— and the odd impulses of generosity which sometimes stir the hearts of tyrants.

The statue was undertaken by Chares of Lindos, a pupil of Lysippus. It cost three hundred talents (£72,000) which resulted from the sale of the siege-train which Demetrius had left behind him in the spring of 30 B.C. Moreover it cost the sculptor twelve years of his life to cast and mount. Its height is variously given but was most likely 105 feet. A prodigious statue, one would think, to work and mount with the available equipment of the day. Pliny does not state how large a staff of pupils and workmen was retained by the sculptor, nor what sort of scaffolding and machinery was necessary to set the statue up. He does say, however, that even when it had fallen down and become a total wreck it was still a prodigy. Its very finger was larger than many of the statues in that city of colossi. The gaping rents in it, the cavities and fractures, revealed the masses of rock and iron which had gone to building an armature heavy enough to support the great construction.

Pliny's account is the most circumstantial. Writing three hundred years after the earthquake which overthrew the statue, he was still in time to see the ruins as they lay upon the ground. For those who enjoy scholastic ambiguity and polemic however there is an inscription attributed to a certain Simonides which claims the work as executed by Laches of Lindos. The portly Sextus Empiricus has offered us an intellectual compromise on this burning question by producing a not unlikely story that Chares, the designer of the statue, having offered his estimates for the work, was told to double its size; this he did, but as he had already spent the money given him he took his own life, and left Laches to carry on the work. The statue, then, took twelve years to build, and enjoyed a life of fifty-six years before the earthquake of 227 overturned it.

The site of the Colossus has never been determined with any accuracy, nor has the pose been described for us by reliable eye-witnesses. Argument over possible sites and poses is likely to go on until the next earthquake, in which presumably the whole island of Rhodes will sink into the sea and leave behind it legends as tenuous as those which make up the myth of Atlantis. At any rate the story that it stood straddling the harbour with its huge legs is a medieval confection. And here it must be confessed that the greater part of the Colossus' fame dates from the Middle Ages. 'In ancient times it attracted little notice; it did not rank among the masterpieces of Greek sculpture, and in size it was rivalled by earlier and surpassed by later statues.' It was, it is true, placed in the catalogue of the Seven Wonders—and to this, no doubt, it owed its great celebrity during the Middle Ages.

For fifty-six years the Colossus stood as a tribute to the magnitude of the siege, and then came one of those sudden earthquakes to which much of the Aegean area is still subject. The town was shaken to its foundations. The temples, the arches, the statues—in the space of a day they had been swallowed up. And in the forest of falling statuary the Colossus was only one of a number of casualties sustained on that memorable day in 227 B.C. An inscription recently unearthed by Sand positively forbids the Rhodians to add another statue to the temple of Aesculapius. The earthquake must have more than regulated such questions of votive overcrowding; the echo of tumbling statues and falling public buildings reached every corner of the civilized world. For nine centuries the figure of the Sun-God was to lie prostrate in the town it had adorned. It was not until the VIIth century that the shattered remains of the piece were knocked down to a Jew from Syria and transported in camel-loads to the Middle East for boiling down. Presumably the statue was formed once more into the implements for a fresh war. This is the kind of inverted poetry by which we live. At any rate the amount of the successful bid has not been recorded; the Jew probably got it cheap; the story goes that it took him 900 camels to load and carry it off. 'The twenty tons of metal,' says Torr coldly, 'would not, however, load more than 90 camels.'

It says something for the veneration and love with which Rhodes was regarded in the ancient world that though the city was razed to the ground the island's allies at once began to send presents of money and food. Ptolemy, that perspicacious hunter of fine books, was deeply moved by the disaster, while the Kings of many other neighbouring states bestirred themselves to help the Rhodians. Treasure flowed in—the greater part of which, no doubt, was intended to help with the restitution of the Sun-God. The Rhodians themselves were anxious to set up the great statue once more, but a curious fact prevented them from doing so. The Oracle of Delphi pronounced against the idea. Worse evils might follow, it said, if the Sun-God were to be set up again. The Rhodians, recalling that *hubris* always carries its ugly reward, desisted.

A good deal of ink has been shed in an attempt to elucidate the problem. Why should the oracle of Delphi, the centre of Apollo-worship, transmit so unfavourable an omen to stricken Rhodes? Insinuating tongues have suggested that the Rhodians found better uses for the donations of neighbouring states, and even that they came to some underground arrangement with the priests of the oracle in order to provoke such an announcement and be free from the irksome necessity of rebuilding the Colossus. It is also hinted . . .

but here again the evidence becomes, in Torr's phrase, 'flimsy,' and in Gideon's 'rather thin on top.' I must leave the reader to worry his own way through the alleys and loop-holes of the argument. As for ourselves, we have spent days arguing about it; afternoons diving in the harbour for fragments of it (in pursuit of some mad theory of Gideon's that it was situated upon the easterly mole, and that some of its shattered fragments must surely have fallen into the water): and now the historical impact of its name is mixed with memories of this pure sunlight, these dancing summer days passed in idle friendship and humour by the maned Aegean. Who could ask for better?

CHAPTER V

In the Garden of the Villa Cleobolus

It is difficult to convey the extraordinary silence of this garden, for it is true that the main road runs along the length of it, and that the noises of motors can be heard; but so dense is the packing of oleanders and small pines and so heavy the shadow in which the house is set that sound itself becomes blurred and mingles with the hushing of the sea along the beaches to the eastward. Here in the evenings we gather for drinks and gossip, sitting in cane chairs around the little painted table, hearing through the dusk the shallow strains of some forgotten fugue wafted to us from the old horn-gramophone which is the Mufti's special pride. Here Gideon and Hoyle play out those interminable games of chess, which always end in a wrangle (and the discovery that Gideon has been cheating). Here, sitting on the ground, the grave detached Huber is whittling at the hull of a ship or the bowl of a pipe.

Presently the servant comes swaying down the dark path with a rosy branch of candles shielded in the coarse red coral of her hand: to sweep up the ash-tray and discarded books and set our supper-places. The little dog shakes itself, yawns and stands up to sniff the premonitory odours of the kitchen. And Mills, dripping wet from the sea, comes panting down the path to change for dinner—from a wet bathing-costume into a dry one.

Gideon has unearthed a peasant legend which purports to explain why the juice of the oleander is so bitter. The Virgin, says the tale, was walking towards Golgotha distracted by her grief when the hem of her dress was caught by an oleander; impatiently she cursed

the tree saying: 'May you harbour forever the bitterness I feel today.'
Immediately the sap of the plant turned acid. Today the peasant uses ·
it as a styptic for cuts—when he cannot find a cobweb.[1]

Gideon's preoccupation with his livestock is assuming the proportions of a mania. 'Every time a cow coughs on the island,' says
Mills bitterly, 'I receive a signal from this bloody old agricultural
fool and have to motor forty miles to see what has happened. It
won't do, Gideon. I shall complain to the Brigadier.'

Gideon sighs and gazes round him for sympathy. 'Unamiable
fellow,' he says mildly. 'I am being inspected next week by the G.O.C.
Cows. As it is half my damned cattle can't stand up. You don't want
me to lose my job, do you?'

'Yes,' says Mills, 'I do.'

'Come,' says Gideon reproachfully, 'Take the larger view, old
boy. Don't let your horizons be limited by a petty outlook. Expand.
Be generous. Be large. . . .'

'And as for that milk. . . .'

'My dear fellow, an administrative oversight. . . .'

'Wasted in pig-swill.'

'Be just.'

A large consignment of powdered milk, long and anxiously
awaited by the maternity hospital which Mills runs, disappeared last
week from the quay. An officer, whose signature on the bill of
lading was quite undecipherable, had carried off the consignment in a
truck. Careful enquiry proved it to have been Gideon; but by the
time Mills caught up with him he was forty miles to the south of
Rhodes, where the precious consignment had been mixed into the
swill of a dozen 'host pigs' imported from Cyprus.

'Like Cellini,' Gideon explains, 'I threw everything into the furnace.
The battle against undernourishment must go on. My job must be
kept at all costs.'

The forthcoming inspection of his department has certainly been
preying on his mind. His cherished 'host-pigs' were suffering from
sea-sickness. What was one to do?

'I should pour your whisky ration into them,' says Mills bitterly,
hovering between genuine fury and laughter.

[1] A few peasant remedies are given in an appendix.

Gideon adjusts his monocle with an air and says:

'What an uncommonly good idea. I never thought of that. I shall do it.'[1]

Three afternoons a week we invite the monk Demetrius to teach us modern Greek. He is a delightful character with an immense beard and a beguiling repertoire of stories—not all of them in the best taste. After a few desultory attempts to find a set book on which to work Gideon has selected 'Pope Joan',[2] that delightful albeit rather salacious novel which we translate together, amid shrieks of laughter from Demetrius. Hoyle, whose Greek is too perfect to need the same attention as ours, enjoys taking part in the conclave, but is occupied on a translation of 'Daphnis and Chloe' with which I help him, in a vain attempt to learn some earlier Greek than demotic. These books at least canalise our enthusiasm which has been, up to now, dispersed over a wide area. Among sporadic translations Gideon has given me his rendering of the one poem attributed to Cleobolus of Lindos, an epitaph on Gordius, King of Phrygia. It is not bad.

> *I am a bronze girl sculptured*
> *And set up here on Midas'* [3] *monument.*
> *Believe me, so ever long as water*
> *Flows in the plains and the sunrise*
> *Delights men as the brilliant moonlight does:*
> *So ever long as rivers rush*
> *Between steep flanks, so ever long*
> *As oceans surge on beaches I*
> *Shall be seen reclining on this*
> *Old unhappy tomb to tell the passer-by*
> *'Midas lies here interred.'*

Huber places the ancient school of the orators on the little plateau near Rodini. It has the precarious look of having been created in something which any puff of smoke might dissolve. A landscape as perishable as a smoke-ring. Here, then, came Cicero to study peror-

---

[1] He did. The inspection was a great success, and the sangfroid of the host-pigs was much admired by his inspector, who was, it transpired, himself a teetotaller.

[2] I have completed his draft and hope one day to publish this witty and improper novel in England

Midas: hereditary title of the kings of Phrygia.

ation, adjuration and bombination. Apollonios Molon's rhetoric had seduced him when the great orator had been representing Rhodes in Rome as Envoy. After Cicero came Caesar. Sand has unearthed some notes on Rhodian oratory from the Museum. I am indebted to him for these scraps of history which make our walks more pleasureable and our arguments, if anything, less pointless.

Legend states that when Pompey visited the island he patiently heard all the resident sophists and presented each with a talent as a mark of his esteem. (Torr declares the talent to be worth £240.) Brutus and Cassius both studied rhetoric in Rhodes. Indeed the mark made by the Rhodian orators appears in every way to justify the praise of them by Tacitus. They are still, of course, great orators. Only last Sunday, at the unveiling of a plaque to commemorate some notable feat of allied arms, a certain Mr Gongorides, clad in morning-coat and sponge-bag trousers, in pince-nez and a cravat, held the floor for something under three hours, until two boy scouts fainted from the heat and the Greek garrison colonel's wife burst into floods of irrepressible tears and had to be dosed with sal volatile. Written in the classical language of the day (*katharevousa*) which is a little more intelligible than Sanscrit to the average peasant, it was an unqualified success. No wit broke the unruffled flow of those serpentine sentences. As Greek speeches go it was remarkable for the restraint of its delivery. Apart from sawing the air sideways as if he were lancing a boil Mr Gongorides employed few gestures. His pitch was uneven: for even the strongest voice cannot maintain the rapid staccato yowling note with which he began, without feeling the strain. By the time Mr Gonorides ended our throats were all sore in sympathy with him. In the Officers' Club there was much growling and swearing at the length of it—but then oratory is hardly likely to find admirers in the Army where the average officer's vocabulary is restricted to monosyllables. The waste of time was considered deplorable, and the naval lieutenant whose permanent hangover has given his face the expression of a man trying to lift a sideboard, declared that he would run Mr Gongorides to earth and dash his brains out with a bottle.

It is not clear what Theodorus of Gadara would have had to say to this speech; as Tiberius' teacher of rhetoric he would be, perhaps, the best qualified to judge it on its merits. But though Rhodes was the home of rhetoric its cause abroad was often pleaded by foreign speakers. When Artemisia occupied Rhodes it was Demosthenes himself who delivered a speech advocating Rhodian independence. Cato saved Rhodes by his speech in the Senate after the war with Perseus, and a few years later the alliance between Rhodes and Rome was the result of Tiberius Gracchus' golden eloquence. Indeed when Claudius restored to the Rhodians their much-prized independence it was in response to a speech delivered by a fattish adolescent of fifteen, who was as much admired for his learning as he was later to be execrated for his crimes—Nero.

In the great catalogue of powers which in ancient times held the sovereignty of the seas Rhodes stands sometimes fourth and some-times fifth. For some twenty-three years about 900 B.C. the Rhodian fleet maintained a reputation for boldness and skill which could rival any other nation afloat. But the Rhodians were great colonisers as well as traders, and their ships covered the distance between Rhodes and Spain; as colonisers they perhaps gave their name to Rhodos, a town at the north-eastern corner of Spain, while legends suggest that the river Rhone took its name from another Rhodian colony founded near its mouth. In Sicily the great city of Gela was founded by them, as was the city of Apollonia in the Black Sea.

The great dockyards were maintained long after the Thallasacratia had passed from the Rhodians. And the spirit remained unimpaired until today, as anyone may judge whose daring is equal to a trip with the Kalymniot sponge-divers to Benghazi or further west. When Heraclides set fire to the dockyards in 204 B.C., thirteen sheds were burnt up and each had a three-banker in it under construction. Rhodian shipwrights built not only for themselves but for foreigners too. Herod of Judea is said to have ordered himself a Rhodian triere, while after the earthquake which overthrew the Apollo great quantities of ship-timber were among the presents sent to Rhodes by foreign kings. Torr adds that among the other presents were numbered items which suggest that other states wished to restore the shipbuilding trade in Rhodes: namely iron, lead, pitch, tar, resin, hemp, hair and sailcloth. He adds that once the Rhodian women had to cut off their hair and give it for making ropes; and that these ropes were for many years afterwards shown as curiosities to visitors. There is a story of a Rhodian captain muttering while expecting to lose his ship in a storm. 'Well, Poseidon, you must own I'm sending her down in good trim.' And they were fine swimmers. . . . When they went out to burn the siege-engines of Demetrius they simply swam home if their own vessels took fire.

From these fragments of reference and legend the picture of the Rhodian seafarer becomes clear; you will see him today, if you have eyes, sitting in the crooked taverns of the old town rolling dice and hissing through his curling moustaches: or slapping down lucky court-cards and grumbling, while his free hand gropes absently for the bottle of mastic. And when the sponge fleet puts out you will see him, a small jaunty figure, sitting loosely over his tiller, as perfectly in tune with the bucking sea as an expert rider with his horse, steering for the coasts of Africa. He hardly ever turns to look back at the dazzling white villages on the rocks of Simi or Kalymnos, or lift his hand as he passes the last cape which will hide the little dots of scarlet, white, blue, yellow and grey, which stand upon the quay and chatter like starlings.

At six these early summer mornings I rise and cross the garden barefoot to wake E by throwing a pebble at her shuttered window; and together we bathe in the cold sea before breakfast. The Mufti has taken to calling on me every morning at this hour. He has discovered that E can make real Turkish coffee. In a Rhodian Turk such behaviour is positively forward. He can have no further doubts about my suitability as a tenant. We arrive back in our bathing-costumes at seven to find him sitting on a chair under the willow-tree, resting one elbow on the little painted table. While Maria sets the table for breakfast he hums a little tune to himself, waiting for his coffee. The sunlight splashes through the rafters of the huge baobab tree which shades the house, picking up the coloured pottery, and lighting his sad preoccupied old face with a warm rosy tint reflected from the red tablecloth. Often Hoyle drops in from the hotel across the way, and all four of us settle down to breakfast in that sunny coolness. Days that begin like this cannot help carrying their perfection forward—as sums of money in a ledger are moved forward under different headings—to lighten the office-work, to persuade even the dour Manoli to sport a flower behind his ear. Idle conversations, leading nowhere except perhaps to the confirmation of a happiness as idle as this shadowy garden, with its heavy odours of flowers, coffee, and tobacco-smoke, mingled with early sunlight.

The peasant girl from Cos makes an admirable servant but she shares the superstitions of her people. It is unlucky, for example, to be the bringer of bad luck or bad news. Telegrams almost always contain bad news. Therefore rather than give me the telegram which arrived this morning she tore it up and put it down the lavatory. 'I was afraid it was bad news,' she says. When I scold her she throws her apron over her head and roars like a bull. What is one to do?

Dry friction of cicada from the palm-tree across the road. Eucalyptus leaves breaking their wrists with a small click as they begin to plane down over the tombstones. The maceration of pebbles by seawater, mingling with the noise of coffee being ground, and the shearing noise of a pot being scoured. An inventory of sounds from a late morning walk.

Torr has some amusing facts about the little Turkish graveyard which I have come to think of as the garden of Villa Cleobolus. During the Middle Ages it was part of the Grand Master's garden. 'In 1496,' says Torr, 'an old ostrich and two young were kept with their wings clipped in a walled enclosure here. They laid their eggs in sand and hatched them by simply looking at them: they fed on iron and steel. There was also a sheep from India and various other strange animals: particularly a hound given to the Grand Master by Sultan Bajazet. It was about the size of a greyhound, mouse-coloured, with no hair at all except about the mouth, and it had claws like a bird. From this last fact comes the story that the Grand Turk had a bird that every year laid three eggs; and from two of the eggs came birds, but from the third a puppy. It was necessary to remove the puppy as soon as it broke its shell: otherwise the birds pecked it.' Not the shadow of a smile disturbs the dry exposition of the scholarly Englishman who has given us the best historical monograph on the island. But then history for Torr was a serious business. I have not been able to discover whether he visited Rhodes. Perhaps he thought it wiser to stay out of this sunlit landscape whose wine and fruit could only lead a man to laziness, procrastination and even to mendacity. From a commanding position on Exmoor he consulted 'every known authority' and pointed a long quivering finger at the bulging rhetoric of the Abbé Cutlet. We are all very much afraid of Torr. Read him and you will see why.

Rhodes, like the rest of Greece, has clung to its belief in Pan. Elsewhere he is known as the kallikanzaros and those who have been lucky enough to catch a glimpse of him have described him as a small edition of the Devil, with horns, hooves and pointed ears complete. The Orthodox Church is partial to the association, and perhaps this accounts for the name he goes under in Rhodes. He is called a *Kaous*. The word seems to be related with the verb 'kao' which means 'to burn'. Combustion, after all, is of the nature of devils, and the name suggests fire and brimstone in equal parts. But if you study the habits of the Kaous as recorded in the popular literature another association will come to mind—the creature is 'on hot bricks'. He is a troublesome visitor to the village, turning things upside down, making women miscarry and cream turn sour. He is worse still: he is a kidnapper.

The peasants believe that if a husband and wife sleep together on the 25th of March the child must be born on Christmas Eve—and this child will inevitably turn out to be a *Kaous*.

Its habits? It circulates mostly after dark croaking over and over again: 'Feathers or lead? Feathers or lead?' People who encounter a *Kaous* and give the wrong answer find themselves suddenly seized. The *Kaous* mounts them like a horse and rides them at breakneck pace across country, beating them with a stick. The annoying thing is that of the two possible responses to the question *either* can prove to be the wrong one, according to how the *Kaous* feels. A certain Basil of Kremasto was once taken for a ride in this manner. He asserts that the *Kaous* galloped him all over Anatolia for the space of a night. He arrived at the tavern exhausted at daybreak and was only able to prove the veracity of his tale by producing an apple which he had plucked from an Anatolian orchard in the course of this head-long gallop. Another man, from the village of Siana, was met by a *Kaous* on a dark road. He did not speak to it but caught it by its long pointed ears. This seemed to render it helpless. He carried it home and burnt a hole in its legs with a branding-iron. Out of the wound crawled hundreds of devilish little snakes and the *Kaous* was healed. It shuddered, came to itself and said: 'Deeply I slept, lightly I waken,' and with that it disappeared up the chimney as the first cock crowed.

Manoli the linotypist has been at it again. He has dropped into the habit of inserting small advertisements in the Greek newspaper for his friends. I do not know what they pay him for it, but it must be less than the space-rates we charge for such items. This evening I was interested to see the advertisement of one Tsirimokos, Cartomancer, Geomancer and Coffeemancer (as he described himself) offering reduced rates for fortune-telling from some obscure address in the old town. Enquiry into this item and others equally odd produced consternation at the office where my Greek editor had faithfully read final proof upon the copy before sending it down to the printing-room. Manoli had cleared himself a small corner of type by subediting an article on St Paul by the Vicar of Rhodes, and had proceeded to lino his advertisements and find room for them in the bed. We have a painful interview. Thrusting aside the basket of pomegranates which he brings with him as a peace-offering I wave the paper under his nose and ask for explanations. 'I was only helping my friends,' he says with an air of ridiculous contrition, his eyes filling with tears. 'Well, you must pay the full space-rates from your next month's salary. We can't have the paper tampered with after it is made up. What will the Brigadier say?' The Brigadier is the latest dragon. We have diligently built up his personal myth to such a point that we are quite afraid of him ourselves. The printers believe that he breathes fire, and lives on a diet of nails and broken glass like one of the Rhodian dragons of the Middle Ages. 'You won't tell the Brigadier,' says Manoli, his sense of logic overcoming his contrition all of a sudden, 'How can you? Such a mistake would reflect on you as much as on me! After all you are responsible for the paper. You should see it isn't tampered with.' I try to kick him downstairs but he is too quick for me. He returns to his linotype with a swagger. After every row with Manoli I know that we shall have twenty-four hours' first-class work from him, and this knowledge is useful. If we have to make up a special number for a feast-day or for some special calendar-date I always pick a quarrel with him the night before, in order to feel sure that he is docile and tractable when the heavy

IN THE GARDEN OF THE VILLA CLEOBOLUS

burden of an extra two pages is added to his daily task. The Levant demands a very special diplomatic approach of its own to human problems.

There is one special convention mirrored in the newspaper which is pleasing. A patient too poor to pay his doctor's fees after an illness will invariably put an advertisement in the daily paper reading as follows: 'I, George Chorakis, feel in honour bound to thank Dr Gongorides publicly for his skill in curing me during my recent dangerous illness.' It is both good advertising and good manners. Sometimes, of course, an unscrupulous doctor will use this method of congratulating himself publicly on a series of purely imaginary cures—but never in a small community like this, where he would be found out very soon.

The first autumn rains came belatedly; this warm green rain does not belong to the beginnings of winter. The Pleiades have gone below ground, daughters of Atlas and Pleione. Hoyle tells me that they are seven in number, but that we only see six because one, Sterope, hides her face on account of a misfortune that befell her; others say that her name was Electra, and she hides because of her grief at the fall of Troy. Gideon rejects their etymology from the verb 'plein' meaning 'to sail'. They were obviously called πέλιαδες in ancient times, he says, which means a flock of pigeons; and to do him justice they are known as 'the birds'[1] in demotic Greek even today. A New Year festival connected with and determined by the rising of the seven seems to have been a wide-spread custom in ancient times.

The rain cares for none of this erudition. It sweeps down among the tombstones with a dull threshing sound, blows open the window at my elbow and splashes me with its warmth. It rattles like sparrow shot in the old well, now choked with autumn leaves. The sky has become soft, melting—as if this were a premonition of spring and not of winter. But we shall have frost to follow, says the calendar, after this momentary exuberance is over and the hollow drumming of water in the runnels and drain-pipes has stopped. Sadness of the year's ending. Autumn is lengthening into winter slowly but surely. As yet there is no snow on the mountains across the channel, though

[1] Note. τα πόυλια.

the air is faintly spiced with cold. In another week we shall have to forsake the baobab tree for dinner and go indoors. 'It won't be too soon for me,' says Hoyle, who feels the cold. 'I call this embalmer's weather.' The grapes are over and the empty vineyards have turned the colour of burnt chestnuts.

Once or twice we walk out to the thermal springs of Calithes where Gideon drinks pint after pint of the sulphurous water trickling from the rock, and falls into a vein of sentimental reminiscence about Baden and Vichy in the days before the war. Hoyle is suffering from hernia, and Mills proposes to perform a minor operation on him when the weather gets colder. 'I shall have to poke a hole in your middle and let some of the sawdust out, Hoyle,' he says. Hoyle hates the idea. 'Can't I die in peace?' he says testily. 'What would happen if you didn't operate?' Mills sighs and swallows his wine. 'You would soon be going about with that tummy of yours on a tray. How would you like to hold up a tray all day?' 'I should have a servant to hold the tray,' says Hoyle with dignity.

The Rhodes we talk about so much—the marvel among cities of the ancient world—what remains of it? Nothing. Today, after lunch we walked, the four of us, up the gentle slopes of Monte Smith, past the little light-house where the Indians are quartered, and along the broad and lovely road which leads to Trianda. Beneath us the blue carpet of sea stretched away to Anatolia where, say the peasants, you may still see the claw-marks of marauding dragons graven in the mountains; stretched sinuously along the capes and faults of Marmarice to where, in the northern corners, the first faint silhouette of islands rose; like stepping stones, pointing to Cos.

Beneath us on the landward side stood the old stadium and the temple, now much-restored by the misguided Italians. In this green and sleepy hollow an old shepherd kept his flock of sheep, standing under the great oak-tree which crowns the amphitheatre. Descending the terraces slowly Sand points out all that remains of the ancient city—a few outcrops of stone-carved tombs on the crown of the promontory: and turning his finger like a compass completes the half-circle at Simbulli and Rodini. Yet the ground is still choked with red pottery and the delicate handles of lamps and oil-jars. Gideon everywhere turns them up with his stick and we wash the clay from them in the ditches, trying to assemble the fragments again, but in vain.

Down on the mossy turf of the stadium the sheep browse and tinkle, looking like so many gold and silver insects in the sunlight, while their keeper comes slowly towards us to pass the time of day. He is an old man, with a deeply wrinkled face, and black sloe-shaped eyes which seem to have had all the good humour worn out of them. He speaks the Rhodian Greek with its clipped sing-song accent and pastoral vocabulary. Sitting around him in the grass, smoking and talking, we hear the history of the last few years, of the privations endured under the Germans, and of the ugly reprisals exacted from the Italian forces which tried to rebel after the fall of Italy.

Below us in the great amphitheatre where once the white city of Hippodamnus lay, with its sacred groves and temples, its dazzling statuary and teeming dock-yards, the Crusader town lours, with its gross bastions and keeps shining through the evening mist, topped by the minarets and the turning windmills of the Turkish quarter.

How far all this is from its Greek setting, from the main current of its landscape tradition—this old swarthy peasant and his sheep on the green hill; the reclining figures of his daughters by the old well, raiding a fragrant violet-bed, and for their daily meal un-wrapping from a dirty piece of paper a dozen sour olives. Against this backcloth the towers and buttresses of the Knights rise into the sky, dark with the premonitions of an alien age, of alien ways. Yet the patient landscape has almost succeeded in domesticating the gothic north; it has sent wave after wave of tangerine-trees to assault the dark stone cliffs of the castle. It has choked the moat with almond and peach-blossom. It has coated the stern ravelins with the iridescent sheen of moss kept moist from some invisible spring seeping through the stones. . . .

After a series of protracted and laboured evolutions Gideon has at last found himself a suitable house to live in; as it is large enough for them both, he has persuaded Hoyle to join him in the bachelor venture of sharing house until the spring, when their wives will arrive in Rhodes. The Villa Mondolfo lies some way from the town on the Trianda road, and for the whole of the last four days the two of them have been away there, spending a long week-end wrestling with the domestic problems which face them. This afternoon I received a note from Gideon with a characteristic postscript in Hoyle's minute handwriting.

'The days of bargaining are over. I am rather sorry. We sat on a slab of marble outside the front door for nearly six hours, drinking excellent wine under a fine mulberry. The present caretakers run the adjacent farm. Their livestock swarm in our courtyard. A turret of blue pigeons make their warbling narguileh-like sound. Partridges reared in coops are as tame as the hens which scribble everywhere. Our host is out of Hesiod—a portrait done bristly on pig-skin. Reddish pigment face, pig snout, somewhat plethoric—but with wonderful curling hair like the waves in a statue. This isn't very good English. His wife is more pug than pig, but lovely and very fat. Two small children: one voice dactyl, one voice spondee. But apart from this fifty pear-trees, seventy apple, ten plum, ten fig, and two hundred rows of wine. . . . My dear boy, a property of size.

'Hoyle has moved in with Croker and a shelf of Latin classics. Can you see how we are going to live? Royally, nobly. We have bought a lot of wood and today, in the first soft providential autumn rain (like catkins), we set up a crackling fire. Stone floors full of nice echoes. You call in a friend to supper: shout to the wife to roast some kidney-beans and lay out some figs and perhaps a bit of hare or partridge: the children are sent to bed: you call in the old man from the field—for he cannot strip vines any more in the rainy dusk: he comes, wrinkling up his eyes to the fire, his dusty old cheek printed with rain-drops: he takes up a glass of wine in that cavernous hand: presently we dine with fruit, salads and chestnuts from our own land. . . . The red Kalavarda wine is strong and coarse. . . . I must leave room for Hoyle who wants to add a word. *Come and visit us.*'

Hoyle's postscript says: 'Gideon must be mad. We *could* live like that a year from now. At present we are living on Spam, sleeping on camp beds, and are tormented by fleas and bugs. Horrible mess.'

CHAPTER VI

The Three Lost Cities

The function of history in all this is a small but precise one: as in some renaissance painting where the hermit occupies the foreground, seated in his drab ochre-coloured cell, but where, over his shoulder, set like a jewel in the rock, his only window gives on to a limitless panorama of smiling country, exact and glittering in its perspectives, symbol of the enamel landscape on which he has turned his back. So here I would like our own idle history of conversations to open like a sally-port, and throw into relief the many-coloured background of the island's own history. Only in this way can one nourish the other, so that the landscape may be evoked from both, before the eyes of a reader who is not free to touch the living grass of Cameirus with his own hands, or to feel the waves of sun-light beating upon the rocks of Lindos. What, now, of the three ancient cities which once dominated the politics and government of the island before the foundation of Rhodes, the capital? Of Ialysos alas! little remains, but their situation has preserved the two others, while the hundred or so miles of modern motor-road which en-circles the island places them within easy reach of the present capital, their child. They lie, too at roughly the same distance from the tip of Rhodes, one upon the northern shore, the other upon the southern. While they are easily reached by road, however, that is not the best way to see them.

I am thinking now of that fine August afternoon when Gideon and I set out on foot to explore the ancient cities, fortified by the knowledge that a long week-end lay before us. Our plan of march was an ingenious one, for we had arranged that Hoyle and Mills should run out by car and meet us at the end of each day's march to share the pleasures of camping out. Time and distance did not permit us to walk the whole way, so we planned to walk to Cameirus in two stages and thence to travel by car over the eastern end of the island to Lindos where we would spend our last night.

Leaving the town we chose the upper road because, if I remember rightly, there was some site whose location Gideon wanted to identify among the rock tombs which cluster round the nape of Monte Smith; but the sun was hot, and the steep hill was enough to set him puffing and blowing by the time we reached the crest overlooking Rhodes. Below us the sea sat perfectly still, cold as jelly; the old grey fort, its walls stitched and cobbled, resembled the pelt of an aged elephant. Neohori (Newtown) by contrast glittered softly in its plaster walls and red roofs. (At one time, says an ancient writer, it was known to the vulgar as Keratohori or Cuckoldville owing to the questionable morals of its inhabitants.) We sat for a while in one of those little rock-tombs where the temperature of the stone, as Gideon observed, made one think that the occupant had just left it for a stroll by the sea; and then, shouldering our packs, climbed up past the last villas and the dismantled battery where dark-skinned Indians lay about in the grass chattering, and took the high road which runs over the crown of the hill and along the glittering cliffs. It was cool here and windy. Westward along the shingle beaches around Trianda the sea was laying down its successive washes of prussian blue and violet, and thinning them out as they touched sand to green and citrons and the innocent yellows you can see on the ripening skins of tangerines. Here too we sat to get our breath and to watch, directly below us, the traffic moving along the main road. Mills emerged suddenly at the wheel of his car, bowling along to some urgent appointment, trailing a puff of dust behind him like a cherub's cloud, and skilfully negotiating the long caravans of mules moving in the opposite direction, carrying produce for the Rhodes market. Here, too then my companion's attention was taken up for a while with the professional appraisal of some sheep. Since his appointment as agricultural officer, he had developed a ridiculously proprietary air whenever any livestock came within his field of vision. 'Now, that's a fine cow,' he would say, or 'There. How's that for a sheep? Fattened up by the Gideon method.' So now, while I sat under a pine-tree and drank some wine, he took himself off to discuss a flock of sheep with a ragged shepherd-boy who was guarding them. He came back looking rather gloomy and took a savage pull at the wine-bottle. 'Their bowels are out of order,' he said at last. 'I hope to God it's not contagious enteritis.'

We set off across the plain with some caution, for the ever-present danger of mines was a constant preoccupation, and no detailed map of existing mine-fields had been published. Indeed the Italians during the earlier part of the war had mislaid their own defence plans, so that when the Germans moved into Rhodes they were forced to re-mine many areas. Maps of the latter fortunately were in our hands. But there were still large mined areas of the island unaccounted for, and Gideon had more than once been in danger of his life as he was forced to tip-toe on to an apparently 'live' field to rescue Homer, his dog, whose curiosity was always leading him into undesirable places. A maze of dry paths led us across the valley, through silvery groves of olives, and pastures richly scented with thyme and myrtle bruised by the hooves of goats. The little cottages here were encircled with walls of hibiscus and oleander, and we stopped once or twice to knock at a strange door and ask if the area was mined. But nobody seemed to be sure. One old lady in a red handkerchief assured us that there were no mine-fields here, but that the other side of the main road 'among the archaics' there was a large field. Gideon groaned. 'This incredible talent the Germans have,' he said, 'for choosing valuable antiquities as gun-sites—such vandalism.' But it is really only Teutonic military logic. What commander could choose a better defensive position than an acropolis?

We were fortunate in not having to carry provisions, for a message had been sent to Peter, the warden of Phileremo, to expect us; and from what little I knew of Peter's habits and temperament—he combined the trades of poacher, guide and family man with perfect harmony—what I knew of him led me to expect nothing less than a whole lamb on the spit. I told Gideon so. 'Lamb?' he said irritably, 'He mustn't kill lambs. We've forbidden that by proclamation.' 'Wait till you taste it—the sage and garlic, Gideon, the sauce.'

Gideon cannot resist licking his lips, but he wags his head reproach-fully at the idea and strikes an olive-tree in passing with the flat of his hand—as if to chastise the forbidden thought.

The village of Trianda stands on the level ground at the end of the fine valley which bears its name; the houses stand off the main road which passes through it, for the most part hidden in groves of olive, fig and orange. They are the summer-houses of the wealthier Rhodians, and the ambition of every man of men is to have a little house at Trianda where he can sit in the cool shade of his own fig-tree during August and September, when Rhodes is hot. It was here, I am reminded, that Lady Hester Stanhope lived during her short and dramatic stay in the island—in one of these small blind-looking Turkish houses with its barred windows and shadowy interior, with its grove of orange and cherry-trees shutting out the view of the sea: it was here that she took to trousers—or the Turkish equivalent of trousers.[1] Here we set our backs to the sea and the village, and our faces to the bulk of Phileremo, the flat-topped mountain which was Ialysos once, and which has offered a first-class defensive site to a hundred armies, Greek, Frankish, Roman, Turkish, German. It is little wonder that no traces of the ancient Acropolis remain. To our right in the valley, as we reach the first upward curve of the road, we see the 'archaics' which the old woman spoke of; a series of trenches and parapets cut in the red soil of the valley to form a square.

How much is archaeology and how much military workings we are unable to gauge until we break the back of the mountain ahead of us, following the sinuous road which now leads through a dense forest of young pine. Here on a shoulder of hill Gideon called a truce to the pace I was setting and we sat for a while to look down over the valley which now lay spread beneath us, its squares and oblongs of cultivation picked out in russet browns and green until the whole prospect looked like some fine old tweed plaid, much darned. The sun was sinking behind Tilos, and the mountains across the way had become wine-dark and bony. A light wind siphoned up the water in the shallows beyond the town and kicked up spray around a caieque heading south. Trianda drowses among its silver-grey olive-trees. Directly beneath we can see the slight tump of excavated ground

[1] I am wrong. It was at Lindos or perhaps Malona.

where the city of Ialysos once stood, and can even discern among its
scarred furrows traces of ancient wall. Of the minefield, however,
there is no discernible trace from this range. Westward the torn gun-
emplacement of Mount Paradiso (an almost exact replica of Phileremo) flares for a moment as the sun picks up fragments of glass and
metal to play upon. We shall, I calculate, have about half an hour of
light in which to potter about the ruins on the crown of the hill.
We turn away from the prospect and climb the long steep road to
the summit. The air has become colder, and spicy from the pine-
forest which surrounds us. From time to time we shout Peter's name
aloud, and the echo of our voices plays back upon us from several
sides at once. But there is no answering call. He must be up at the
monastery, waiting for us.

But then his laugh came out of nowhere and startled us. It was as
if the trees laughed. Homer barked. We turned about, looking now
here, now there, like characters in the Tempest, while Peter's tittering
laughter sped from tree to tree, from rock to rock. Finally he had
pity on us, and climbed down from the branches where he had been
hiding. Brushing the dust and bark from the battle-dress of which he
was so proud he came towards us, a short stocky man, with yellowish
eyes, a snub nose, and an irresistibly comic expression on his round
face. 'Did you think I was a *kaous?*' he asked. We shook hands and he
expressed himself honoured to meet Gideon of whom he had many
favours to ask. Together the three of us left the road and followed a
narrow turning path to the summit, walking deep in anemones
across the shadowy glades and mossy brakes which crown Phileremo.
'First,' said Peter, 'I shall explain all the archaics to you without any
charge, and then we will go to my house where I have a splendid
dinner for you.' Gideon grunts.

'I suppose you have a sheep?' he said in an off-hand way, torn
between duty and a hunger which Timocreon would have sym-
pathised with.

'A sheep?' Peter sounds outraged. 'For six people, not including
my family? I have two sheep.'

The others are supposed to be coming on to join us later in the
evening, and to be bringing blankets and mattresses for Gideon and
me.

There is precious little to explain about Phileremo today; the monastery has been thoroughly bombed, and the image of the Virgin, which was the object of so much veneration in the time of the Crusaders, has long since vanished. Once more, however, we found ourselves walking among shattered field-guns and a metal harvest of cannon-shells, for Phileremo had been the site of fierce action between Italian and German troops shortly after the fall of Italy. The Italians, though they outnumbered the Germans by six to one, and held the crown of the hill, only lasted out a week of Stuka bombardment. They left behind them mounds of live ammunition and a small pyramid of tin helmets. The little monastery is a ruin. In the garden a few fragments of Byzantine and Hellenic stone lie forlornly about. But the view is incomparable from the little monk's walk, tree-lined and shady, which has been contrived to cross the summit from end to end. From here you can stare down landwards at the gutted aerodrome of Maritza, now dotted with abandoned aircraft, some wingless, which lie about among the fields like charred moths under a lamp. Beyond that green bowl the hills rise again and lead away to the green-spires of Monte Profeta.

'In old times,' says Peter, 'the image of the Panaghia was the patron saint of the island. In moments of trouble it was carried in a solemn procession to Rhodes, and all round the town. Even before the last siege of the Turks they did this, but it had no effect.'

'Where do you get your information from?' asks Gideon.

'There is an old monk in the village who told me.'

'How does he know?'

'Books,' said Peter, 'he has many books. Before, there were many relics in the island, but now none.' He is right there; Torr has preserved a list of them which for sheer variety takes some beating. I quote: 'Chief among the many relics preserved at Rhodes were the right hand of John the Baptist: one of the three bronze crosses made by the Empress Helena from the basin in which Christ washed the Apostles' feet: a cross made from the True Cross: a fragment of the Crown of Thorns, which budded yearly on Good Friday: and one of the thirty pieces of silver; wax impressions of which, if made by the priest in Passion Week, were efficacious in travail of child-birth and in peril by sea.'

Cameirus

While Gideon and I went to make a further exploration of the hillside, Peter sat down under a tree to wait for the rest of the party. As we returned we heard voices among the trees. Mills, to the alarm of his wife, was already busy collecting souvenirs from among the cannon-shells that littered the paths. Hoyle sat in Sand's old German car, quizzing the view through his glasses, while Sand himself and E were climbing the staircase to the monastery tower with Peter. After a good deal of ferocious banter from Hoyle and Mills, Gideon was permitted to announce himself more than ready for dinner, and the cavalcade started off down the hill to Peter's house, Hoyle taking his little rests every fifty yards with the punctuality of a Swiss clock, and Mills singing at the top of his voice.

The house of Peter the guide lies off the main road some two hundred yards before it breaks up through the pine-forest and reaches the crown of the hill. It is built in a cutting sheer against the mountain-side. Its forecourt is shaded by an enormous plane-tree, while a stream runs thickly out of the side of the hill, so that the air under the great tree is a perpetual mixture of shadow and spray. To the noise of cold running water the children shout and play all day, the seven cages of canaries slowly swing in the arbour under the terrace, while their occupants chirp to the note of the water. To live so close to a powerful stream is as good as living by the sea; the noise of it—black water squirting down upon stone—provides a background, a momentum for one's life. The air vibrates and wavers round one as if from the hum of a great dynamo. Even when you enter the house, and the noise of the water is stilled, you have, as if within the canals of the middle ear, a deep echo.

Peter's house boasted a precarious balcony overlooking the valley —an extremely dangerous-looking wooden arrangement built along the first floor. The feeling of height, the great expanse of country below one, and the fear that at any moment one might fall through those crazy planks of wood into the valley, gave a strange character to that first dinner-party in Phileremo. Hoyle said that he felt he was up in a balloon. Peter's own feeling for metaphor was not far behind Hoyle's as he added proudly: 'Sitting here you know what the bird feels when you hang its cage in a tree.'

The house abounded in livestock and small black-eyed children.

Visitors to the table included a tiny and immaculate lamb, with a coat as soft as moss, and an eye like a live coal. It drank wine from a saucer with the utmost concentration, its chevril ears crumpled upon its flat and woolly skull. Two tortoises walked about with a blameless clockwork air; and Gideon was kept busy buying up cicadas from the smaller children and setting them free. The peasant children have a nasty habit of catching a cicada and tying it to a piece of string. It makes an admirable bull-roarer, for if you swing it round and round your head it lets out a dull creaking sort of protest. Needless to say this is a habit which Gideon dislikes intensely, and no sooner does he see a cicada trussed up in this way but he must buy it and set it free. 'Let me see,' I remember him saying, 'Six children, six cicadas at five lirettas a head. . . . Philanthropy is an expensive game, Hoyle. Don't have anything to do with it.' But Hoyle, who was carving the lamb with an infectious air of approval, was too occupied to give much thought to this animadversion. 'I was afraid,' he said, 'it was going to be a *leetle* bit tough but,' putting a segment in his mouth, 'praise be to our Lady of Phileremo, it isn't.' It wasn't.

Lamps had been lit by now and perched on nails. They cast a frail radiance over the balcony so that, seen from the ground-floor, where Peter's wife was still busy cooking a dish of octopus in a metal cauldron, the balcony looked like some lighted ship sailing upon a canal perhaps, or the unruffled waters of some great lake. A comparison I thought poetical enough to express to Mills, who had come down with me to inspect the octopus. 'Yes,' he said, standing beside me and gazing up at the scene. 'And Gideon is lifting his glass to his mouth with the regularity of a Varsity oarsman, rowing.' Gideon, indeed, had become as ruddy as a lamp himself. He glowed. His monocle was misty with good cheer. The fourth bottle of wine had brought its customary loosening of tongues. The octopus when it appeared looking like a boiled motor-tyre was greeted with shouts of applause. Gideon proposed a toast to it. The octopus was in no condition to reply to these courtesies. It lay bubbling in a rich red sauce flavoured with garlic and peppercorns. Hoyle once more constituted himself taster and repeated 'I was afraid it was going to be a *leetle* bit tough but,' putting a piece of the sucker in his mouth, 'praise be it isn't.' It wasn't.

Mills slipped down to the car and brought up his guitar. The wooden house proved an extraordinary sound-box, mellowing the note of the strings, and making it louder, more resonant and authoritative. Voices too had a curious ebbing volume over that blue valley with its darkened border of sea. We sang for the most part the traditional Greek folk-songs, tasting once more their extraordinary purity of line, and the marriage of words and music in dance-measure which is their supreme quality. Later Peter felt emboldened enough to sing us some of his Anatolian songs, with their sharp quarter-tones and strange lapses from key to key. In order to achieve this kind of singing you must put your head back and let the voice become pliant, soft, almost undirected. Peter's voice bubbled in his throat like rose-water in the bowl of a narguileh as he followed the windings of these old melodies with their intricate cross-references of rhythm and accent. It is the singing of a bird, apparently haphazard and undisciplined, but demanding far greater voice-control than European singing does. The songs, too, though they resembled those of Crete and of Macedonia, had a hint of something else in them—the flavour of Arabia, of Persia. Their melancholy was not wild and savage as the Greek mountain melancholy is: it was softer, more quaintly flavoured.

Gideon by now was asleep with his head upon the table. Hoyle, whose capacity was normally a minim of wine per meal, had poured himself a whole glass and was sunk, I could see, in his own memories of the East, the songs he had heard in Beirut and Damascus before the last war. E sat with her black eyes fixed upon the singer's face following every supple turning, every sour change of tone and key. By her side Chloe petted the lamb and tried to interest it in a slice of octopus. Mills and Sand were cracking walnuts in the palms of their hands, expressing an over-exaggerated solicitude whenever the noise seemed to border upon rudeness to Peter. But the singer himself was lost. He held the guitar lightly between his knees, his blunt fingers folded about it with the repose that comes from long familiarity: and as I hold this picture for a moment in my mind I see him singing with his black eyes fixed on the darkness of the valley below us, his sleeves rolled back, his collar open, and the sound of his voice wobbling in his throat like a second pulse.

From there to the roaring of cars, the loud good-nights, and the yellow swathes of headlight cutting the pines, and diminishing with the noise of engines in the valley—from there the transition is immediate. Yet it must have been late. We were left with the roaring of the mountain spring and first whoop of owls. We settled down to sleep in flea-bags on the balcony, Gideon and I. 'We must be up at cock-crow,' he cried once, indistinctly, in the voice of one leading a charge against hopeless odds—and then fell asleep with his head buried upon his arm. I blew out the lights and lay for a long time, listening to the wind stirring the pines, and the faint noise of cars crossing the valley below us. The children were long since in bed, and only Peter sat upon the deserted balcony, drinking a last glass of mastika before turning in.

On the landward side of Phileremo, no doubt, the early moon had risen above the horizon and set. Meanwhile without ceasing the stream flowed on from the heart of the mountain, its water ringing steadily upon the stone still of the fountain before it disappeared among the mosses and cresses of its underground track again. But already our ears had become so accustomed to it that we should not have recognised the silence that might follow if it should suddenly stop.

It was already dawn when I awoke. Gideon had rolled out of his flea-bag and was lying on his back snoring like a clockwork toy, his face smoothed out and juvenile, the round circle of his eye scored out by his eyeglass gleaming white as a scar.

In order to reach the privy at the back of the house one had to pass through a ground-floor room whose furniture would have delighted a surrealist. There, standing upon the earthen floor, without any attempt at premeditated arrangement, I saw a sewing-machine, several Louis Quinze pieces, a Sheraton sideboard, desk, a type-writer, and a very handsome grand piano. The piano had been white-washed. The reason for this accumulation of treasures is a simple one; during the period of acute starvation in Rhodes the peasants refused to trade their vegetables for money because they were afraid of fluctuations in value, or even of the Italian liretta being recalled in exchange for some valueless occupation currency. They would accept articles of value, however, in exchange for vegetables; so it was that one saw caravans of carts setting off from the town every morning for the interior loaded with furniture, pictures, typewriters, plate, linen, etc. In the remote villages these objects were freely exchanged, and now the peasant houses are crammed with them. And the whitewashed piano? Peter's explanation has a certain nobility about it. 'Of course we whitewashed it,' he said, 'You know as well as I do that black is the colour of mourning. We did not wish to attract a death to the house. So we painted the piano white.'

The air was sweet with the damps of night as we set off, and we walked steadily until we reached Kremasto, where we explored the church with its holy well and immense cypresses; and where the vicar, who looked like a dispossessed earwig, conducted us from ikon to ikon with great circumstance and a wealth of pointless detail. Afterwards we took a glass of sticky liqueur with him in the sunlit courtyard whose floor was paved in pure white sea-pebbles, dusted spotless by the brooms of two old women who seemed to be nuns. Kremasto is the scene of the greatest festival of the year, held on Assumption Day, and on the ninth day after that date, in honour of the Panaghia. Here, as in Tenos, the holy ikon performs its yearly miracle of healing, and here come crowds of foreign visitors from Turkey and the islands round about. Along four sides of the monastery are the cells in which they are accommodated during the festival. Despite the prevailing dislocation of traffic with the mainland a good crowd of suppliants is expected, says the old man. During the war years everything was at a standstill, the narrow straits were mined, everyone was starving. Now . . . peace is here. He leaned forward and took one of Gideon's hands, pressing it warmly between his own. 'England has brought us white bread,' he said, nodding that rusty old head on his shoulders.

We moved off in good order down the sunny main street of the town which was lined with barrows full of bright vegetables, for Kremasto is the nearest market-town to Rhodes, and it is here that the peasant unloads his stocks if he does not feel like travelling to the capital in search of a buyer. Needless to say, keeping a vegetable stall is one of those occupations which do not take up all one's time; there is plenty of time to drink, to gossip and play cards—and these seem to be the major occupations of the stall-owners, who sit in the little cafés lining the main street and while away the hours in this manner. Here we bought some apples, not without difficulty, for the owner of the stall was engaged in a game of backgammon and sent us a message with a friend to say that he was indisposed; he was sitting in full view at the time, his big coarse face bent over the board, his coffee cup beside him. We entered the café and after a long argument prevailed upon him to serve us. He did so with hauteur.

We made good time in the direction of Villa Neuova along the broad motor-road for it was early as yet. Gideon chatted amicably as we walked, pausing from time to time to cross the hedge and peer anxiously into the features of a goat or a cow. By the early afternoon we had reached a hollow in a hillside beyond the town of Villa Neuova where a number of sources broke from the mossy banks of a hill and created a shady pleasaunce—I do not know how else to describe it—encircled by some tall plane-trees, forming a sort of pavilion around the little whitewashed tavern where we proposed to halt and eat. The sunshine was, by this time, fierce enough to have turned Gideon's thoughts in the direction of a siesta. There was no food to be had beyond a boiled egg or two, so we were glad of what we had brought with us. There was, however, plenty of good red wine, served in generous tin cans which had originally been intended as measures for oil. The tavern-keeper was a tiny emaciated man in the last stages of consumption. He served us deftly and quietly, and paused with pride to indicate the superb view from the little earth-terrace upon which we sat. It was indeed worth looking at—that sloping foreground of mulberry-trees, thinning away to the bold blue of sea and the violet-cloud of mountains opposite. But it was not a view that one 'saw' in the strict sense; it radiated over one, dancing in that brown heat, pouring into the eyes and spreading within the five senses—as light enters the pin-hole of a camera's lens but floods the whole gelatine surface of the negative; so that we sat in a kind of dark inebriation, tasting the sweat and wine mixing in our mouths, and breathing in the whole landscape with every breath we drew like a perfume.

The wine was ice-cold, for the pitcher had been hanging down the well all morning on the end of a rope. Our host came timidly to the table and sat down with us to watch us eat and to ask the inevitable questions. He accepted some bread and lamb with a dignified air, stretching out his thin talons in a way that reminded one of something fastidious and small—a cat, perhaps: and this impression was strengthened by his thin black moustache which grew limply enough, but whose ends were waxed and turned up like a cat's whiskers. He was called Panayotis Porphyrogennis. 'But,' he added modestly, 'they call me Pipi here.'

You have guessed it? The inevitable happened. Gideon, animated by his own excellent conversation and the weather, drank more than three glasses of wine, which turned him the colour of brickdust, and sapped his stamina as a walker. There was nothing for it but take a short nap on the mossy bank under the planes until the sun had westered a bit. This we did, and it was not until four that we mustered up enough energy to strike the road again. 'We shall never make Cameirus,' groaned Gideon, as he stumped along. 'We shall be picked up by Mills and he will jeer at me, I know it. He always swore we should never reach Cameirus if we found a tavern on the way.'

We did however manage to get a tidy way across the Kalavarda valley with its long flat grape-orchards, and its hundreds of metal windmills imported by the Italians to draw up water from the artesian wells. Despite the fact that each of these rather crude contrivances bore the legend MADE IN CHICAGO they looked very poetical in the greenish afternoon light, slowly turning their metal flukes in the north-wind. The roads were shaded too and everywhere there sounded the noise of water flowing out along the irrigation channels on to the parched red soil. Storks had built their crazy muddled nests in some of the water-wheels and we heard their cracked voices as we passed, mingled with the bubbling of water, and the swish of wind in the silver-grey olives that stretched away in clumps towards the receding hills.

We passed through one or two dirty and dilapidated villages— Gideon religiously averting his face whenever we were confronted with the word 'Kapheneion' written on a wall or lettered out on some crude signpost. By the time Mills' little hornet of a car came whizzing up we had good enough reason to be pleased with ourselves, for we had covered a good part of the way to Kalavarda. To Gideon's surprise and relief Mills was full of admiration for our prowess. He had collected the mattresses and flea-bags and proposed to go on ahead to Cameirus. As there was no room for us in that tiny car—which barely accommodated Chloe and himself on two seats shaped like egg-cups—he roared off again along the dusty road, and left us sitting in a dry river-bed among a clump of vivid oleanders to wait for Hoyle and E. Gideon was much relieved at Mills' respect for his day's walk, and felt disposed to boast a bit, and he was still in this vein when Hoyle's old German Mercedes came into sight. Hoyle, however, seemed surprised to see us so soon. 'What?' he said, 'I thought you people told me you were going to walk?' He commented briefly on Gideon's partiality to tavern life, adding dark asides about the lower nature of man, until Gideon was quite out of humour, and pretended that a sprained ankle had prevented him from walking as far as he might have done.

We climbed into the car, and swept down the long straight road into Kalavarda. Here the country changed abruptly, very much as it does when one enters the valley of Epidaurus, and the change was like a premonition, a quickening of something inside one which only the sight of Cameirus itself could satisfy. The hills were low here, and the road ran along the sea-shore. A sense of something definite and pre-arranged, as in the landscapes contrived by those ancient Chinese gardeners for the rulers of old China. Or, as Hoyle put it, 'Limestone formations, with a thinnish topcrust of green. Look here, Gideon, holm-oak and juniper.' Gideon was still disposed to be testy. 'My dear Hoyle, that's not holm-oak, it's barbed wire from a gun-post.' At last we came to a fountain set in a circle of young plane trees, and here we found Chloe washing great bunches of grapes against dinner, while Mills, who had run his car off the road under the pines, was lovingly tinkering about in its entrails with the air of a surgeon performing a delicate operation.

Leaving them to fill the water-jar, we climbed the tree-lined way which leads up the hill to Cameirus, the car groaning and panting in second gear at the steepness of the slope. Beyond the swaying tips of the pines somewhere lay the city, and in ancient times this gracious tree-lined approach to it from the little harbour of Mylantia was made more lovely by the population of statues that stood beside the road to welcome the newcomer. Now the fleshy scalp of the hillside showed the ugly workings of anti-tank gun sites. This had been part of the defensive system manned by the Italians. We deduced this from their refuse which always contained a high percentage of empty hair-oil bottles and discarded clothing. The road wound higher and still higher, passing the ugly cemetery for German troops (pitched with such vandalistic accuracy slap in the glade below the town) and breasting the green hummock which cuts Cameirus from the world.

You arrive in the centre of the ancient town almost before you know it; it is as sudden as a descent from a balloon. The whole thing assembles itself before your eyes like a picture thrown upon a cinema-screen. It lies there in the honey-gold afternoon light listening to the melodious ringing of water in its own cisterns, and the faint whipping of wind in the noble pines which crown the amphi-theatre. The light here has a peculiar density as if the blue of the sea had stained it with some of its own troubled dyes. The long sloping main-street is littered with chipped inscriptions. One can make out the names of city fathers long since dead, of priests and suppliants; they rise in a long progress up the chalky pathways of the town to the red earth wall beyond which the archaeologist has not trespassed, to the rather over-poetic votive column which, one can guess without being told, is part of the most recent Italian restoration work. Nevertheless Cameirus is beautiful in a way that persuades mere ugliness to conform to its grace of air and situation; even the curator's Nissen hut, now crammed with verminous filth, smashed bottles, shed equipment, and bandages—even this cannot intrude upon the singing beauty of this ancient town uncovered by the spade of the archaeologist. If such a city, you find yourself thinking, if such a landscape-out-of-time was not able to strike the right chord in the human heart by its appeals to clemency, truth, and intellectual order of life, what chance have we with our unburied cities to do so? And when you see the grave-stones from the little necropolis of Cameirus stacked up in our museums (it is inevitable that the treasures of towns like these are hoarded up in Museums) it is the so-often repeated single word—the anonymous Χαῖρε—which attracts you by its simple; obsessive message to the living. It is not the names of the rich or the worthy, not the votive reliefs and the sepulchral epigrams, but this single word, 'Be Happy', 'Be Happy', serving both as a farewell and admonition, that goes to your heart with the whole impact of the Greek style of mind, the Greek orientation to life and death: so that you are shamed into regarding your life, and realising with bitterness how little you have fulfilled of the principle behind a thought so simple yet so pregnant, and how even your native vocabulary lacks a word whose brevity and grace could paint upon the darkness of death the fading colours of such gaiety, love and truth as Χαῖρε does upon these modest gravestones.

The party was not nearly as riotous as the one we had enjoyed the previous night. Cameirus, glimmering whitely below us, was perhaps the reason. Its silence and its utter self-possession forced themselves between our sentences like the blade of a knife, separating thought from contemplation, and filling one with self-consciousness by their volume. So it was that for the most part we ate silently, staring out from the dim circle of wavering yellow light to where the late moon had quicksilvered the marbles of the old town, and picked up the three small promontories which jutted into the sea below Cameirus, one of which contained, in ancient times, a temple to Pan. But if our conversation was desultory it reflected in no way upon the humour of the company; Gideon had recovered from his fit of pique—a bottle and a half of white Kastellaneia had seen to that. Hoyle himself was disposed to be complimentary about our walk; he was always slow to reach what he himself called 'a considered opinion', and perhaps by now he had realised that Gideon's annoyance at his teasing was genuine and not simulated.

Mills and I walked about the ancient town for a while before turning in. The moon was all but gone, yet the light brimmed the whole amphitheatre, casting a surface of glittering aluminium over the white houses, and blocking in great masses of shadow on the seaward side. Despite the light frost, and the thick nap of dew which had fallen over everything, we were only mildly cold; a few moments of walking about, and we found ourselves warm again. In the silence we could hear the water gurgling somewhere down there, below the earth.[1] An owl whistled once, twice, and we heard its creaking flight

[1] The bat-infested underground water-conduits of Cameirus I never had the courage to explore until one memorable day when Paddy and Xan and the Corn Goddess shamed me into following them down its dark tunnels.

from one tree to another, like the rustle of a linen skirt. I suddenly remembered other moments of time spent in this landscape, time printed upon silence with all its real colours up: the faint burring of honey-bees in Agamemnon's tomb: one glittering spring day, the noise of snow melting among the meadows at Nemea: a bird singing stiffly at noon like a voice on stilts from the bushes where we had slept: the crash of a falling orange in an island: all isolated moments existing in a peculiar dense medium of their own which was like time but not of it. Each moment to itself entire, populating a whole continuum of feeling. Coming over the ridge into Sparta, bursting through a cloud to see the lime-green Eurotas gushing into the valley carrying with it a multitude of tinkling spots of ice. . . . And these separate moments, quite loose, not stitched together except by their parentage in the same quality of feeling, suddenly added themselves to this quiet second of time spent with Mills, sitting in the frail moonlight of Cameirus, tracing an inscription on a votive stone, feeling the chisel's edge hard through the moss, spelling out Χαῖρε. 'Be Happy,' 'Be Happy.' Then the owl whistled once again from a different quarter, and someone struck a match up there under the trees. We rose by mutual consent and walked back up the long main-street of the town.

Next morning I awoke with a start to see Mills on his knees pumping the Primus stove. The sun had risen, but was still behind the hill. Its warmth, however, penetrated the crust of the island, warming the statues back to life, drying the dew from the houses of Cameirus, and offering us the auguries for another lovely day. A green lizard had crawled up to a favourite stone, and was warming itself in the indirect light of the sun. Its satin throat quivered as if with song.

Today we intended to complete the circuit of the island, and spend the night at Lindos—a journey which would put us within striking distance of Rhodes for the morning following; when we were due back at our respective establishments. We started off together, but the sedateness of Hoyle's driving soon wore out Mills' patience, he passed us on a corner and disappeared across the valley in a cloud of dust. 'It'll be a case of physician heal thyself one of these days,' remarked Hoyle sadly. His own driving technique, while accurate enough, would perhaps have been more suited to a landau. It was as

if he had carried over his tendency to have 'little rests' into his driving
—or else as if he had infected the engine of the Mercedes with some
of his own heart-trouble. At any rate, when a new idea struck him,
it was his habit to slam on the brakes, stop the car, and sit awhile to
consider it from every angle.

The sun was up now. I sat behind with E while Hoyle and Gideon
shared the front. We ate grapes and watched the valley unroll itself
before us. Hoyle and Gideon were still deep in the subject of vampires,
I remember, a subject which sounded more than ever fantastic in that
clear air. The road from Cameirus runs along the flat sea-line,
dotted with beaches. Shallow hills like green tumuli stretch away
landwards, studded with bushes of myrtle and thyme—a haunt for
the red-legged partridges and the rock-dove. The road is a bad one,
so that we were quite surprised to catch Mills up by the time we
reached the little harbour of Cameiro Skala. As we lumbered up
across the plain we saw why he had stopped. Three yellow fishing-
boats had just put in and were piling up their catch. In the middle of
a chaffering crowd of Symiot fishermen Mills was standing, blond
and stocky, bargaining for half a dozen red mullet. Gideon's re-
sourceful eye had already noticed a tavern by the roadside, and here
we waited for the deal to be closed, drinking a mastika that tasted
like horse-embrocation and listening to the squibbling of a clarinet
played by a fisherboy. Here, too, we met the inevitable American
Greek who made the inevitable comparison between Detroit and
this 'lousy country', and complimented us on speaking our mother-
tongue as well as we did. Gideon flew into a temper with him: 'You
stinking empty-headed son-of-a-bitch', he said, with an excellent
imitation of a New York accent, 'why the hell do you come back
here and poison the air of your mother-country with your cheap
snarls and your passion for Coca Cola?' The man recoiled as if he had
received a push in the chest. Hoyle clicked his tongue against his
teeth. 'Really Gideon,' he said. 'An officer and a gentleman simply
doesn't, you know.' Gideon adjusted his eyeglass. 'Perhaps he doesn't,'
he said mildly. 'But I do, old man. I definitely do. The cheek of these
people.' Mills by this time had concluded his business and stowed the
fish in the tool-box of his car. We set off pursued by the cries of
'Good journey' 'Come back soon'. Greeks adore partings.

The road winds steeply uphill, past the old Frankish fort called Castello today, and then turns abruptly inland: and rising out of the cluster of hills before us, we saw the frowning crags of Atabyron, the chief mountain of the island. Its massifs of shining black towered up into the sky from a green vegetation-line marking the site of Embona. Atabyron in that lucid morning air looked more like some invention of man than a natural phenomenon, it was as if some prodigious rough model for a statue had been abandoned here. The wind and rain had eroded it. The winter snows had polished its slippery black surface until it glinted with a bluish light, as charcoal does. It lay with all the massive pregnancy of a liner at anchor among the lesser hills, and as we climbed towards it the air became thinner, and bluer, while the mountain-villages glittered in its rareness like clusters of lump-sugar.

Up there on the final crag, from which one could faintly see the mountains of Crete, had once stood the little temple to Zeus where the great sacred bull had uttered its oracles. There is evidence to suggest that the sacred bull cult had not concerned itself with the worship of a live animal but with a gigantic bronze representation of it, in which the bodies of human beings had been placed, to roast over a fire. Their cries and groans, it is suggested, may have been taken for prophecies.

Tasting the blue refinements of that air, and watching the geological structure change to granite, we felt the first pangs of hunger steal upon us, though we were far from our objective—Monolithos. We stopped in an orange-grove outside Embona and nibbled some bread and fruit, while Gideon cracked a bottle of wine. He had got into the habit of 'fining' himself for little errors of taste or judgement. 'Damn,' he would say, 'I fine myself two glasses of red.' Or else 'I simply can't let that pass without fining myself a glass of white.' Needless to say he derived a certain pleasure from this odd method of self-punishment. Now he fined himself for his rudeness to the American Greek of Cameiro Skala while Hoyle watched him with all the weight of his unexpressed distaste apparent in his expression. 'Your liver will have to pay up in the end,' he remarked sourly.

We passed the road to Embona and turned right, to circle the great charred butt of Atabyron, whose stony ramps of black rock made

it seem more than ever medieval—like some old black-letter bible
rotting away in a Museum. . . . Gideon showed some disposition to
try and climb it but we shouted him down. Monolithos lay ahead,
and we pushed on across this razor-back landscape of rock and thistle,
punctuated everywhere by springs gushing out of the side of the
mountain, and giant walnut-trees, Artamiti . . . Saint Isidore (whoever he may be). The air was thickly scented with pines now, for we
were descending gradually.

To reach Monolithos you must crash over the brow of a hill and
think that you are falling into the sea. Miraculously, however, you
see that the dirt road continues, and the great hump of rock stabs at
you, rising out of the sea like a pointing finger. You crawl down
almost to sea-level before you reach the pine-glade lying at the foot
of the castle. 'How Mills ever got down here without breaking his
neck I don't know,' mutters Hoyle as he eases the big Mercedes into
the hollow with circumspection. But Mills is sitting in a cleft of stone
at the very top of the castle, tossing pine-cones into the sea, and singing at the top of his voice.

There was everything to be said for singing. In that dry clement
sunlight we climbed the grassy staircases to the summit. Everywhere
there were tiny dells dense with anemone and daisies. Chloe had flung
herself down between two knuckles of rock, and when she sat up to
welcome us we saw that she was covered with bright yellow pollen.
The summit of Monolithos is like some great sculptured lion's paw;
between the claws thick mossy carpets have grown up, fed by some
underground spring, no doubt, and here you may lie down in beds
of flowers for all the world as if you were still in the lowland glades
around Rodini. It was in one of these that we had lunch and talked,
idly watching the kestrels dip in the blue gulfs beneath us, and the
little coloured lizards scrabble about among the crannies of the rock.

Afterwards Mills and I went off together and climbed the tower
of the Byzantine chapel to see if one could spit directly into the sea
from this vantage-point. Mills was of a distinctly competitive turn of
mind. He was always thinking up feats of this kind to test his native
skill. Spitting over bridges, playing ducks-and-drakes upon a calm
sea, diving for pennies—there was nothing that he would not do
for the sheer pleasure of doing something active and, if possible,

slightly irresponsible. In the intervals of spitting over the cliff he said: 'I say, have you ever looked at Gideon's monocle? I picked it up yesterday while he was asleep, to see how weak his eye was. Do you know what?'

'No. What?'

'It's made of ordinary glass.'

'But what's the point of that?' Mills sighed and dusted his blue pea-jacket with his hands. 'Humanity is so constructed that when it wants to hide something it is forced to accentuate it, to throw it into relief: I doubt if you'd notice Gideon's glass eye at all if the poor old thing hadn't drawn attention to it by wearing that monocle.' I had not noticed any signs of shyness about Gideon, I must say, and the idea came as rather a surprise to me. 'But Gideon could carry a couple of glass eyes and a pair of wooden legs with ease,' I exclaimed. 'He bluffs his way through life like a tenth century man-at-arms.' Mills jumped down from the rock and began picking flowers. 'Have you never heard Gideon's own definition of an Englishman?' he asked. 'It fits him perfectly. An Englishman may be defined as a soft-centred creature with a tough and horny shell, through which two sensitive antennae (humour and prejudice) explore the world around him.'

The journey down into the flat and featureless valley to Cattavia was uneventful. Gideon discovered Hoyle's copy of the Abbé Cutlet in a pocket of the car and regaled us with quotations in an exaggeratedly correct French accent. '*Après Lindos, Cattavia,*' he intoned, '*paysage plus riant.*' It wasn't really 'riant'—simply a stretch of alluvial marshland, poorly cultivated, and lying at the back of the eroded mountain we had crossed. After an hour or so we hit the nondescript, flattish, amorphous coastal belt, with a few villages fast asleep in their flea-tormented isolation. Here sunlight was a drug.

Nearing Lindos, however, it all changed abruptly and rose up into a gnarled rock-hewn landscape—a coast bitten out in huge mouthfuls of metamorphic rock, gleaming dully with mica, and shot through with the colours of iron and trap. It was as if a storm at sea had suddenly been solidified and compressed into these frowning capes and fastnesses of coloured rock. The sea boomed upon the sand of the long beaches, while everywhere the rusty wire and the skull with its legend 'Achtung Minen' spoke Prussian to us. To the east tiny figures knelt in a frieze along the thundering coastline, as if engaged in some obscure rite. They were lifting mines. Even from this great range one could see the tense preoccupation that convulsed them, kneeling there within the sound of the sea, burrowing in the sand with their nervous fingers. Later at a bend in the coast-road we saw the little island where Lady Hester Stanhope was washed up. It is called 'the biscuit'[1] on the charts today.

Doubling back a quarter of a mile before Calato you come upon Lindos through a narrow gulley of rock. It is as if you had been leaning against a door leading to a poem when suddenly it swung open letting you stumble directly into the heart of it. The road bores through a blank wall of rock and turns sharply to the right, running down an inclined plane. Lindos with its harbour lies below you—as if at the bottom of a pie-dish. The configurations of the promontory, upon which the town is built suggest something like the talons of the crab. The little harbour is all but land-locked and the blue of it drenches you like spray. The beach-shallows are picked out in lime-green and yellow, against the reddish, deckle-edged surfaces of stone. In the air above it rides the acropolis. It does not insist. It can afford not to presume, so certain of the impact which it must make on everyone who comes upon it through the gulley in the rock. Is not Lindos the official beauty-spot of Rhodes? The contrast with Cameirus is remarkable—for where Cameirus is refined, turned in upon itself in sunny contemplation, Lindos is bold, strident. Cameirus has all the stillness of an amphora in a Museum, with its frieze of dancers caught in a timeless dancing; Lindos, under the sweetness of its decoration, is like a trumpet-call, beaten out in gold-leaf and vibrating across the blue airs of time.

The little modern town which lies at the foot of the acropolis is perhaps a quarter of the size of ancient Lindos. Its beauty is of a scrupulous Aegean order, and perfect in its kind. The narrow streets which rise and fall like music are paved with clean sea-pebbles, and criss-crossed with little inter-communicating alleys. Their width is enough to accommodate two mules abreast, but no car can enter them. Everything is painted white, a dazzling glitter of plaster and white-

[1] Paximadi.

wash, so that if you half closed your eyes you might imagine that Lindos reflected back the snowy reflections of a passing cloud.

We had intended to sleep on the summit of the acropolis, but the women declared that they would prefer beds, so we accordingly did what all travellers in Greece must sooner or later learn to do if they explore areas where there are no hotels. In the sunny tavern of Lindos we asked for the mayor of the town, and when he arrived, introduced ourselves and set him down to drink a glass of wine with us. He was eager enough to help, and without much difficulty managed to find rooms for us. The nature of Greek hospitality is such that no traveller who flings himself upon the mercies of a village 'demarchos' will ever go bedless.

The sun was low, but there was still time to admire the little Greek church, inspect samples of the famous Lindos ware in some private villas, and admire the four or five Crusader houses which were still standing, and in excellent repair. All the latter were inhabited by Greek families who offered us cups of coffee and the polite possibility of a political discussion. Mills did his 'Florence Nightingale act' as he called it, and visited the sick. By the time he came back to the tavern we had sorted the baggage and prepared such food as we had to carry up the acropolis. The sun was westering rapidly as we walked up the winding paths of the Acropolis behind Markos, the guardian of the site. He was a slow-spoken, lazy-looking man, with a fine head set well back on broad shoulders: his broken nose gave him a slanting quizzical expression. He had been a commercial traveller and regretted that we spoke Greek, for he would dearly have loved to conduct the party in French, which he said he knew well. He was as breathless as we were, however, by the time we reached the carved rock-relief of the ship which marks the entry to the fort, and which had been executed in ancient times as a trophy—perhaps even to celebrate the long Thallassoocratia of the Rhodians, which endured some twenty-three years of naval competition about 900 B.C. Markos sat him down on a stone and waited for his breath to come back as he rubbed his hands along the stone bows of the vessel. He accepted a cigarette from Mills who had completed the ascent at record speed, and who betrayed no signs of strain. 'You're too healthy,' said Gideon.

Hoyle had been left miles behind, resting on a convenient rock and staring down into that blue circle of sea whose outer end is marked by a stone tomb rising out of the sea which, say some authorities, is where Cleobolus is buried. I walked back to accompany him. As we toiled up the hill, he chatted knowledgeably about Athene Lindia who had been worshipped in Ancient Lindos with 'flameless sacrifices'. It was at the remains of the temple of Athene that we found the others. They were lying on their stomachs and gazing down six hundred feet into the eye of the sea—that peacock-green twilight eye, glimmering with caverns and deeps where only enough light penetrated to print the diffuse markings of rock and seaweed. Markos, the guide, was in full flight. 'This is Athene Lindia's temple. There.' He picked up a pebble and threw it. 'There the temple of Zeus Policus.' Nobody, I am sorry to say, was listening to him. Down there on that darkening water lay a tiny fishing-boat like a model. 'Listen,' said E. In the silence, like the voice of an insect, came the thin strains of a fisherman singing. The sound slanted up at us through the canyons of coloured rock. We stared down it, watching the curdled greens and reds of the seaweed wavering under it. From this height we could see fish moving under the boat which were invisible to fishermen, travelling in little phosphorescent sparks of light. 'Athene Lindia' I was repeating to myself, like an incantation. Somewhere there had been a grove of sacred olives dedicated to her. Pindar's great ode on Diagoras of Ialysos had been graven on tablets and placed in the temple. In the height of her glory strangers had sent her offerings from Syria and Egypt.

The sun had been sucked down into the sea; dazzling spokes of silver spread out for a moment on the blue, as if from some great lighthouse. Then the uniform dusk. 'Cleobolus was a remarkable old thing,' Hoyle was saying, for the stream of classical evocations which had seemed to dwindle away had suddenly come to life again. The fisherman was out of sight, his singing out of sound. 'Tell us about him, Markos.' Markos took a deep breath and fired out his knowledge in demotic. 'He travelled in Egypt, was very beautiful, and wrote thousands of lovely acrostics, distichs, and other verse. He was one of the Wise Men, and a close personal friend of Solon. He lived to be seventy years old. His famous epigram 'Nothing in excess' is one which the Greeks have treasured to this day.'

'But haven't lived up to,' said Gideon dryly. Markos avoided his eye and pretended that he had not heard the interruption. 'He was, with Pythagoras, one of the first to admit women into the circle of knowledge,' he said amiably baring his teeth at E. 'His daughter Cleobulina was also a writer and left many beautiful poems.'

It was getting chilly. We made a leisurely circuit of the battlements, peering down into the little inlet where, says popular tradition, St Paul was shipwrecked on one of his many voyages. Out at sea the light was fading upon four little islands which Markos pointed out to us: the fourth was a mere shaving of rock awash when the sea was rough. 'Look,' said the guide, 'those islands they call Tetrapolis.'

'Who does?'

'Everybody. The people of Lindos. In ancient times, they say, four cities were there, and all of them sank in a great earthquake.' Gideon was getting restive. He preferred sharper lines of demarcation between legend and attested fact. 'Who says this?' he demanded— and to do him justice you will not find the story of Tetrapolis in any of the authenticated histories.

'Since before my grandfather they say so.'

'But who says so?'

Markos became a trifle impatient. He waved his arm like a wand over the dusky village beneath us. 'Everyone,' he said with a trace of sulkiness. 'Is it true?' said Gideon. Markos nodded vigorously. 'Once,' he said, 'the truth was proved to me by sponge-divers. Every summer they worked this coast and every day I drank with them in the tavern. They had seen columns of marble and statues under the sea when they dived for sponges. Once they gave me some coins which they had brought up and I sold them to a German for bread.'

We slept well that night at the tavern, and next morning did the run to Rhodes in good style, wheeling up through the rock-face where the road turns at right angles to run down to the green plains by Calato. The jagged ruin of Pheraclyea lay on the coast to our right, but Gideon had assured us from an earlier visit that nothing remained of the fort but rubble, and that extensive minefields thereabouts made it hazardous for tourists.

We lumbered through Malona and past the sunburnt farms which the Italian government had subsidised and settled with Sienese farmers—one of the richest agricultural areas in Rhodes. Here Gideon stopped for a brief chat with his Italian overseer. Many of the families had stayed on to wait for a passage to Italy, and they still worked the fields as they had always done, singing and smiling.

The road curls around the shaft of the mountain called Tsambika and through a pass, so that the entry to this second valley is nearly as sudden as the entry upon Lindos.

But at last we ran out along the final spine of the island and saw, at a turn of the road, the spires and turrets of the capital come into view. Here there was time for a final cup of coffee before separating about our various business. We took it under an olive-tree, on dry grass already waking up to the drumming of cicadas.

My heart sinks as I think of the mass of proofs, of correspondence, of files, which await me.

Mills starts up his car and gets into it slowly. 'We have a little while yet,' he says. 'Before they scatter us all over the world.'

The dust rises on the road as the cavalcade sets off.

CHAPTER VII

The Age of the Knights

XV mile the See brode is
From Turky to the Ile of Rodez
At the begynning of this Ile
Wit in but a litell while
Is a thorp that hight Newtoun:
And on a hull there alle alonen,
Is a Castell stiff, and strong,
That some tyme was a cite strong.
The Castell hight men saie soo
Sancta Maria de Fulmaro . . .[1]

A strong toun Rodez hit is,
The Castell is strong and fair I wis.
MATTHEW PARIS: *Purchas His Pilgrimes*

When in the sweltering July heat of the year 1099 the city of Jerusalem fell at long last to the Crusaders, the Rhodians might have claimed a share in the victory, though they played no part in the appalling massacres that followed it—when some seventy thousand human beings were butchered in the streets, and when the Crusaders who had despatched them, knelt upon the blood-stained cobbles of the Redeemer's shrine, 'weeping from excess of joy', to give thanks for their victory. The sea-transports of Rhodes had helped to provision the besiegers. But even before this the island had sent out supplies to the Crusaders when their forces were encamped about Antioch. In this they exercised a religious rather than a political preference, though it is hard to distinguish between the two in the affairs of this age.

[1] The present Phileremo.

Yet the direct connection between the Knights of St John and Rhodes can only be treated tentatively, episodically, because it is only a small part of a larger story which clean overlaps the boundaries of time and place. For a long time Rhodes itself lay, so to speak, in the back areas of that enormous battlefield. Its importance only began to grow when the Knights were expelled from Jerusalem and retired to Cyprus in 1291. At this time, though nominally a dependancy of the Emperor of Constantinople the island was in fact very much at the mercy of the Genoese who administered it, and who, as allies of the Byzantines, exercise a sort of pirate's licence over its harbours and coves when they fitted out their galleys for expeditions against the rich commercial traffic of Venice in the Mediterranean.

High in the catalogue of these rogues, who dignified themselves with the title of Admiral, stands Vignolo de' Vignoli. It was he who first suggested to the Grand Master of the Knights of St John the idea of an attack on Rhodes and the surrounding islands. The island was his base of operations against Cyprus, and it is possible that he had become increasingly conscious of the Knights as a power lying across the path of these predatory raids. More than this, the Turks themselves were a constant nuisance, operating from the creeks and inlets of what is now Anatolia. They had virtually despoiled all the islands off the mainland. They disturbed Vignoli's whole-hearted concentration on the exercise of his craft. Every time he returned from a raid on the Venetians it was only to hear how, in his absence, the Turks had made an incursion, fired a town, destroyed some galleys, deforested an island. . . . Why not, thought Vignoli at a single blow perform a triple feat of skill: neutralize the Knights in Cyprus by an alliance with them: persuade them to consolidate the Dodecanese islands against the Turks: and leave himself free to operate as he pleased?

Fulk de Villaret, the Grand Master of the Knights Hospitallers, was a grave and cautious man, deeply conscious of his order and of the faith in which it was founded; Vignoli was both bold and persuasive. The strategic value of the plan itself was obvious—for the Dodecanese islands, as they are now called, offered something like a deep second-line of defence to the Crusaders, who were no doubt already aware of having over-stretched their lines of communication with the Europe on which they depended. With Jerusalem lost, Cyprus was like some precarious stepping stone around which the water was already lapping. While they sternly maintained their charge it must have been obvious to them that it could not be held indefinitely against the rising tide of barbarism. It was not as if the sea itself was safe; marauding privateers of every colour were abroad. The Knights were like castaways, adrift on the stone rafts of their fortresses, in a sea alive with sharks; these precarious religious enclaves they had founded—each castle which even today seems clenched like a mailed fist—depended on blood and stones for their maintenance.

They moved across this enchanting landscape, dedicated to impulse, like strange automata, these iron men: bringing purpose and direction to places where only appetite and disorder had reigned: sustaining themselves on the iron rations of a discipline and a moral purpose which awoke something like a half-hearted admiration even in the breasts of their enemies. They burned with a self-dedication which could withstand every temptation—save at last the languorous airs of the Levantine landscape they dominated for so long.

But Vignoli's plan offered something new; a string of island fortresses from which the whole variegated coastline of Anatolia could be surveyed and ravaged; a string of stepping stones pointing north to Constantinople. Yet Fulk de Villaret was worldly enough to demand precise and determined articles of the voluble and friendly pirate. The success of their joint attack would give each what he wanted most: to the Knights a defensive barrier, and to Vignoli that treasured peace of mind which was so necessary for the exercise of his talents. The plan was as follows:

Rhodes was to go to the Knights except for two villages which were to be held by Vignoli. Leros and Cos, which the pirate already held under the terms perhaps of some Golden Bull, he was prepared to cede to his allies. One third of the revenue of such other islands of the group as might be conquered was to be payable to Vignoli, and two thirds to the Knights. Vignoli reserved the right to be vicar of all the islands save Rhodes itself.

It is perhaps not without significance that one of the witnesses to this document was a member of the great Florentine banking house of Peruzzi. There were after all perquisites to be thought of in an expedition of this kind, for trade followed the Order as in later times it was to follow the Union Jack.

The Grand Master fitted out two great war-galleys and four smaller vessels for the expedition. He embarked thirty-five chosen Knights and a force of infantry, and on the 22nd of June the convoy set off in a freshening wind for this new adventure. They watered at Castel Rosso for a month while Vignoli went ahead on a reconnaissance. On his return the fleet set sail for the Gulf of Makri where it waited upon a plan of Vignoli's, who nourished some hopes of a speedy and bloodless conquest of Rhodes. Two Genoese galleys were ordered to enter the harbour and surprise the Byzantines holding the city, but they bungled their work. Their captains were arrested by the authorities, and only managed to escape by a feat of prodigious lying which puzzled their captors. On their return Fulk de Villaret gave the general order for the attack with the whole force. It was not after all going to be as easy as Vignoli had promised.

The city was attacked by both land and sea, yet by the end of September only Pheraclea, that mountain of useless rubble, had fallen to the Knights. Phileremo was surprised early in November: a Greek servant of the commandant, to revenge himself for a flogging, showed the invaders an unguarded postern. Here a disgraceful massacre of three hundred Turkish mercenaries took place. The Byzantines themselves claimed sanctuary in the chapel on the mount.

But by now the winter was setting in. The first light falls of snow whitened the grim butt of Atabyros and swelled the mountain torrents. The north-wind drummed day and night upon the north-eastern flanks of the island. It became obvious to Fulk de Villaret that his resources were inadequate for the task of reducing Rhodes. His infantry had been badly mauled in the campaign and many of his Knights wounded. Now they had made what shift they could to bivouac on the windy slopes of Phileremo, but watching them shivering round the flapping pine-fires they had kindled the Grand Master knew them inadequate for the task ahead. Spring came and summer. The stalemate dragged on. But the Knights had learned the lessons that only long campaigns can teach: patience, tenacity. Their numbers had been increased, it is true, after the bitter fighting around Phileremo, by a fresh body of Knights summoned in haste from Cyprus. But even their present forces were not enough. Worse still, the coffers of the Order were empty.

The delay was to last two years during which time Fulk de Villaret tried to strengthen his arm, first by an appeal to the Emperor of Constantinople to grant him the island and accept his Knights as vassals on the tenure of military service to be performed by three hundred of their number. This appeal met with point blank refusal. Then he had been forced to turn to the Pope for further aid which was only forthcoming after de Villaret himself had made two summer journeys northward in order to kiss hands and plead his case in person. By the spring of 1309 however he had gathered a large body of troops under his command and could muster twelve galleys, all in his pay. But by now the long wait had sapped the morale of the Byzantines, and when a Genoese transport bound for the garrison with corn and arms, was captured, Fulk de Villaret told its captain to go to Rhodes and open negotiations for the surrender of the island. He was fairly sure they would treat, and he was right.

On demanding and receiving suitable guarantees the defenders of the island surrendered on the 15 August 1309. The Knights soon acquired a number of other islands, Chalce, Simi, Telos, Nisyros, Cos, Calymnos and Leros in the north and north-west. Castel Rosso also fell to them, and while they made some tentatives against Casos and Carpathos, they quickly withdrew when the Venetians intervened, not wanting any trouble from that quarter.

Historians have remarked on the gradual change in the character of the Order after it had conquered Rhodes, and had also succeeded to the vast estates left it by the defunct Templars. The accumulation of vast material wealth, say some, was gradually sapping the moral structure of the organisation. Secular interests had begun to compete with the spiritual.

At any rate Fulk de Villaret put on one side all the old statutes which had determined the limits of his powers as Grand Master and after the conquest of Rhodes began to act for all the world as if he were a sovereign. Nor were his Knights slow to resent this and already in 1317 there was an abortive attempt to seize him while he was travelling in the interior of the island. For a while he was besieged in the fortress of Lindos and his deposition was decreed; yet the matter was somehow compromised for his successors continued to exercise much the same power in Rhodes as the Doges themselves.

Meanwhile however the Rhodians gained immensely by the presence of the Order in the island. The Turks did not dare to attack them as of old; justice prevailed in the law courts; commerce boomed. The harbours of the island offered safe anchorage to merchant ships. The Order found little difficulty now in raising substantial loans abroad—among the great banking houses with which they dealt was, of course, the house of Peruzzi. The frequent forays against the Turkish vessels plying in the Levant brought them immense booty which more than offset any budgetary deficits incurred in fortifying the islands. Rhodes basked in this transitory peace and plenty. Vignoli went about his unlawful business with a quiet mind—loading his privateers to the gunwales with gold and silver, precious stones and silks which he captured from the Turks, and sailing home with whatever would float behind attacked to his blameless rudder. Were *they* not infidels? Was *he* not a Christian?

The Knights were hardly less sure of themselves in this context, and took every opportunity of slaughtering the captured infidel. Some horrible massacres are recorded to their credit—or discredit: depending on one's angle of judgement. But a history of these early years is too thickly planted with detail for us to do more than skim it.

Irregularities began to grow up within the walled garden of the Order of the Knights Hospitallers. By constitution the member Knights were supposed only to live for the service of the poor and the defence of the true faith. They were supposed to live under the three vows of chastity, poverty and obedience. But by now the Order itself was by repute as rich as all the rest of the Church put together while many of the Knights owned immense estates in their own right. They had began to dress with the utmost luxury, to spend improvidently on gold and silver plate, on rich hangings and carpets bought from the traders of the mainland. They kept strings of richly caparisoned horses. They hawked the island. They neglected the poor. It is true that sumptuary laws were afterwards passed from time to time but it is clear that the rich living no less than the delicious airs of Rhodes had begun to etiolate their characters. How else is one to account for the stories, vague enough perhaps, but for which evidence could be produced, of the Knights themselves indulging in piracies? There were stories, for instance, of Knights disguising themselves and their men as Turks in order to plunder the passing Venetian traffic; while only a few years before the siege of 1522 it was charged that one of the captains serving under a Spanish sea-robber who haunted the coasts of Corfu, was a knight.

Nevertheless these moral lapses had not as yet impaired their fighting powers, as the two great sieges testify; and doubtless viewed through the average townsman's eyes the Order was still what it always had been—a tower of disciplined strength rising steeply out of a raging sea. It is indeed said that, so great were the dangers and hardships of the life they had chosen, hardly one in twenty of them lived to reach the age of fifty. The youthfulness of many of the Knights was remarkable. One could be admitted to the Order at the age of fourteen, and enjoy the privilege of residing in the fortress and wearing the full dress of the Order, though the admission to full privilege in arms could not be conferred before the age of eighteen. The sons of the nobility and the gentry, however, could gain admission into the Order as students and undergo instruction in the science of war.

The civil dress of the Order was black with the eight-pointed white cross, instituted before their sad expulsion from Palestine. Their battle dress was red with a square white cross, as shown in so many of the old paintings. In the sombre surroundings of their forts these uniforms in their simplicity must have glowed with all the warmth of Christian reassurance in the eyes of their patients who crowded the great hospitals for treatment. The semi-monastic nature of the Order impressed the Orthodox islanders very much, for military discipline was never at any period lax. The Castle itself was stringently guarded by night and day. Even during times of general relaxation, as during Carnival, nobody in a mask was permitted entry to the fortress on Rhodes. Generally speaking the Knights themselves were not permitted to enter the town unless on horseback or walking two by two. In the case of the Hospital in Rhodes the warehouses facing the Sea Gate formed the endowment of the prior and chaplain. The physicians were bound by order to visit their patients not less

than twice a day. Two surgeons were standing by under their orders
to perform whatever operations were found necessary. A large store
of herbs and drugs was maintained as part of the charges of the
establishment, while the patients were fed upon all kinds of nourish-
ing food. But dicing, chess, and the reading of chronicles, histories,
romances or other light fiction of the kind was strictly forbidden.

The dead were carried out into the town for burial by four men
wearing black robes which were set aside specially for that purpose.
The townsmen watched them come through St Catherine's gate,
their faces solemn in the flapping yellow torch-light, their solemn
strides measured perhaps by a single kettle-drum, walking symbols
of a faith which took death as sombrely as it took life on earth.
Watching such a procession the peasant crossed himself and sighed
as he watched these iron men, torn between admiration for their
humanity and discipline and distaste for the rigidity and excessive
formalism of their lives. Ah! for the good old Byzantine days when
everyone had his own opinion—provided he owned a dagger with
which to enforce it!

The Order itself was composed of tongues, eight in all, and the
defence of the fortress was parcelled out to the various nationalities
with due regard to their numbers and prowess. At first the Hospitallers had been mainly French; for the Knights of Provence and of
Auvergne were as thoroughly French as the Knights of France were.
But in 1376 a Spaniard was elected Grand Master. His tenure of
office lasted twenty years, and both his successors were Spaniards.
The lattter of these took the step of increasing Spanish influence by
expanding the tongue of Spain into the tongues of Castile and of
Aragon. This was an important step, as voting in the Councils was
based not upon the number of Knights but upon the number of
nations represented.

This, then was the organisation which made itself responsible for
the safety of Rhodes and its inhabitants. Chronicles and studies of
this packed and ample age abound, and while the sour Torr in his
notes on the bibliography of this period, finds this chronicler wanting
in taste, that in judgement, and all a little wanting in 'factual veracity',
nevertheless for my own purposes more than enough material is
available to the student; there is no need for the brief and popular

account so much in fashion today to bridge the gap between the joyous pages of Bosio and any of a dozen studies published since.

The two great sieges by the Turks which occupy the central panel of the medieval picture are no less marvellous than the siege of Demetrius; but so much rich and confused colouring is available with which to paint them that it would be cruel to devote less than a whole book to them. And that must wait. Suffice it to say here that the Order, which for so long withstood not only the genius of the landscape but the momentum of history itself, at length succumbed. In December 1522, after bitter fighting in which 3,000 of the garrison and 230 of the Knights perished, Rhodes surrendered to the infidel.

The terms of the capitulation were not unduly onerous. The Knights were free to take their arms and property and to depart: the Sultan himself would provision their ships. Any civilian might leave Rhodes if he wished at any time during the next three years, with all his possessions. Those who stayed would be exempt from all tribute for the next five years; their children too would be forever exempt from conscription as janizaries. Freedom of Christian worship would be guaranteed.

So, on New Year's Day, 1523, the Knights entered their battered fleet, and set sail once more for Cyprus.

Little enough remains now save the chain of ruined forts, and the names of famous battles petrifying slowly in the history-books. The culture to which the Knights were heirs took shallow roots which barely outlived their departure. It never penetrated to the heart of the Mediterranean way-of-life—that mixture of superstition, impulse and myth which so quickly grows up around whatever is imported, seeking to domesticate it. The landscape puts her nymphs arms about human habits, beliefs, styles of mind so that imperceptibly they are overgrown by the fine net of her caresses—paths choked with weeds, wells blocked by a fallen coping-stone, fortresses silvered over with moss. Decay superimposes its own chaos, so that standing on some heap of stones today, watching a shepherd milk his goats, hearing the drizzle of milk in the cans chimed by the whizz of the gnats which hover round him, you wonder whether this mauled assembly of stone is Frankish or Mycenean, Byzantine or Saracen. Often enough the answer is: all of these. But only the eye of a specialist can read it like a palimpsest, text imposed on text, each dedicated to its peculiar folly or poetry.

As for the Crusaders, you must hunt for them today in the folk-songs, in the superstitions. Here and there, too, you may find gleams reflected from their chivalry in the border-ballads of the country; or their influence in the workmanship of old weapons—styles borrowed by the smiths of Constantinople and adapted to their own style. Pottery, too. In the pottery-styles of some periods you may see the influence brought to bear by heart-sick Turkish or Persian prisoners, who solaced themselves in their exile by painting plates which even today give back an echo of their oriental homesickness.

Even this garden of the Villa Cleobolus where I write these lines. . . . Though it still lies on the site of the Grand Master's garden, its appearance must have changed at least a dozen times since those days. Nevertheless the little groups of tombs like sentry-boxes, the marble gravestones with their flowing Arabic inscriptions, make a not ineffective monument to that lost epoch; even though to the eye of an initiate they are of a later period—the graves of Turkish civil servants who died of boredom and over-eating in small consular posts, or of political exiles who wore out their hearts waiting for an amnesty. The grove of eucalyptus trees towers over them all, the drifts of autumn leaves rain down on them. Each year they have to be dug out afresh from the mounds of leaf-mould, to be renovated. And even now as I write these dry sickle-shaped leaves are breaking off and planing down, spinning like propellers as they fall upon the blue table.

CHAPTER VIII

Lesser Visitations

Hoyle has been seriously ill after his operation and poor Mills has been almost beside himself with anxiety. However after a relapse and a blood transfusion Hoyle has rallied and is now permitted visitors. He lies in the dazzling white room he chose for himself at the Hospital, his hands folded on the red counterpane, staring out at the cypresses and the sea. I am touched by the pathos of his glance, by the magical composure of his face. The room is full of violets gathered by Chloe and dressed in green china bowls made for Hoyle by Huber. Here he lies like a mandarin with a few choice dictionaries beside his bed.

'As you get old,' he says, 'it gets harder to grab hold of life. This time my fingers nearly slipped.'

He is still rather weak and we take it in turns to read to him. 'Thank God it's you this afternoon. I am beginning to hate Gideon. Yesterday he ate all my grapes and insisted on reading a book I didn't want to read at all—just because he was in the middle of it himself. He gave me such a muddled synopsis of it, too, that I could hardly make head or tail of it. Then he borrowed my Turkish dictionary and brought it back full of breadcrumbs and grease marks. What is one to do with the fellow?'

We read or chat away the afternoons.

Deep-scented groves of Profeta with those magical carpets of peonies; and everywhere in the dense tree-scapes of the mountain the breathless promise of deer. The deer you see on the vases, perhaps, with the liquid melting almond-shaped eyes. Great bundles of conglomerate rise out of the green glades. Rock and grass. But the Germans killed all the deer when they were starving.

Manoli told me a story today which I jotted down in my note-book. It is too good, in a sense, ever to make material for a short-story writer. Sometimes life itself borrows the forms of art, and the sort of story told by life is only fit to transcribe raw: without premeditation.

St Pantaleimon is a tiny village buried so deeply among the foot-hills around Taegetus that for weeks its inhabitants did not know that the Germans had over-run Greece. The occasional aircraft they saw only made them wonder what celebrations were going forward in Athens. Had Greek troops entered Rome? The village consisted entirely of grey-beards except for three small boys aged about ten who kept the flocks. The oldest of these was Niko, a spade-bearded patriarch of eighty, tough as holm-oak. Well, one day the news came (Manoli talking), and Niko summoned a conference. Apparently Greece had fallen and they were surrounded by Germans. Doubtless these would soon appear. It was up to St Pantaleimon to resist them. Accordingly all the old men furbished up their flintlocks, and looked to their ammunition. There was little enough of it. Enough for one good volley, perhaps, but they were determined that the Germans should have it. Weeks passed and nothing happened. Then a runner came up from the valley to say that a German patrol was on its way.

The village elders took up ambush positions at the mouth of a defile—the only entry to the village. They heard noises. Presently a strong patrol of Germans came in sight—but alas! They were driving before them the whole flock of sheep and the three young shepherds whom they had captured on the hill. In a flash Niko saw what was going to happen. He drew a deep breath and hesitated. The am-bushed Germans were unaware of the rifles pointing at them. Then Niko commended his soul to God and standing up roared 'Fire'. The children fell with the rest.

The 'evil eye' is a well-known Mediterranean superstition. Most children, all valuable beasts of burden—and by extension all motor-cars, wear the familiar blue beads which can avert the malediction of anyone who has what Ovid calls 'the double pupil of the eye'. This week there was rather an amusing crisis involving this deeply-rooted belief. The seven refurbished taxis of Rhodes had just been licensed to circulate and great was the rejoicing when it was announced that from Tuesday next the taxi-rank on the pier would contain seven road-worthy vehicles. On Tuesday however nothing happened. It seems that there were no blue beads to tie on the radiators. The vehicles were in hourly danger of being blighted by the evil eye if they should circulate without this precaution. Moreover there seemed none available for sale in the town. The Administration was nonplussed. The Brigadier sent for me: 'Is it true,' he said, 'that these bloody lunatics won't circulate without lucky charms tied to their bloody bonnets?' I explained what I knew of the terrible powers of the evil eye, of how in the past innocent taxis had been struck dead in their tracks by the power of a witch: had developed carburettor trouble or the pitiful state of wasting away known as 'slow puncture'. He was not impressed by this. 'Honestly,' he said, 'they really drive one crazy. I can't think what you see in them. Now the Swahili. . . .' When he had finished telling me how superior the Swahili were he said: 'Well, I suppose we'll have to signal Cairo for some blue beads. They'll think I've gone out of my mind. Sometimes I think it won't be long before I do.'

The situation, however, was saved by Martin, the young South African who is virtually mayor of Rhodes. He came into the room at this moment and said 'It's all right, sir. I've issued them with saints.' The Brigadier threw up his hands. 'You've done *what?*'

'I got them an issue of saints from the Archbishop. They're quite happy now.'

It was a happy stroke, Martin had prevailed upon the clergy to provide seven 'assorted saints' as he called them—those little tin medallions with a coloured saint on them. These they had happily tacked on to the dashboard of their taxis.

If you should happen to admire a pretty child or a beautiful animal in the presence of the mother or owner, it is only common politeness, as well as firmly established custom, to turn your head aside, spit thrice, and mutter the charm να μην άβασκαθῇ ('may it not be blighted'). This is not merely a nostrum against the evil eye, though it serves its purpose in this context as well. Huber tells me that this is a custom of the greatest antiquity: in fact the πτύειν εις κολπον of the ancient Greeks, who warded off the vengeance of Nemesis in this fashion. Conversely if you see someone afflicted by some terrible illness you can guard yourself and your own family against it by the same charm. Gideon has contracted the habit in the course of his cattle-appraising and spits with great abandon whenever he stops to discuss a prize hog or pat a peasant's child. Perhaps the old English custom of spitting on a silver coin before pocketing it is a remnant of the same belief.

Mills has been away in the south of the island with Chloe, who combines the roles of wife and nurse with equal skill. It is his habit to scribble me a few lines from time to time, asking me to convey messages to his hospital, or to arrange for drugs to be motored out to him. Here is a typical passage from a letter: 'I was called out some days ago to a village near Siana, unpronounceable name. A farmer's pregnant ass had been gored by a bull. It had aborted, poor thing, and stood in the middle of the field beside the dead foal with its intestines hanging down to the ground through a wound eight inches long. An attempt had been made by the villagers to sew up the rent with silk but it had broken down at once. I gave the patient 3 grains of morphia and had it lifted off its feet on to its side. Chloe and I then bathed its guts in salt water to clean out the dirt. We popped them back into the abdomen with plenty of sulphonamide and did a complete surgical repair to the laceration. This took over two hours, terribly exhausting. At the end of it the donkey got to its feet and took some water out of a pail. I ordered it water and milk for a day and then a normal diet. The farmer's pent-up emotions were now free to devote to the bull. He chased it round and round the field hammering its behind with a huge rock taken from the wall of the field, swearing marvellously as he ran. As I did not want to perform the same sort of operation on him (the bull showed signs of annoyance) I thought it better to retreat, which we were allowed to do when everybody had had a chance to kiss our cheeks or our hands.

'The ass did quite well for a day or two. Then, alas, its abdomen began to swell—inevitable peritonitis—and to our great grief it died. The farmer cried, and all the villagers; and Chloe cried, and I was hard put to it not to do the same. It was not the personality of the ass that made it seem so heartbreaking. When you realise how these people live and what a beast of burden means to them the loss is far graver than the loss of a pet. It is a setback in the battle against starvation.

'Today the farmer has sent us a beautifully worked goatskin knapsack, fit for a baby Pan.'

Omens of our impending departure are in the air. There seems a fair chance of the Peace Conference coming to a decision which will involve the fate of the islands. The Greeks have appointed a Governor designate who will for the time hold a watching-brief with a small military mission. Gideon's delight is marked when he hears that this exalted functionary is to be the redoubtable Colonel Gigantes,[1] an old friend of his. We meet the little party at the airstrip near Calato and soon the two monocled soldiers are shaking hands with each. 'Gideon, you rogue,' growls Gigantes grasping him by the hand. They go off together arm in arm, their conversation punctuated by roars of laughter.

That evening we celebrate a new addition to our ranks, and the conversation takes on an added animation, an Athenian zest. The General brings with him a pungent whiff of politics and warfare from the north to enliven the *taedium vitae* of a territory where sobriety and firm government have allowed little free play to the typical Greek character with its talent for political intrigues.

The war completely destroyed the livestock, and thus stopped the manufacture of raw materials for clothes. Long before this, however, the influence of western dress had driven the peasant in the direction of the shapeless cloth cap, the trousers and open shirts which so many of them wear today. On feast days, perhaps, the elder men would open their oak chests and lay out the traditional eagle-winged bolero, the blue Turkish trousers and the sashes in which they carried their silver-knuckled pistols or daggers. The craft has not died, but the materials are sadly lacking today which would enable the wife of the family to trick out her man's costume and her own with delicate gold embroidery and scarlet piping. Nevertheless while no new costumes are being made the old have been carefully preserved, and at festivals the women once more emerge from their everyday

[1] Of the Greek Sacred Legion.

147

clothes and dance in full costume. This is something worth watching. The best dancers of the island are the girls of Embona, the village which lies at the foot of Atabyron; after them those of Soroni.

General Gigantes before settling in has decided to make a royal progress through the islands with the Brigadier, to show their respective flags. Gideon says that his privately confessed intention is to leave no wine untasted in the fourteen islands—and from what I know of the Brigadier he will fall in with this plan without demur. Gideon, needless to say, has succeeded in getting himself invited. 'As chief of Agriculture,' he says, 'I am more or less responsible for the wine and food. Besides, old Gigantes can teach us all a thing or two.'

The new proclamation on censorship has vested the responsibility in me; but the wording of the text runs: 'All printed material must be submitted to the Information Office before issue,' and the Rhodians have taken it all too literally. My office is crowded now with a variety of people asking me to frank beer-bottle labels, cartons, theatre-advertisements and handbills of all kinds. In this way I have increased my acquaintance a hundred-fold. It is very seldom, however, that a writer strays into my net. Nevertheless today my door flew open and standing before me was a large cadaverous individual with corn-cob teeth and curling moustaches, clad in a blood-stained smock. He turned out to be a butcher-poet from one of the outlying villages. 'Is it true,' he said with a ghastly grimace, and in a tone of such hollowness and resonance that I recognised at once the village speech-maker. 'Is it true that the *democratic* Anglo-Saxons impose censorship on works of art?' I admitted that it was true.[1] He sighed and cast his eyes to the ceiling. 'Sir,' he said, 'what a disappointment after seeing the Italians run like hares.' He produced from under his smock a wad of the ruled scrap paper that tradesmen use for their business jottings and held it out to me, saying simply. 'I am Manoli the butcher, and this is my epic.'

I cannot read the cursive hand easily, though the text was fairly written, but I was reluctant to let my visitor go without getting to know him better. 'Read me a little of it,' I said. His eye brightened

[1] In fact my brief was political and not artistic. Later I founded 'Techni' the first Greek literary weekly in the islands to which Manoli tried often to contribute.

and drawing himself up he launched into his epic without a trace of embarrassment. It was comical, but it was also impressive, his utter self-possession. The poem itself was a portentous piece of doggerel, written in thumping sixteen-foot lines, and entitled 'The Miseries and Trials of Rhodes under the plague of the Fascists'. I longed for Gideon to be there to enjoy it with me. Manoli the butcher was rapt. The truth was that he did not read very fluently and the monotonous cadences of the poem demanded the utmost attention if he was going to get the scansion right. He picked off each accent with a slight nod of the head. The whole performance took him about twenty minutes. The sound of all this powerful declamation attracted attention; first E tip-toed in, then the Greek editor Kostas, and finally the Baron Baedeker, clutching a handful of soiled prints. Manoli was not put out by this addition to his audience; he continued his monotonous chant, but inclined himself towards the newcomers slightly, to give them the benefit of the performance. As he came to the end of each page he allowed it to drop to the floor with a superb gesture, so that at last he stood before us empty-handed with his epic littering the floor around his feet.

Kostas humbly gathered up the pages, stifling a desire to laugh. Manoli stood there with a queer mixture of humility and pride, clasping his large hands. 'It is very remarkable,' I said. The rest of the audience muttered suitable praises. The butcher inclined his head modestly, though he obviously held himself in good conceit. 'I wish to print it,' he said, 'So that there should be some record of our sufferings.'

'Kostas,' I said solemnly, 'Hand me the rubber stamp.'

Kostas breathed on the article reverently and gave me the shadow of a wink. I gravely stamped the manuscript and handed it back to the butcher who replaced it in its hiding place under the bloody apron. 'Sir,' he said, 'I thank you,' and shaking my hand warmly he withdrew.

Later that morning when we set out in the brilliant sunshine to walk back to the hotel a breathless child ran up to us and thrust a blood-stained paper parcel into the saddle-bag I was carrying over my arm. 'It is from Manoli, sir.' he piped. For a moment I was nonplussed. There are so many Manoli's: we have three among the printers. Then I remembered. Inside the parcel were some lamb-chops, a true poet's gift.

Timachidas of Rhodes was an epic poet the loss of whose work only Gideon mourns. It was a single immense epic pregnantly entitled 'The Dinners'. Was it simply a catalogue of dinners he had enjoyed in the past—or a poem devoted to ideal dinners which he would have liked to enjoy if he had had the means? We shall never know. Parmenon of Rhodes was famous for an early cookery book which is also unhappily lost. It might have given us some help with the vexing questions raised by Lynceus of Samnos who goes out of his way to praise Rhodian delicacies among which he lists the aphye (anchovy?), the ellops (sword-fish?), the orphos (sea-perch?) and the alopex (shark?). The conjectures are not mine but Torr's.

Among an unsorted mass of crumpled notes I came upon a few lines about a visit to Calithea last week with Mills and E. A few random impressions of swimming in a dark sea under a clear and moonless sky: 'All around contorted hefts of volcanic rock snarling immobile dragon-snarls. Smell of bitter creeper and cloying jasmine. The dark water warm and salty from a day of south wind. Occasional draughts of cool air and colder currents curling in snake-like from the rock-entrances of the harbour. Hanging there in the sea as if in a web, webbed feet spread, webbed fingers parted, to look back and upwards through wet eyelashes at the star-flowered sky, huge pieces of which slide about like glassy panes, so one can reach up and knock aside the planets. A silence palpitant with quiet voices and the aberrant crunch of oars. This silence was not absolute, as if the membranes of the air, damp and sticky mucilage, were glued together with the warm sticky night, reminding one that silence, after all, is only sound in emulsion. Later in an orchard of pears above the harbour a fugitive happiness: thin sweet grapes and mastika.'

The royal party has returned rather the worse for wear. It was not however the carousing which caused the trouble—though both Gideon and the Brigadier seem a trifle chastened by their experiences. It was the tireless walking imposed on them by Gigantes who insisted on inspecting every island in detail and showed an utter disregard for distances and natural obstacles. Honour dictated that where he went the Brigadier must follow; and where the Brigadier went, Gideon must go to. 'God, what a jaunt,' said my friend. Up the dizzy crater of Nisyros, perched on barbaric eructating mules, round the crumbling coves of Patmos and Astypalea, the sinuosities of Cos and Leros—wherever there was firm ground the Greek General marched firmly, gleaming monocle in eye, pausing only to utter good-humoured taunts at their dilatoriness. Each day there was some prodigious excursion to undertake to some unvisited corner of an island where the startled peasantry (having caught sight of their visitors from distant peaks and crags) had already set out a table in the main-street and broached the best wine. And now Greek hospitality set in like a Trade wind, and glasses were clinked and emptied in response to numberless toasts—the native genius of Gigantes, like that of Gideon, lent itself to the creation of toasts. More than once they were carried back on mules from these outposts in a state of exhilarated exhaustion. Once Gideon was deposited in the sea by his mule. He suspected that Gigantes pushed him. And one of the younger liaison officers, declaring that he saw a mermaid, set off swimming after it in the direction of Asia Minor, calling upon it in eloquent terms to stay and talk. He was placed under close arrest, and was so indignant that nobody believed his story that he challenged Gideon to a duel on the sand-beaches of Cos. The Brigadier's uniform was eaten by a goat while he was bathing. . . . 'Altogether,' said Gideon, 'there is a wealth of local colour about this excursion which can only be discussed in the privacy of the club, as between officers of equal rank.' The only member of the party who was not prostrated was the indomitable Gigantes himself who declared that the excursion left him feeling 'remarkably fresh'. Among the spoils of the raid were several casks of what Gideon called 'alcoholic booty' which will enable us all to study wine-production in the islands in the detail such a subject deserves. I have agreed to give style and tone to the report which Gideon is writing, on condition that I share some of the research.

Most of the Government experimental farms will be closing down, for despite their own apparent prosperity they never formed an integral part of the island economy. Nor, unluckily enough was much learned from them by the peasant farmer who might have profited by Italian experience. For example, the Rhodian peasant has not yet learned to grow his own forage crops; yet the government farms have been growing their own stocks of vetch, lucerne, trifolium incarnatum, and so on. A knowledge of this skill would have had an important effect on the Rhodian economy in its effect, not only on the rotation of crops, but also on the fate of the heathland and forest—at present grazed promiscuously and indiscriminately. The present day village rotation is variable but in general consists of 1 to 2 years straw crop and from 2 to 4 years fallow.

Soil-erosion, too, is far advanced, though the Italians did much to preserve the top-soil of the greener areas of Rhodes. The peasant is intransigent, however. One of Gideon's problems is to persuade him that all the soil-preservation measures initiated by the Italians were not baleful infringments of Fascism upon human liberty.

By the post of England on the medieval walls—so broad that six horsemen could gallop abreast upon them—we spend the afternoon lounging. We can overlook the whole town from here, as well as the shrill private lives of a dozen families who live directly under the towering walls, in gardens picked out with palms and bushes of red hibiscus. A windmill turns, creaking, and from the invisible market-place rises the surf of human bartering—the vibration of business. On the wall itself two armies are fighting with wooden swords—a dozen children in paper hats against half a dozen bareheaded ones. They are not Knights and Saracens, as one might think, but British and Germans. The battle sways backwards and forwards. Nobody dies or is hurt, though one of the shock-troops has started crying. Their shouts marry the thin keening of the swifts by the walls, darting against the blue. High up against the sun an eagle planes above us, watching history plagiarising itself once more upon these sun-mellowed walls.

CHAPTER IX

The Saint of Soroni

'A village without an ikon: a head without an eye,' says a proverb more comminatory than most, for the psychic life of these small Aegean communities is healthiest where it can be focused upon some such arbiter of fate. Lines of force radiate outwards from the shrine of a patron saint like holiness from a halo and, none the less real for being invisible, they play their part in the common adventures of the fisherman, herdsman and farmer, easing the burden of his conduct—not in the narrow theological sense, but in the sense of faith in acts.

A journey by water may be dedicated to the protection of the saint, just as an illness may be placed, so to speak, on his knees. He is a help against the brute adversities that face simple folk in these islands. But it is not only in adversity that one turns to him, it is also in joy. One's precious male child is dedicated to him. After a successful harvest, who can forget to offer the shrine a measure of oil for his lamps? Oaths both good and bad are uttered in his name; while no material object is too small to commend to his care—a sick child, a sickly lamb, or a tattered fishing net. He stands at the confluence of those two great rivers, man and the unknown, and his job is to domesticate each for the other. He remits the temporal pains.

I am not speaking now of the more famous ones whose medicine has become a cult, and whose sphere of influence is no longer regionalised—located in some small tumbledown church, whose cracking gesso backgrounds bear the half-obliterated faces of forgotten Byzantine divinities: I am not thinking of Tinos where the little hanging offerings of crutches, bandages and paintings testify to the miracle having taken place, and remind one once again that here, as in the ruined and forsaken shrines to Aesculapius, healing and divination are one.

The little saints of local fame are those who keep the broad current of everyday life flowing in the right direction. Often they are only names without a pedigree the peasants understand; their faces are kissed with no less reverence for that. Often fragments of contemporary history have become entangled in the legend.

The Aegean saint is not an object for contemplation, of self-enquiry in the western sense. He is not remote enough for that. His role is like that of an ordinary mortal over whom he enjoys the advantages of several special faculties; he is in touch with God on the one hand and man on the other—standing between them rather as a Platonic *daimon* than as anything else. He is an extra-terrestrial being domiciled on earth as a sort of heavenly vice-consul with the powers of a chargé d'affaires. This is a status that suits him perfectly for in it he commands reverence without servility; prayers and petitions to him have a man-to-man quality. And it is right that he should wear this half-human aspect—for has he not taken up his position upon the very altars of the Greek gods he supplanted and has he not inherited some of their more human and endearing characteristics? Sometimes like them he may find himself ever so slightly disposed to accept a bribe for his services—a silver dish for his altar, a candelabrum, a taper the size of a human limb. And where is the harm in all this if the influence he exercises is over a journey which does no harm to anyone, over a marriage prejudiced by illness, over a small business deal in contraband tobacco? Somebody has to lend us a hand with these problems.

The three most venerated relics of Rhodes—the hand of St John the Baptist (cut off by Luke who found the exhumed body too large to carry off whole): the cross made from the True Cross: and the picture of Our Lady of Phileremo—were carried off to Malta, whence the last Grand Master took them in 1798 to Russia. Of these I have little doubt that the wonder-working portrait of Our Lady was the most famous. Its history, unlike that of St John's hand, is obscure; the Knights apparently found it in place on their arrival in the island

and its reputation antedated the more general publicity it enjoyed when the eyes of all Christendom turned upon the famous Order's battles against the Saracens. Phileremo, to judge by the accounts of earlier travellers, was a well-established place of pilgrimage before the time of the Knights, and the picture had doubtless served generations of petitioners before the standard of St John flew over Rhodes. In times of danger it was customary to carry it into the city, where it lay in St Mark's, a church which had been founded by the Venetians; here, during the siege of 1522 a cannon-ball burst over the altar where the picture stood, killing several people, and the Grand Master, fearing for the safety of the relic, ordered it to be placed in the chapel of St Catherine which was inside the palace. As far as I know, nearly as much mystery surrounds it as surrounded the Colossus: there does not seem to be any record of how she looked—this latter-day Artemis, nor have any details of her miracles been preserved.

The little modern chapel on the summit of Phileremo is a ruin today, its battered walls still heaped with mountains of discarded Italian ammunition, water-bottles, bayonets and grenades; a few heavy carcases of anti-tank guns lie about forlornly under the trees, already so thickly overgrown that one might believe them to be all of a piece with the few fragments of Hellenic and Byzantine stone in the once sacred precincts. The architecture of the modern church is adequate but uninspired. In the single habitable room of the monastery lives a solitary Franciscan—a strange bird-like youth who rides a borrowed motor-bike and uses a piercing hairoil. He peddles a leaflet setting forth in brief the history of the church and carrying on its cover what purports to be a representation of Our Lady of Phileremo. But the whole business smells of premeditation and of unction. One feels the long arm of the propaganda office on one's shoulder, as one does in Capri.

Nevertheless in Greece there is room for everyone; travellers have already noted that in the neighbouring village of Cremasto the church is dedicated, unusually enough, to the Panaghia Katholiki, and there seems little doubt that the great panagyri of August is a faded memorial to the powers of Our Lady of Phileremo. Our Lady *in absentia* she should be called.

Is she descended from Artemis or from Athene Lindia—who was

once the most venerated Goddess of the island? It is hard to tell. Artemis crops up quite frequently today in the folklore of the peasantry, and I am reminded as I write that not far from here, beyond the grey stone slopes of Profeta—the road winding upwards through clement forest-land carpeted with red and white cistus, anemone, and great peonies—there is still a small monastery-site called Artamiti where, to judge by an inscription found thereabouts, once stood an ancient temple. She, like Athena, was a daughter of Zeus, and the loveless puritanism of the one perfectly matches the qualities of her step-sister, the giver of the fruitful olive.

But if Rhodes has lost her Lady of Phileremo she has gained another local saint whose fame is growing daily and who is well on the way to supplanting her in the general veneration. No literature has grown up around this new figure as yet, and no critical apparatus; the Orthodox Church itself seems a little puzzled as to where he fits in—at any rate no hagiographer has come forward with an explanation as to how Saul, a footsore apostle of Paul, managed to win himself a shrine in the shallow hills around Soroni.

Saint Soulas (as he is called in demotic) is supposed to have been a member of the party which, headed by Paul, was washed up in Rhodes on the way to Palestine. (At Lindos a little cove is still pointed out to one today as the actual landfall. During his short stay in Rhodes, Paul walked for miles each day, expounding the scripture to whoever would listen. His disciples followed his example, and among them Saul, who must have been something of a walker to reach Soroni, which is by no means near to Lindos. At any rate, here he found an ancient shrine with a warm spring—though unluckily legend has not preserved the name of the original tutelary God. The neighbouring villagers seemed to him in need of testimony as they were all heathens of the darkest dye; he tried adjuration, exhortation, and peroration without any success at all. They clave to their folly. He talked till he was hoarse, but they regarded him with the unmoved scepticism that we should all feel if a small, hairy foreigner with a beard, dressed poorly, with dusty feet and a funny pronunciation, tried to undo in one afternoon what had taken centuries of pious mumbo-jumbo to create—a complex of belief, comforting, homely as a salt-lick. Saul was at his wit's end to know how to cope with these obstinate and semi-literate peasants. Much against his will he was compelled to resort to a miracle. There were a number of people with sores about. He healed one out of hand by dipping him in the spring. 'Can your God do that?' he asked. The villagers took his point and came over to the true faith in a body.

I am not happy about this story; in the first place it seems to me that peasant belief has really muddled the issue. It seems to me that St Paul himself must be the hero of this widely-held belief—for his name was Saoul, or, in its ancient Greek form, Saulos. That the warm spring was already famous for its cures there is little doubt. Even today the locality is called in Greek στοῦ ψωριάρη. Furthermore the most common kind of sore in the Aegean seems to be caused by a parasitic substance which is contained in the bag at the root of the sponge; it is a common enough affliction among sponge-divers and can be cured only by bathing the sores in some mild astringent. The spring *could* have been famous for these cures long before St Paul appeared on the scene. In this context we should perhaps remember that Heracles was the common patron of hot springs and his name is connected with Lindos from times of the remotest antiquity; according to the ancient legend he, like Paul, arrived in Lindos one day, hungry after a long journey. With him was his son Hyllos. He asked a passing husbandman for food for the latter but met with curses. He therefore helped himself to one of the oxen with which the man was ploughing and breakfasted thereon with Hyllos, while the infuriated owner watched the pair from a safe distance and cursed them. This is said to have been the origin of the strange form of Heracles worship which once prevailed at Lindos. While the actual sacrifices were offered the officiating priest heaped curses and abuse on the name of the Hero, not haphazard but according to a fixed ritualistic order. There was apparently nothing like this in the rest of Greece and the saying 'Like Lindians at their sacrifice' became proverbial for all who used profane language in sacred places. Does a tenuous thread run through these detached fragments—or is it just that history itself, conditioned by place, repeats characteristic and familiar gestures, as a friend might?

It was however something more than the spirit of disinterested enquiry which led Gideon and I to embark on an expedition to

Soroni on the day of the saint's panagyri. For one thing the whole of
Rhodes town would be there, and certainly all those among our
friends who were not bound by administrative preoccupations. We
decided to travel in the old town bus with the staff of the printing-
house, who had all booked tickets one way, intending to sleep or
dance away the night under the pines.

By nine o'clock the first buses have begun to rumble off down the
blue road to Trianda, each loaded to the brim with holiday-makers,
laughing, gesticulating or singing songs. Three big lorries, packed
with Italians who are due for repatriation to Italy next week, pass
through the town with streamers flying. These are Sienese farmers
from the state farms around San Benedetto and they sing beautifully
as they rumble by; a sharp, poignant singing which has something
almost valedictory about it. This will be their last fiesta on the island,
and the buses travel so slowly that one imagines they want to draw
out their last view of Rhodes, to pack their memories with its green
landscapes which will continue to haunt them perhaps in their own
graceful homelands. Italy is beautiful, but it lacks the wild pang of
the Greek landscape; it is tamed and domesticated—an essay in
humanism. It is not the cradle of tragedy.

Our departure is not until midday. In the far corner of the square
behind the market-place stands the machine in which we are to
travel—a package-like municipal bus which at this moment is
surrounded by an extremely angry crowd. One sight of those
waving arms and flying fingers, and my heart sinks. It is obvious that
something is wrong. Familiar faces loom up out of the dense press.
The Baron Baedeker stands in his severe black clothes, clutching his
step-ladder grimly, and shaking his head. Christ, the author, dressed
in a white boater and a composition collar an inch wide is repeating
something despairingly and waving a ticket. His voice cannot be
heard above the hubbub. On the step of the bus, guarding the doorway, stands the conductor, viciously repelling boarders with his
elbow. The crowd has clenched itself around him like a fist. At the
head of it stands Manoli the linotype-setter, his eyes gleaming
through his spectacles, his hands flying. He is obviously in charge of
the boarding-party. Every few seconds, overcome by impatience,
the crowd gives a lunge forward and he is driven like a battering

THE SAINT OF SORONI

ram into the conductor's side. The conductor, half-turning, fends him off with an elbow shouting 'I tell you no'. The argument is resumed until impatience sets in again and the crowd rears like a wave, only to break in vain against the sides of the dusty bus. Small eddies of violence are thrown off from inside the crowd itself—some of which have nothing to do with the main argument. For instance in one of these frantic lunges a man with a guitar has got himself entangled with his neighbour's coat-buttons; these have wrapped themselves round the guitar strings which are in danger of being broken. The press is so great however that the men cannot disengage and at every lunge they are carried forward in unison, one crying 'My guitar' in tones of anguish and other crying 'You fool'.

Reluctant to get caught up in this battle-scene we hang about on the outskirts of the crowd trying to get a clue as to the nature of the argument. It seems hopeless, so great is the noise and so continuous the flood of invention and rhetoric. Occasional snatches rise above the general uproar. 'I tell you I *have* got.' 'Everybody knows what it. . . .' 'You should . . . police would soon. . . .' Another heave forward and another shuddering impact against the bus. A melancholy long-withdrawing roar of 'I tell you no' from the conductor.

Kostas, the Greek editor, comes staggering out of the mêlée to greet us breathlessly. 'The usual has happened', he says, when he can get his breath. 'There are forty people with tickets and only twenty seats. The bus company is always doing this.' At this a little man, quite beside himself with rage, comes up and shakes his fist at the boy, shouting: 'I tell you that is not true. I am in charge of the tickets. I can tell you that we only issued twenty. Here is my own.' He thrusts a soiled ticket under my nose. Kostas raises his shapely hands deprecatingly. 'Have you no shame,' he says, 'to shout so before foreigners?' The little man swallows and turns purple. 'They must hear the truth,' he splutters.

Christ has been edging his way towards us from the opposite corner of the crowd. He beckons to me, holding his straw boater in his hand. There is something he wishes to confide in me. We move to one side and put our faces together under his hat. In all that swelling hubbub we are like people trying to light a cigarette in a high wind; his voice is grave and troubled. 'May I tell you something in complete confidence?' It seems an unlikely place for an exchange of confidences but there is little to do except to agree. 'Manoli,' he says, 'is responsible for the trouble. You know we print the tickets for the bus company in books of five hundred? Before dispersing the type last week he took the serial numbers of the tickets and printed twenty extra for himself and his friends. He is taking a large party with him to Soroni and they are all travelling free—perhaps he has told them that he bought the tickets for them as a present: but it is more likely,' and here Christ's voice sank to a dark and diabolical register, 'it is more likely that he made them pay *him*.' His dark eyes dilated as he watched my face for reactions. 'If,' he goes on, 'you wish to prove it you will see that he has printed his own tickets on different paper—the coarse Italian newsprint. The bus tickets are on the imported paper.' Having delivered himself of this vital piece of information he replaces his hat and retreats to a far corner of the crowd to see what will happen—like a man who has lit a fuse and wishes to keep a safe distance from the explosion.

Gideon groans when I pass on this piece of information. 'It would be Manoli again. I suppose it's up to you to quell him.'

The problem is how to get at him through the press, for the argument has reached renewed heights of violence. Manoli's grandmother has appeared, a whiskered old lady who brandishes a rolled umbrella over his shoulder at the conductor, and who is backed up by a couple of old beldams—nuns from the convent, carrying baskets. Things are getting lively. The conductor is getting rattled too, and shows some disposition to make use of the starting-handle of the bus which lies behind him on the step. I take a deep breath and wade into the crowd pushing and scrambling breathlessly forward inch by inch until with my outstretched fingers I can just grab the sleeve of Manoli. He shakes me off impatiently once or twice until he realises who I am. Then he grins and turns sheepishly towards me and enables me to shout: 'You have forged the tickets. All is known.' A momentary flicker of astonished anger flits across his face and is almost immediately replaced by an expression of desperation. The crowd heaves once more and we are swept apart, Manoli to plunge into the midriff of the bus-conductor, I to be sucked back into that sea of vociferous holiday-makers. Manoli faces a terrible dilemma

An architectural reconstruction of the Crusader Fortress of Rhodes, by Gabriel Alberti, especially undertaken for the Italian Government. Mandraccio Harbour (The Sheepfold) is on the right

Tongue of England
Tongue of Aragon
Tongue of Auvergne
Tongue of Germany

St. Athanasios Gate
Tower of Spain

St. George's Tower and Gate
Amboise Gate

Mt. Smith (H. Stephanos)

Grand Master's Palace (Castello)

St. Peter's Tower

The Collachium

The Hospital

St. Paul's Gate

Naillac's Tower

Mandraki (Galley Harbour)

St. Nicholas's Fort

Windmills

France

St. John's Tower and Gate

The Burgh

St. Catherine's Gate

Grand Harbour

Castile

Tongue of Provence

St. Mary of The Victory Gate

Windmill Tower

Tower of Italy (or Del Carretto)

Windmills

now, for if his friends find that he has sold them non-existent places on the bus they will most likely dismember him; on the other hand it must be clear that if he persists in his folly Gideon and I will either expose him or call a policeman. For a moment or two he marks time as he thinks over these alternatives, plunging forward with every push from the crowd behind, and shouting just as vigorously. Then the situation is saved as if by a miracle by the appearance of a completely empty bus which draws up alongside with a shriek, while a tousled head leans out and a voice shouts the equivalent of 'Any more for the Skylark'?

This is a bus which has been taken off the road for repairs; but the festival of St Soulas has proved too tempting for the solitary mechanic to whom the repairs have been entrusted. Half way through the morning he has decided to defer the work and to visit Soroni on his own. But a natural generosity of spirit, plus the fact that he has been drinking, caused him, on seeing the surging crowd round our bus, to stop and offer a lift to those who could not find places. Manoli is overcome with relief and joy and loses not a moment to save his face and his pocket. 'This way,' he shouts, and grabbing his grand-mother hustles her in the direction of the empty bus, while his rumpled party of guests follow suit with all despatch. We mount our bus now with comparative ease and sink breathlessly into our seats, to watch Manoli's party swept gesticulating and shouting out of sight. Our conductor expresses his relief by crossing himself. 'Another moment,' he says, 'and I should have had to hit him.'

So we set out. After a perilous journey (for Paul the driver is known for his competitive spirit), we approach Soroni. One by one the lorries rumble forward throwing up a wave of dust on either side. Countless walkers are met and passed on this strip of the road, for the most part peasants bearing baskets of fresh fruit to sell at the fair. Merrily honk the horns. Despite the choking clouds of dust the shouting and banter between those in the lorries and those on foot is continuous. We pass a dilapidated old cart in the back of which Manoli the fisherman lies at ease, surrounded by his family and a few select friends. At one point we are pelted with flowers by a dozen young girls. At another an elderly peasant, with a crate full of turtle-doves on his head, flings a handful of sweets in through the window, one of which cracks a lens in the Baron Baedeker's spectacles. He is most provoked, and for a moment one has the feeling that he is going to say something peculiarly offensive and to the point. He restrains himself however and says: 'What people. What people,' in sad and reproving tones as he turns the damaged spectacles over and over in his fingers.

We bowl over the crown of the last hillock and there before us lies the site of the shrine; the ground slopes away on all sides in a series of thinly-forested hillocks, leaving a level space of perhaps four acres. Here the villagers of Soroni have performed their usual task in digging a dozen large pits which will be filled with glowing charcoal and over which sheep and oxen will be roasted. At strategic points, too, huge bundles of dry brushwood lie piled, waiting for the night. Lofty pine-trees give a good deal of shade, and here out-door cafés have sprung up all round the shrine, which looks something like a small provincial bus-station. Paul jockeys us out of the line of lorries and we bump across the dusty soil toward the cover of the trees where he draws up with a triumphant smile. Everybody piles out of the bus into the sunny afternoon light, eager to see what is going on.

The sky above the eastern hollows is suffused with clouds of pinkish dust kicked up by the heels of mules; apparently some of the races have already started, as one can discern the gesticulating figures who ride them, with coloured scarves tied round their heads. The course itself has been squared out neatly with tent-pegs, and in one corner, on a wooden dais, sit the Brigadier and senior members of his staff, half choked with dust, and busily trying to memorise speeches in demotic which they will have to deliver at the prizegiving. To the westward, under the pines, stand groups of black-coated figures— each looking for all the world like a spiny black hedgehog in the shadow; this must be a cluster of choirs from various parts of the island. The low grumble of their chanting can be dimly heard above the prodigious hubbub of the crowd which fills the middle distance. They too have a dais from which prizes will be distributed, gaily decked with Greek and English flags stencilled all over it in water-paint. Overhead is a roof of plaited palm-leaves which contributes a faintly central-African flavour to the scene.

Around the shrine itself (which resembles an ant-hill) streets have

begun to improvise themselves as if a boom-town were suddenly
growing up under one's very eyes. Yet the streets are lined, not with
houses, but with stalls packed to the sky with sweetmeats, lemonade,
almonds, cheese. There is hardly an unfamiliar face here, for every
itinerant pedlar of Rhodes has made the pilgrimage on foot. Here
for example is the old one-armed man who trundles a barrow about
the town, loaded with chestnuts which he roasts on a brazier; I have
often watched the skill with which he fills the little paper bags,
shouting all the time in a deep croaky voice, 'Chestnuts . . . Chestnuts.' Next to him stand several of the itinerant fresh-water sellers,
each with his little white municipal cart shaded by a cluster of green.
Next again come the sweet-meat sellers, shouting as if their hearts
were broken 'Sweeeeets. . . . Sweeeeets.' There is chocolate, nougat,
almond paste, marzipan, pistachio nougat as well as those heavier
confections like *galactobouriko* and *baklava,* which Gideon claims are
made from waste blotting paper and honey. At intervals too stand
the *loukumades* experts, their long spoons at the ready to seize the
roasted doughnut when it is fried brown and crisp, and then to duck
it in honeyed sauce. Small children stand round these stalls breathing
in the flowery scent of the ovens with appreciation, each holding a
slip of paper on his small brown palm, waiting for the hot sweetmeat
to be plumped into it. Here too pine-nuts are being roasted, and there
spools of mastic (the Aegean chewing-gum) are being wound out
and pressed into shapes, or being merely loaded into spoons and
dropped into glasses of water.

At one end of this gallery of smells and sound is a section inhabited
by a number of ferociously unshaven gentlemen, each stripped to the
buff and liberally coated with soot. They dwell in an absolute forest
of entrails out of which they stick their heads from time to time in
order to utter a shriek before they return to their work at the spits;
all round them on biscuit tins loaded with fine charcoal roast the
entrails of Gideon's luckless sheep and lambs. Every sort of offal is
here accorded expert treatment; tripe is wound round and round a
giant spit, plugged with clove, nutmeg and garlic, and is roasted
slowly; sheep's entrails receive horizontal roasting, being basted
quickly with fat and lemon juice as they turn. Testicles, hearts and
livers are all given an exacting professional attention and distinctive

treatment on spits of various kinds. The cooks themselves carry long knives between their lips which gives them a terrifying look, and they dart from side to side of their stalls, now shaving off a tiny piece of beef to see if it tastes right, now banging a whole cluster of kebab off a spit on to a tin plate. They seem never to stop shouting for a moment, even when their knives are between their teeth. The attitudes they strike are magnificent, gladiatorial. Pools of hot dripping fall in the deep dust beneath the stalls, and here whole colonies of cats and dogs lounge, waiting for tit-bits. The pandemonium which reigns the whole length of this street is indescribable; but set back twenty yards on either side of it, the cafés are less noisy. Chairs and tables have sprung up like mushrooms everywhere, and here the peasant families have seated themselves in bright semi-circles to drink and eat. Here and there, too, small bevies of musicians are tuning up their accordions, guitars and violins, standing back to back to play a few stray phrases from time to time. Somewhere a big drum is banging, slow and paunch-like, which suggests that already a dance has begun, but I cannot see where; meanwhile the upper air is hoarse with the sickening braying of asses and the fever-shrill bleating of sacrificial lambs.

On the high ground where the green grass is thickest and where the line of myrtle and arbutus begins, lorries are slowly straying, like lost camels, looking for good camping-sites. Here whole families have unpacked their belongings, spread coloured rugs and pillows, and have settled down with no intention of moving before to-morrow. Stately peasant matrons are unpacking their squamous litters of small children, and their saddle bags full of bottles and cans and immense loaves of home-made bread. I wander in this forest of human beings with the loving detachment of a child in a familiar countryside, drinking it all in—even the savour of the harsh reddish dust which coats the air and dries the throat: all the weird mixture of smells which together compose the anthology of a Greek holiday under the pines—petrol, garlic, wine and goat.

For a while I sit myself down under a tree, the better to study this crowded canvas, in every corner of which simultaneous and totally disconnected scenes are being played. Mehmet Bey, who has obviously succeeded in running a good cargo into Trianda bay, is

busy unloading an enormous chest into the gaping suitcases of the
dozen or so pedlars who are doubtless his agents; beads, mirrors, rings,
combs, cards of Turkish embroidery, and various childish confections
in celluloid, like small propellers mounted on sticks. (Waved from
side to side, the propellers revolve with a satisfactory furry noise.)
The children have thrown themselves upon the cart like dogs at a
bear. They are beaten off. They return. Mehmet Bey pulls off his
gaucho's hat and makes ineffectual sweeps at them as he tries to
calculate with one half of his mind how much stock he is giving to
each pedlar. A little to the left some children are pelting with crusts a
lunatic, who is doubtless attached to one of the café's as a luck-
bringer: or perhaps he has come to he healed by the Saint. To the
west, I observe the Baron Baedeker working like a beaver. Business
is evidently booming. Everyone wants his or her photograph taken.
The Baron has set up his headquarters against the whitewashed side of
a dais—which makes an admirable reflector. On to it he has put up
his only backcloth which is, I must say, most suitable to the time and
place. It is a garish picture of an aeroplane with holes cut in the
canvas in which the sitter or sitters can insert their heads, and so be
photographed in flight, as it were. The peasants are delighted by this
fantasy and argue furiously with each other about whose turn it is
next. The aeroplane itself is of a very improbable kind: I doubt
whether Bleriot would have dared to cross the channel in it. Nevertheless the whole conception is most successful and attracts admiring
smiles from everyone.

The Mufti is wandering gravely in the crowd clad in a new turban
and his elastic-sided boots; beside him I notice Hoyle and General
Gigantes. They have been buying *kolouria*—bread cooked in
circlets[1]—and each wears two or three of them on his wrist like
bangles. Hoyle is discoursing with waves of his unencumbered hand,
his spotted bow tie behind his ear, his coat flapping loose. If I am any
judge of character I should say that he was hunting for the roast-
pits over which by now a dozen sheep are sizzling, and more than
one whole ox. They lie beyond his field of vision, however, on the
slope at my back. Here the heat has burnt a great shimmering hole
in the atmosphere, for the charcoal is red hot. I am pleased to see that

[1] Stuck with sesame seed.

among the turnspits are some of the members of the printing-house
staff, stripped to the waist. They kneel about the pits, talking
gravely, and from time to time making minor adjustments of height
or speed to the spit. There are about a dozen of these pits scattered
about in a rough semicircle. Two have oxen roasting on them fixed
upon enormous cast-iron bits which are turned by an old-fashioned
spring-winding device such as one sees sometimes in old English
farms. These spits revolve with a slow dry clicking sound until the
spring runs down—a process lasting perhaps three hours. In this
little corner there is not noise—or comparatively little; a heavy air of
professional preoccupation hangs over the scene. The turnspits all
wear piratical handkerchiefs round their heads, and lounge about
outside the range of the heat, talking gravely to the sound of the
ticking spits. Occasionally a volunteer approaches a pit, shielding his
face, and cuts a slice of meat from the animal; this is gravely eaten
by the jury of ruffians who sit around, shaking their heads, and
offering ripe comment and advice. Once in a while the oxen are
basted, when a terrific hissing is heard and a column of charcoal dust
rises into the air, rich with the scent of fat and blood. 'Ah!' cries
everyone with satisfaction.

Prolonged cheering and clapping to the east now suggests that the
mule-races are over, and through the clouds of dust vague figures
can be seen to mount the dais and bow as they accept something from
the hands of the Brigadier. It is too far to hear the speeches and the
toasts. Gideon emerges from the press, panting, with a celluloid
propellor whirring in each hand. He sinks down beside me to mop
his brow and to grope in his pockets for some nougat. 'Not bad, is
it?' he says. 'There must be fifteen thousand people here. Kostas says
that Manoli's bus ran into a tree and they all had to walk.'

There is, after all, some justice in the world, to catch up with the
wicked. Luckily, however, nobody seems to have been hurt—at any
rate Manoli at this moment is having his photograph taken, with a
baby on each knee.

Two more big drums have begun to beat with punctual emphasis
and one circle of dancers is beginning to form below me on the slope.
They are gathered round a cluster of music-makers, drummer,
violinist, clarinettist and guitarist, who stand back to back, heads

inclined towards one another. The dances always unfold like this from the centre, in a flower-like pattern. For a moment or so the participants stand in a semi-circle about the musicians, listening with lowered heads and nodding to establish the time: then they begin, slowly, hesitantly, to dance, the subtle meshes of their footwork calculated, deliberate, matching itself to the scribbling of the strings. Then, one by one, they appear to catch fire; their heads rise on their shoulders, their tip-tilted chins begin to carry upwards from the very ankles the smiles of recognition which light their faces. As the circle moves slowly about its centre—the little statuary group of musicians—it begins to establish the authority of the rhythm, rising, you feel, as much from the warm dust of the earth as from the music that is being made. In a little while too, the musicians begin to feel the established circuit, and raise their heads with a sort of pleased relief; they relinquish the melody to its own created momentum and allow it to be carried away on the tide of the dancing feet. Meanwhile the circle itself is growing as new dancers break into the circumference at every point, taking up the rhythms from the twinkling feet of their neighbours', smoothly as candles taking a light from one other. Soon the whole organism has developed its own life and swallowed up the individuality of each of its members, accepting it into the rhythm of the whole, which now moves round and round the live hollow centre of music with the queer archaic peristaltic movements of the *kalamatiano*—the most graceful and earth-coaxing of all Greek dances. From where I sit I cannot hear the highly syncopated jabber of the violins with any clarity: but the spicy afternoon air begins to tremble at the thump of the big drum which marks the end of each bar with a cavernous wallop. The circle wheels and sways, ever-widening as new dancers surrender to its magical appeal.

I am about to go down and get a closer view of the dancing when my attention is distracted by a new development. It is apparently time for the litany to be read at the shrine, for across the dry brown sward from the direction of the trees comes a small straggling procession of villagers, some holding aloft ikons painted on banners. They are headed by the dark figures in clerical robes and tall hats. Ten paces before them walks a small boy, diligently tapping a triangle. The priests are perhaps chanting, for their lips move; but

so great is the hum of the crowd that the remain as yet beyond ear-
shot.

This little procession advances in measured fashion towards the
shrine, at the door of which a dense crowd has gathered—like the
shapeless clotting of bees at the entrance to a hive. From time to time
it is shaken by internal convulsions which throw up the figures of
those (either the most curious, or the most in need of the Saint's
magic) who wish to station themselves before the iron grille which
marks the entrance to the grotto. But by the time the priests approach
a pathway clears itself in the dark mass of bodies and a hoarse murmur
rises. The doors open and the procession descends; and I am close
enough to them now to hear the hollow resonance of voices echoing
in the cave, amplified by the hollowness and the presence of water.
Candle-light flickers warmly where there was lately nothing but a
dark hole; and the sour spiral chanting of the monks begins in a lower
key. Question and response, separated by a semitone. Draughts of
incense sweep up through the gloom, over the water. A shiver runs
through the crowd. Lips move in prayer. Everyone makes the sign of
the cross. With a bitter struggle I succeed in elbowing my way as far as
the iron grille. From here I can gaze down the steps into the grotto.
The incense clouds rising from the water gives one the impression
that it has issued, boiling, from the earth. Yet two or three elderly
women, clad in white shifts, are standing dispiritedly in it, and beyond
them I catch a glimpse of a mongoloid youth being held by two old
crones dressed like nuns. They form a strange bedraggled group as
they stand thigh-deep in the concrete basin, the candle-light flickering on the whites of their eyes. The chanting goes on punctuated by a
series of respectful groans and sighs from the crowd—though whether
they express religious emotion or annoyance at the heat I cannot tell.

I feel a touch on my arm. It is Mills, who has fought his way into
the crowd to see the saint at work. 'All my patients,' he says in a
whisper, 'I want to see if the old man can do better than I can.'
'Materialist,' I whisper back. The immersions have begun within
the grotto. The swishing of water almost drowns the chanting of the
priests. The mongol is making some semi-articulate protests but the
two old nuns have him fast in their talons; all three subside in a
scrambling heap in one corner of the bath.

'I do not know why we are standing here,' says a hoarse voice, 'The miracles take place two days after the service, you all know—never on the spot.' I recognise the butcher-poet who once read me his epic in my office. He has a bunch of spring onions in one hand and a propeller in the other; he seems a trifle intoxicated. 'At least,' he continues, baring his teeth in a grin, 'so the priests would have us believe.' Several people turn their heads and hiss for silence. He eats an onion loudly and puts on an air of scornful scepticism. For villagers today this attitude (so far from what they really believe or feel) represents, so they think, intellectual emancipation. It has come down to them through the village schoolmaster and lawyer, those heirs to the vague radicalism and agnosticism which is poisoning the whole source of our culture. In the butcher-poet I recognise the kind of sceptic who, while he is busy telling you that God does not exist, nevertheless is the first to cross himself if someone would mention the death of an acquaintance. . . . And yet, as Mills says, the real trouble with both reason and mumbo-jumbo is that they are equally suspect. They are both fogged mirrors, badly in need of cleaning. But the ignorant man can get nothing from either—not even a reflection of his own stupidity.

The suppliants have emerged from the pool now, and are drying themselves briskly with towels, their faces still turned in the direction of the altar from which the sounds of prayer still issue, accompanied by great draughts of incense. No miracle appears to have taken place, yet as my butcher-poet says, the effects of the service are often not felt for a day or two afterwards. It is as if the saint needed perhaps time to think things over—to convince himself of the validity of the claims made upon him.

Outside the shrine the shades of evening have begun to fall. The sun is westering behind the mountains, plunging slowly down into the sea beyond Tilos. The sky is beginning to take, softly, wash by wash, the subdued violet tones of evening which slant across the leaves of the trees, and begin to fill out the shadows of objects with darker volume. A light breeze springs up, scattering the dust raised by the brown feet of the dancers and tilting the smoke which rises from the pyres of roasting flesh. We make our way slowly across the violet slopes, so plump and rosy now from the encroaching night, both of us consumed by conflicting curiosities. The dancing-competitions have begun in earnest now. Three hissing carbide lamps fling down a chalky blaze of light upon the brown earth floor where the champion dancers are to compete. A dense crowd has formed a semi-circle, almost engulfing the raised wooden dais upon which we can see the long-suffering face of the Brigadier, flanked by various mayors, dignitaries and churchmen. Other dancing circles have sprung up all over the valley now, but this is the central one; and as we reach it we can hear the heralds shouting aloud the name 'Embona', which raises a great hail of clapping and cheering—for the Embona dancers are reputed to be the finest in Rhodes.

They plunge out of the shadow of the trees with a queer jigging movement—a long line of brightly dressed girls like circus ponies, tossing their heads. Each holds the girdle of the one before her. The line is led by a tall and graceful young man, clad in a white shirt and in tapering trousers, cut something like our riding-breeches, who shuffles a tambourine. The girls wear high boots of calf-skin, and their dark blue pleated dresses are picked out with concentric rings of brighter colour which throw into relief the white shirts they wear and the vivid looped head-scarves. The long line flows out into the arena with this curious loping shuffle to the jingle of the tambourine. Then it halts and dresses itself by the right. The young man steps forward, holding the hand of the endmost dancer and raising the tambourine above his head, pauses, watchful, tense. Then he cuts the air downward with vivid emphasis and the music bursts into life. The dancers drink in two bars before they follow it, each springing forward and backward with the queer see-sawing movement of the dance called 'the cradle'. It is taken at top-speed by these practised village-girls and is something out of the ordinary—though perhaps not the most graceful of the Greek dances I have seen: it has strange elliptical figures which fill in the main structure of its form—a swaying, cradle-like jig, and the formation they adopt is that of a half-moon. This, it is true, gives them a certain mobility and enables the chain to break the measure and flow from side to side of the floor with small shuffling steps, to take up the dance-position in a new corner. But always at the head of the line, capering like a satyr and jingling his tambourine, dances the young man in his soft jackboots.

The dust, too, has begun to rise in clouds from the hard floor of baked earth, so that the crescent of dancers seen from the shadows beyond the plane-trees look like some coloured planet whirring on its course, and surrounded by its own dense atmosphere. 'Come,' says Mills, 'Let's go and see what old Gideon's doing. I've seen the *susta* often enough.' But it is easier said than done, for the dark press of faces behind us offer no hope of an easy egress. We are walled in by the bodies of the crowd. The critics follow the dancers with a passionate intentness, some beating time with their heads. The whole dance-floor has become one swelling cloud of reddish dust by now in the centre of which (their faces preoccupied and remote) ride the dancers, their flower-like bodies carried forward on the music like river-narcissus. The warm dust-cloud has risen to the height of their top-boots, giving them the ghostly appearance of goddesses being born from the earth itself, and aided only by their struggles, and the unearthly music of the fiddles which torment them. The young dance-leader alone raises his feet above the dust-cloud, capering and shaking his tambourine, proudly showing his twinkling heels. His goat-like eyes glitter.

I am reminded, as so often in Greece, that dancing is never a performance so much as a communal rite—the transmission of an enigmatic knowledge which the musician has summoned up from below the earth. It flows outward through the dancing feet which are building the dusty circle, stitch by stitch, like a fabric being woven: step by step like a city being built: and the darker circle outside, the lookers-on, gradually absorb the rhythm which triumphs over them by sheer repetition—being laid down on the consciousness like successive coats of a thrilling colour. One can watch the crowd being drawn into such a dance man by man, impelled by something like that gravitational law which decrees that autumn windfalls should plunge towards the centre of the earth when they are ripe. The vivid circle of the dancers is the centre towards which the audience leans, its blood quickened by the notation of the music—itself (who knows?) a transcription in terms of cat-gut and wind of profounder melodies which the musician has quarried from his native disenchantments and the earth.

But while we have been watching, the darkness has fallen in

earnest; westward the pines still describe themselves against the sky, but very faintly. To those lucky couples who lie about on the grassy slopes it must seem as if they were looking up at the heavens from the bottom of an inkwell, so deep is the blue darkness, yet striped here and there like a leopard's skin with the sulphurous patches of yellow fire from the great bundles of dry gorse and twigs which have now been set alight all along the circumference of this sunken valley. We walk across that dark hinterland, Mills and I, stopping from time to time to watch other teams of dancers in action, some dancing in the eerie light of lanterns, some by these crackling furnaces of thorn and light brush. Everywhere the light scoops out rosy pools in which the dancers swim, as if in an element lighter than air, while the pink puffs of dust which flow upwards seem as light as foam beneath their feet. And everywhere the thumping of the drums only underlines the sullen vibrations of the earth itself under so many moving feet. Everywhere outside lie pastures of ink, where movement is small, individual, owing nothing to the group hypnosis of these dancing circles. Candles flicker in the bushes where the peasant families are making their arrangements for the night; some of the children, after being put to bed, have escaped again into the magical darkness to join some rapt circle of dance critics. Their mothers' plaintive voices can be heard calling 'Spiro! . . . Pavlos! . . . where are you?'

Once we blunder into an untethered mule, and once Mills trips over a prostrate body which groans and curses in accents jocund with garlic and mastika. The light is better in the long main-street of the boom-town, which by now resembles an oriental bazaar lit by pressure-lamps which have the same ghastly brilliance as old-fashioned gas-lighting. Here Mehmet is busy haranguing people from a stall covered with carded embroidery. Business is still brisk, but it is chiefly the old people who are still busy arguing, assessing and buying goods. The young have been drawn off by the dancing. Christ is busy before a pastry-cook's stall, buying some sweet cakes for his old mother who is sitting at a table on the slope peering into the gloom eagerly with those cataract-covered eyes which somehow look abnormally keen and clear-sighted.

On one of the dance-floors Sergeant Croker is in action, dancing with a comical stiffness, but with faultless accuracy, cheered on by an

172

appreciative crowd. I have heard that he is engaged to a Greek girl now and has learned the language passably well. His fellow-dancers are a queer mixture; some are tradesmen from Rhodes town, and some villagers from one of the remoter villages. Croker's cap has fallen off. Prolonged shouts and cheers. 'I've never seen old Croker dance,' says Mills with admiration. 'He must be as tight as a drum.' It is true that as the Sergeant swings round into the light one notices a distinct glassiness of expression, but this may be accounted for by the intricacy of the evolutions he is performing. They need some concentration. Hoyle suddenly appears at my elbow, gnome-like, panting, delighted. 'I've been looking for you everywhere,' he says. 'This crowd is rather far gone. Isn't Croker wonderful? When he went on to dance people began to jeer and shout at him. All of a sudden a Herculean figure bounded into the ring—Gigantes. He took Croker's arm and they danced together for a while, and of course the jeers changed to cheers for the General. Don't you think that was a graceful and delightful thing to do—typically *Gigantesque?*' Croker is by now having his full meed of cheers. He looks as if he could go on until morning. The General, by showing him public favour, has endeared him to everyone. 'Where the devil is Gideon?' says Mills irritably. Hoyle has lost track of him. 'He said he was going to get his fortune told. Which means that he was going to hunt for a good wine.'

So we turn our steps towards the cafés under the trees, and it is not long before we run Gideon to earth in one of them. There is not very much light up here, but our friends seem to know where we are; within a few minutes of our arrival little gifts of food begin to arrive for us. They are handed to the waiter in the darkness outside and he places them before us, whispering in our ears the names of the donors as he does so. Mehmet sends us a platter of black olives and some paprika which has been steeped in vinegar—a favourite appetiser of Hoyle's. Christ sends us a noggin of black wine and some white roses, while Manoli unexpectedly appears in person bearing a wooden bowl piled with crystallised fruit and green apples. 'What a country,' says Gideon. 'One only has to look hungry, to sit around for a while, and people just send you things.'

After a while we are joined by Sand and the Baron Baedeker, who

173

converge upon us from opposite directions. Sand is his usual taciturn self, but the Baron is a man transformed; he has a very weak head, and has been given a glass of wine by one of his clients. He will normally only speak English when his courage is at meridian. Now he refuses to speak anything else. 'Ah, if I had *flesh,*' he keeps repeating, 'If I had *flesh* I could take a picture of you all . . . piff.' It is too dark, alas, for his camera, though he climbs his step-ladder rather unsteadily and peers at us through a finder-lens once, just to be sure. His grave and gentle face bears an expression of unwonted animation. He accepts a small glass of wine with a simper and says to Hoyle: 'I have my circumcision in Turkish town tomorrow—you wish to see?'

We are well into the second can of retsina when a messenger comes panting into the circle of light with a message from the General. We are urgently bidden to the village banquet which is being given in honour of the representatives of Greece by the mayor and aldermen of Soroni. Gideon and Hoyle gaze at one another with some misgiving, for a banquet means toasts and probably speeches; however, if Gigantes has sent for them, go they must. For my part I am loth to be tied down by any one entertainment on a night like this; I prefer to remain free to wander. And Mills makes some excuse which must be truthful, for he gets up and disappears into the darkness.

After parting from the others, and wandering round for a while, I stumble upon a little group of figures whose immobility in the midst of all that noise and movement is almost shocking. I am drawn by something like as sense of impending danger towards the little construction of reeds and plane-leaves—a makeshift shelter—inside which, posed as if for the crude Nativity of some medieval painter crouches a group of peasants. A horn-lantern with one feeble candle alight in it stands upon the ground, throwing its waxen light upon a half-circle of faces whose blank uncomprehending anguish, devoid of recognition, seems trained downwards, as if eternally fixed, upon the figure of a small child lying upon a dirty peasant blanket which is drawn back over his knees. He is dressed in a shirt of vivid whiteness open at the throat, and he gazes out beyond the circle of faces at the sky with some of that gentle vagueness which the human face wears at the approach of death. At the fringes of that puddle of sallow light crouch the patient sleeping forms of goats and a rough-coated sheep-dog. To the left a kneeling woman with her bright scarf drawn across her face and her head bent. But dominating the foreground is a figure I recognise, clad in much-patched blue trousers and a dark open jacket which is barred across the chest by the heavy woollen vest of the fisherman. It is the other Manoli—the old sailor whom I visit every day on my way to work. Those toil-swollen fingers are resting on his knees as if to spare his rheumatic joints some of the strain of kneeling on the hard ground. I say that I recognise him, but the truth is that the figure I know to be his, bears to the Manoli I know the resemblance of a plaster effigy.

His features seem to have been stripped of all meaning—the gesture, mobility, or repose, which alone give an accidental significance to the inert structure of flesh and bone, and which carry on them the index of the human personality, its masks. He crouches there like a figure stamped on some old leaden seal; and while my own startled senses clearly interpret his physical attitude as one of pain and misgiving, to someone else casually passing, he might seem to be like a man who has just been deafened by an explosion which has scattered the whole sum of human expressions by which his face might register some idea of its magnitude. The very earth seems deaf around the little group, fixed in the attitudes of a forgotten tableau around the flickering lantern. As I come nearer I understand the meaning of this graven immobility. They are holding their breath for the child, trying to stare out of countenance the death that they can seen on his face; which rises noiselessly within him like a column of water rising in a well. A little circle of villagers have closed in about the actors, forming a web of human heads, a circle of compassionate helpless witnesses. All are silent. The whole scene has the veridic fixity of an old master—though the figures breathe, and though one recognises the brush which has so thoughtfully, so masterfully painted them in as the brush of pain itself. Some of the men have the faces of those whom shock has somewhat sobered; one holds a mattress, one a bottle of wine, and even these objects so listlessly held in hands whose very pose suggests the uselessness of all action, seem somehow lost to common context. They are like the wreckage left behind after an invasion of the senses by all the armies of the unknown.

The child himself wears a cold original chalky bloom; he breathes, but there are long spaces between each breath, during which he gazes with an expression of almost voluptuous detachment and purity at the outer night, giving little visible sign that it is exactly here—in the spaces between breaths, that the intrusion of something so unforseen as death is to be feared. Yet each sip of the spicy air is drawn to his lungs with a languorous burden—a deep sigh, hanging like a bead of water to the lips of a pitcher: it trembles and falls; and after a long wait another is drawn from the inexhaustible treasury of the darkness, to fill his veins with oxygen. It is scarcely visible, this process. He breathes as a flower is said to breathe. I can see the white tip of a pointed ear above his collar. His hair has been cropped close, like that of all village children in summer, to guard him against ringworm. The two dark eyes—one cannot say that they are expressionless: it is rather that their range of focus, the depth of their experience, has suddenly widened to include a new horizon, a wealth of new preoccupations based in a magical stillness, a terrific but unstudied world-weariness.

In the earlier darkness and confusion which reigned during the setting up of the outer encampments on the slope a lorry had swerved aside and passed over him as he lay asleep. The little fringe of faces moves slowly, heavily from side to side—like the movement of a shelf of seaweed in some submarine calm. In the face of that terrible considered breathing the breath of these frightened peasants has itself become shortened—too precious to waste on the usual whispers or lamentations. As for the child, he seems already to be entering that class of material objects whose context has been torn from them by the force of the tragedy—all these bottles held half-empty in still fingers, the idle propellor of celluloid which his brother still holds in a thoughtless fist, the burning candle-stump. His mother repeats his name from time to time under her breath but without conviction— as if she were trying it for the first time. Though she crouches with lowered head most of the time there are moments when she will straighten her back and, as if to knock the memory forever into her reason, as one would drive a nail into an oak, she bangs upon her forehead twice with the knuckles of a clenched fist, uttering a hoarse cry of pathetic incomprehensibility, which fades out into the deafness of that death-divining circle of faces as soon as it is uttered.

The official Italian Road Guide to Rhodes, an accurate production of the year 1939

It is strange how passion held in restraint burst, so to speak, upwards into the very musculature of the human body, as if it must at
all costs exteriorise itself. The heavy rope-like muscles of Manoli's
body, already swollen and contorted by rheumatism, have further
tightened under the pressure of unexpressed feeling and of shock. It
is as if in some old house, ruined by damp, the arterial system—the
plumbing—had been revealed by a fallen wall, or by the incursions
of damp or snow. Yet he crouches limply, hands unclenched, gazing
with a dumb and sightless longing at the boy stretched under the
blanket. It is as if someone had drawn a wet sponge across everything else in the world leaving only this circle of fading light and
the characters which peopled it as the whole content of his thoughts.

All this, which takes so long to describe in words, is seen and
apprehended in the space of a few seconds—for in a dozen short
paces I have reached the crowd, which has the curious (sour earth-
bound) smell that I recognise as the smell of human beings suffering
from anxiety. Mills is already there; but he is crouching on his knees
and is hidden by the onlookers. Those quick sensitive fingers have
already explored his subject with the tact and deftness that is their
special gift. He kneels for a second to watch the child, his chin on
his hand, his face puzzled. Then he rises to his feet and turning
catches sight of me. He clears his throat and shoulders his way through
the crowd to me, to take my arm and lead me into the darkness
beyond the tableau, saying: 'Good. You can help.' We were already
hurrying down the slope when he adds: 'Someone's gone to phone
for an ambulance, but I don't trust them. Or the phone may be
locked. It may take ages. Will you take the car and go up to the
Hospital and see that they get the message? I think the kid's had it.'
He stops in surprise for we are suddenly bathed in the moonlight,
which has brimmed over and is filling the dark bowl of the valley,
dredging up solid objects and giving them shape—as if some great
lake of darkness were being slowly drained: cars, shining bicycles,
tents and hoardings are being reclaimed one by one. 'I needn't come
any further. You can see the car under the trees there. Take the keys.'

The wheel of the little racing-car is slippery with dew, but she starts
readily enough. In a moment I am bumping and chattering down
the coast road towards the sea, which swims up towards me in the

moonlight, glittering and peaceful. The hills begin to skim away on
every side now, taking up new positions to the north and south,
until at last I clear them and reach the coast road which turns sharply
right and runs along through the mulberry-groves and sleeping
villages towards Rhodes. On the long road leading to Trianda I
catch sight of a white floating object out there on the coast road,
flickering between the hedges as if recorded on a strip of old moving-
film. It is the ambulance. I draw across the road and hear the sweet
tinkle of its bell gradually becoming louder as it approaches through
the trees. It flutters towards me like a great white moth and stops.
The driver and the duty-nurse are perched up in the front seat waiting for me. The message got through. I tell them as briefly as I can
what they are to expect and they nod curtly. The driver crosses himself. Then I stand back and the ambulance plunges off down the road
to Soroni, its sweet cloying bell ringing it away into the distance like
a messenger from the stern world of duties and penalties let loose
upon this elegaic God-befuddled landscape.

Between Trianda and Mixi the road reaches the sea for the first
time, and here the beaches have been swept by the moon until the
floor of pebbles and sand glitters as if it were slippery with the mucus
of frogspawn. It is warm and there is not a soul about. In a moment I
have shed my clothes and am swimming out across the golden bars
of moonlight, feeling the soft foamy commotion of water drumming
on my sides—the peerless warmth of that summer sea. The light
filters down a full fathom or more to where, on the dark blackboard
of weed, broken here and there by dazzling areas of milk-white
sand, the fish float as if dazed by their own violet shadows which
follow them back and forth, sprawling across the sea's floor. Or
perhaps it is the blinding shimmer of phosphorus which outlines my
own swimming body as it plunges towards them throwing out
sparks. I swim for a moment or two and then turn on my back to
watch the sky through wet eyelashes and lying there, arms behind
my head, on that resilient tideless meadow of water, I see in my
mind's eye the whole panorama of our Rhodian life, made up of a
thousand different scenes and ages, all turning before me now as if on
the slow turntable of the four seasons.

In Rhodes we have been the willing bondsmen of the marine

Venus—the figure that sits up there alone in the Museum, disregarded, sightless; yet somehow we have learned to share that timeless, exact musical contemplation—the secret of her self-sufficiency—which has helped her to outlive the savage noise of wars and change, to maintain unbroken the fine thread of her thoughts through the centuries past. Yes, and through her we have learned to see Greece with the inner eyes—not as a collection of battered vestiges left over from cultures long since abandoned—but as something ever-present and ever-renewed: the symbol married to the object prime—so that a cypress tree, a mask, an orange, a plough were extended beyond themselves into an eternality they enjoyed only with the furniture of all good poetry. In the blithe air of Rhodes she has provided us with a vicarious sense of continuity not only with the past—but also with the future—for surely history's evaluations are wrong in speaking of civilized and barbaric ages succeeding or preceding one another, surely they have always co-existed—for one is the measure of the other? Everywhere the dualism of the human personality has created side by side profanity and piety, truth and falsehood, hate and love. Time is always aspiring to a dance-measure which will entangle the two in a dance, a dialogue, a duet: dissolve their opposition. The radiance of that worn stone figure carries the message to us so clearly. . . .

Arriving back in Rhodes, I leave the little car in its usual place under the plane-trees and walk slowly down the hill towards the Villa Cleobolus. In a field a horse stands asleep, its coat aglitter with dew. As I reach the esplanade I see that there is a light on in the duty-room. This is unusual except when, for one reason or another, the Cairo plane is delayed, and the mail is sorted at night. I climb the staircase and push open the door to the duty-office. Sitting at a table, facing one another, sit the two Sergeants Manners and Kirkbride, puffing pipes and playing Rummy. They are inseparable friends, and by consequence always elect to share tiresome guard duties together; also as elderly married men they prefer a quiet life to the more meretricious joys of festivals and balls, so that one usually finds them on duty late at night or when the whole administration has had to turn out for some function or other. 'It's come, sir,' says Manners, taking his pipe out for a second and making a sort of token gesture of standing up before he subsides again. Kirkbride, who has some of the middle-aged, matronly spread of a natural beer-drinker, copies his fellow and adds: 'Just come off the wireless room, sir. Order to pack up. I sent the signal clerk up to the Brig's villa.'

So it has come at last. The islands are to be handed back to Greece. I am delighted as I picture the beaming figure of General Gigantes when he hears the news. But my happiness is touched with regret, for this means yet another separation from a country which I have come to recognise as my second home.

I turn and go slowly downstairs and by the narrow gate into the heavy darkness of the Mufti's courtyard—so dark that I must grope my way past the tomb of Hacmet: the goat awakes in alarm and swings out on the end of its cord, scattering droppings with its hooves. In the silent garden the leaves are still dropping. They are not inclined to wait for autumn this year. My thoughts turn to E and I walk across the garden to the hotel to see if there is a light in her room. The shutters are open but the room is dark.

In my familiar room at the Villa Cleobolus I strike a match and the Turkish lovers leap off the counterpane towards me—as if they had been asleep. Yet the serenade has not ceased for an instant. The viol has been playing all the time in the darkness, touched by those long saintly fingers: she has been smiling idly up at him: the bird in the branches above their heads has been on duty all the time, singing as if its heart were broken. The two white vases filled with lilac raise their long graceful throats above the fireplace. I remember so vividly the thump of the clay on the wheel, and the gradual emergence of their fine stems under the broad thumbs of Egon Huber as he said 'Something for you two', trimming them with a fine knife as they turned: and then moving them off the wheel still wet, to the shadowy pottery where they would be given their glaze. They had stood there for two years now, fronting the shelf of sea-stained books and indifferent water colours, the rolled tent, the tinned food, the anchor. I think I have never loved a room so much. Here I have spent all my spare time—a whole winter—working on a play which is never destined to be published or played, stopping from time to time to pitch a resin-scented log on the fire, or look up a reference in a book. 'Here too I have been visited by friends who dropped in like swallows from the sky—Paddy and Xan: the Corn Goddess: John Craxton: Patrick Reilly—all bringing with them the flavour of the outside world: Romney Summers, Tricoglou and Jim Richards, who stayed and remembered: Mary Mollo and Katy P. who nearly died here. And Boris who thought I should get a job with Unesco and said that "This cult for islands was becoming deplorable".'

I sit for a while thinking about it all before undressing. I am half asleep when I notice something pinned to the counterpane. It is a signal adressed to my office. On a corner of the sheet of paper in E's tall handwriting is a message. 'Here it is at last.' The signal reads: 'The date for the handover is to be announced on Saturday. You will complete preparations for winding-up and report to Cairo by the first of next month, liquidating all our press responsibilities in the islands.'

I get into bed and settle down to sleep; but the waning moon has moved over and peers in at me from an unshuttered window, so that after perhaps two hours I am awake again. So radiant is the night, and so rich with the scent of flowers and creepers that I am reluctant to waste it in sleep. The news of our impending departure has made me miserly. I dress and walk rapidly across the little town to the hospital. The white ambulance is parked outside in the drive and a sleepy duty-nurse dozes under a weak yellowish bulb in the ugly stone entrance hall. I leave him asleep and climb to the first floor, tip-toeing through the long sleeping-wards in the direction of Mills's private room, which lies at an angle to the operating-theatre, on the shadowed side of the building. I open the door and make my way through the darkened room to the terrace. It is empty, but turning to my right, I can see shadowy figures seated around a table two terraces away. Very little moonlight penetrates the dense clump of pines which grows out of the side of the hill and all but hides the sky.

I retrace my steps into the lighted corridor and meet my friend as he is about to enter a door. He looks pale and weary, and is stripping his hands of their rubber gloves. 'He's no right to be alive but he is,' he whispers with the ghost of a smile, untying the tapes which meet across his back and pulling off the little sterile mask from his mouth in one deft flowing movement born of long practice. From somewhere to our left comes the faint clink of steel on metal. I imagine that some operation must be going forward in the theatre, but taking my arm he pilots me to the end of a corridor and into a small buttery where Chloe is cutting bread and butter. 'Come in,' she whispers and I sit down on a chair by the sink.

'Manoli and his wife are on the terrace. They've been crying, but they're asleep now, both,' she says. A nurse's head appears in the doorway and Mills jumps up with a muttered apology to vanish through the door. I say: 'Chloe, our orders came through tonight. We'll be leaving in a fortnight.'

She looks up with a wistful and sleepy grace, her face full of sympathy. She looks very beautiful with her hair piled carelessly up on the top of her head, her face unmade-up, her body youthful and candid in the flowered kimono. 'So have ours,' she says at last. 'They came through last week. We are posted to Abyssinia. He wouldn't let me tell anyone before it was necessary. We didn't want to break up all this.'

'Gideon will be sorry. I can see his face so clearly when he hears the news,' she continues. 'He will soon be left with only Hoyle for company.' 'But,' I say, 'their families will come out. A new life will begin.'[1]

'It is not the same,' she says, a little wistfully.

The enamel plate is full of sandwiches now. 'Will you take the plate and go and sit with Manoli, please? I must help Ray. They will be so hungry when they wake.'

I step into a darkened room and cross it on tiptoe to the terrace, placing the plate silently on the table and sinking into the empty chair which stands between the two sleeping figures. Manoli sits in the wicker chair like a waxwork, bolt upright, only his head has fallen a little to the right and his mouth is open. His Italian wife has drawn her head under her flowered shawl, as a bird draws its head under a wing. Their breathing sounds utterly composed, utterly peaceful. Before them stand untouched glasses of cognac on the metal table.

As I sit here between them I find myself sinking into that feeling of

[1] Not for Gideon alas! He was accidentally killed in crossing an unmarked minefield on Nisyros, and left a gap in our lives which could never be filled.

detachment, almost of peace, which visits me when I am alone in a great crowd of people all urgently occupied with their own affairs. Or else when I am an onlooker, at some drama which is going on before my eyes but in which I am powerless to take part. At such times one's individuality seems to focus itself with greater emphasis; one overlooks the affairs of men from a new height, participating in life with a richer though a vicarious understanding of it; and yet at the same time remaining fully withdrawn from it.

Sitting between these two sleeping figures, who will wake to a new meaning of life, a new daylight, I see them as symbols more than as human beings. Italy and Greece, if you like, the lovers: the Italy of the domestic arts, the passionate feeling for husbandry and family order, the feeling of a vineyard built with the fingers, pinch by pinch, into terraces of household wine: Italy that conquers as a wife or nurse, encroaching on nature with the arts of love. Then Greece: the vertical, masculine, adventurous consciousness of the archipelago, with its mental anarchy and indiscipline touched everywhere with the taste for agnosticism and spare living: Greece born into the sexual intoxication of the light, which seems to shine upwards from inside the very earth, to illuminate these bare acres of squill and asphodel. It seems to me so clear that their arts of life are not divergent ones, but the complementaries of each other. How unlucky that here, among the humps of Aegean stone, islets dropped red hot from the trowels of the Titans, among the windmills and the springs curdled by moss-grown cisterns, the truth should not have been made plain. They both belong to this sacred territory, husband and wife, as the myrtle and olive do.

And then again, between the sleeping figures, I saw the dying child, no less a symbol—but of what? Our world perhaps. For it is always the child in man which is forced to live through these repeated tragedies of the European conscience. The child is the for-feit we pay for the whole sum of our worldly errors. Only through him shall we ever salvage these lost cultures of passion and belief.

Then my thoughts turn to complete the greater arc of this small green island, touching my sleeping friends—the sightless stone woman in her cubicle, Gideon and Hoyle snoring somewhere among the mulberry trees of Trianda, Huber tacking for a late landfall at

Mandraccio after a night's fishing, E in her calm bed at the hotel feeling the first faint breath of the dawn-wind from Asia Minor as it stirs the balcony curtains, the Baron Baedeker and Christ snoring under the pines at Soroni . . . all playing an unconscious part in my own inner life, and now, by this writing, made a part of it forever.

The light is growing fast and it has turned much colder; the strip of sky behind the pines has been drained of the violet moonlight and is slowly filling with the new colour of approaching sunrise. I am suddenly beginning to feel sleepy here, alone with my thoughts. When Chloe comes to find us with whatever news the new world of sunlight has to offer she will find me dozing between the two silent figures.

EPILOGUE

The Sporades are lean wolves and hunt in packs; waterless, eroded by the sun. They branch off on every side as you coast along the shores of Anatolia. Then towards afternoon the shaggy green of Cos comes up; and then, slithering out of the wintry blue the moist green flanks of Rhodes.

It is good to see places where one has been happy in the past—to see them after many years and in different circumstances. The child is asleep in its rugs: that long, much-loved, much travelled coastline breasts its way up against the liner's deck until the town fans out—each minaret like the loved worn face of an earthly friend. I am looking, as if into a well, to recapture the faces of Hoyle, Gideon, Mills—and the dark vehement grace of E.

Ahead of us the night gathers, a different night, and Rhodes begins to fall into the unresponding sea from which only memory can rescue it. The clouds hang high over Anatolia. Other islands? Other futures?

Not, I think, after one has lived with the Marine Venus. The wound she gives one must carry to the world's end.

A Short Calendar of Flowers and Saints for Rhodes[1]

JANUARY

In some parts of Greece January is called 'The Pruner' because now the husbandman trims vines and trees. An omen is drawn from the observation of the weather at Epiphany. The following saw illustrates this:

> *Dry Epiphany and pouring Easter weather*
> *Bring us happiness and plenty both together.*

The woods are starred with early anemones of a delicate purple (Mostly *Anemone coronaria* L.) Visit the lush meadows around Casa del Pini.

January 7th is the feast of St John the Baptist and there is mumming in the streets by children in masks.

Glorious pink and white flowers of the wild almond in puffs everywhere. Flowering often begins as early as mid-December (*Amygdalus communis* L.) Loveliest in the hill districts.

The shy winter crocus with its lavender-coloured flowers appears (*Crocus Sieberi* Gay).

The Japanese medlar is in bloom. Its scent is strongest just after sunset. Wistaria blooms.

The weather in this month is often fine, dry and cold (the Halcyon days).

[1] Acknowledgements are due to Dr. Theodore Stephanides for help with this calendar.

FEBRUARY

On the second falls the Feast of the Purification of the Virgin (our Candlemas), and the prevailing weather on this day is popularly supposed to last 40 days.

Anemones still at their best.

The large purple periwinkle (*Vinca Major* L.) begins to flower.

Purple-blue irises (*Iris cretensis* Janka) appear.

The deliciously scented narcissus (*Narcissus Tazetta* L.) appears, esp. in swampy places.

Wistaria still in bloom.

MARCH

The first cuckoo and the early spring winds. (Charcoal-burners dread the cuckoo's note as foretelling dry weather.) Now the first cicadas begin to welcome the sunlight, and swallows start building under the house-eaves. (Destroy their nests and you'll get freckles, says popular legend). On the 1st of the month the boys fashion a wooden swallow, adorn it with flowers and travel from house to house collecting pennies and singing a little song which varies from place to place in Greece. This custom is of the remotest antiquity.

For the first three days of March peasants think it unlucky to wash or plant vegetables. Trees planted now will wither. The March sun burns the skin: and a red and white thread on the wrist will prevent your children from getting sunburn.

Some of the orchids begin to flower, incl. the purple lax-flowered orchid (*Orchis laxiflora* Lam.) which grows in swampy places; and various species of pyramid, bee and fly orchids.

Other blue irises (*Iris attica* and *Iris florentina*) appear.

The bright yellow bog iris (*Iris Pseudacorus* L.) brightens the dykes and other swampy places with its quarantine-like flags.

Narcissi still found: anemones dying off. Periwinkle still seen.

Orange and lemon trees in full bloom.

The arborescent heath (*Erica arborea* L.) shows its masses of white flowers. It is from the roots of this plant that 'briar' (from the French *bruyère*) pipes are made.

EASTER

has been grafted on to what was probably the Lesser Eleusinia in Ancient times—the return of Persephone. It is the period of red eggs and roasted lamb on the spit today and is ushered in by the great 40 days fast of Lent. The two Sundays before Lent are known respectively as Meat Sunday and Cheese Sunday. The week between them answers to our western carnival week and is so celebrated in the cities of Greece with masquerades, black dominoes etc. . . . Scholars hint at pre-Christian survivals saying that these antics suggest the Old Cronia festivals of ancient times while Lent itself suggests a connection with the Eleusinean mysteries—commemorating Demeter's long abstinence from food during her search for her lost daughter.

March 25th, Lady Day comes when peasants hang red coloured sashes and handkerchiefs from their balconies. Eggs are dyed red, and with the first egg the mother makes the sign of the cross on the face and neck of her child, saying 'May you be as rosy as this egg and as strong as a stone.' The egg is then placed near the family ikon of the Virgin until next year.

On Good Friday do not touch vinegar. It is unlucky because on this day the Jews moistened Christ's lips with it.

On Holy Saturday do not wash your hair or you'll turn grey before your time.

The midnight Mass of Easter Sunday is the highpost of the year's festivals and no traveller should miss the impressive ceremony. In villages the gospel is read out in the churchyard under a tree. At the end the news that 'Christ is risen' is announced to the banging of gongs and the explosion of crackers; in the dark church the priest holds up his consecrated candle and calls out to the congregation 'Come and receive the light'; they light each one a taper from his candle and pass the light back into the dark body of the church to the rest of the congregation. If you are lucky enough to get your candle home without it going out you'll have good luck the coming year.

APRIL

In the uplands sheep are shorn and the air is full of the plaintive crying of lambs unable to recognise their shorn dams; about the 23rd of the month (St George's Day, the patron saint of Brigands and Englishmen) the shepherds return to the mountains with their flocks.

Orchids at their best. Irises still going strong. Narcissi ending.

The spring Asphodel (*Asphodelus microcarpus* Viv.) shows its *branched* spikes of white flowers in the olive woods.

Snake-wort (*Dracunculus vulgaris* Schott) shows its huge green, brown and purple blossoms (rather like an outsize arum lily, rare) and can often be located from a distance by its carrion-like smell.

The prickly-pear (*Opuntia Ficus-indica*) begins to show its pretty yellow flowers.

The yellow wallflower (*Cheiranthus cheiri* L.) now in flower.

Various species of cistus begin to show their pink, white and yellow flowers.

The Judas-tree (*Cercis siliquastrum* L.) sometimes begins to bloom towards the end of the month.

Gorse (*Calycotome villosa*) and broom (*Spartium junceum* L.) explode into bright yellow on the hillsides.

The golden marigold (*Crysanthemum coronarium* L.) decks the fields.

MAY

Parties are formed to go picnicking and 'fetch back the May'; the young men of the village make wreaths of flowers and hang them at their sweethearts' doors; but May is unlucky for marriages because, says the proverb, 'In May the donkeys mate.'

Cistus, wallflower, periwinkle, prickly-pear, dracunculus, still in flower.

Judas-trees at their best, in great splashes of magenta all over the countryside. Gorse and broom in full wing. Bog iris still going strong.

Orchids finishing.

The climbing clematis (*Clematis flammula* L.) shows its white flowers. The peasants call it the swallow flower—chelidonia—probably because it appears when the swallows return.

The wild thyme (*Thymbra capitata* Griseb.) begins to flower, to the delight of the bees which produce the Hymettus honey.

White acacia trees in full flower (*Robinia Pseudacacia* L.).

JUNE

In some places called 'The Harvester' because the harvest begins normally in this month. On the 24th June falls the Nativity of St John the Baptist which is celebrated by a great feast with crackling bonfires.

Nigella (love-in-a-mist, alias devil-in-a-bush) shows its delicate pale blue flowers.

The seeds of the ailantus tree (*Ailantus glandulosa* Desf.) show great masses of orange and crimson.

The squirting cucumber (*Ecballium elaterium*) shows its pale yellow flowers. Within the month it is ready for action, and then mind your eye. Active until September.

Thyme in full swing; also mint and sage.

Swamp iris, prickly-pear, still in flower.

The spineless caper (*Capparis inermis*) shows its large white flowers with their long purple stamens. In rocks by the sea-shore.

The leaves of the eryngium turn a metallic blue.

The bright vermilion flowers of the pomegranate are seen; flowers also in July.

The chaste-tree (*Vitex agnus-castus* L.) shows its purple flowers; esp. along the coasts. The Ancient Greeks believed that the scent of its leaves and flowers was an 'anti-aphrodisiac', hence the name.

JULY

In some places called 'The Thresher' presumably because the corn is threshed in this month. In Macedonia farmers make a thin wafer-like cake from newly ground corn which they crumple into wells and distribute it among the passers-by; this is called grasshopper-cake— an offering to the favourite insect of the farmer. The cicada is the insect of this month, and his orchestra fills the long afternoons with deep humming. Often at this time a distant cousin, the locust, moves in for a week or two in the flat land about Malona and causes alarm; so far however his depredations have been successfully checked. He is blown over the sea from Africa, it is surmised. On the 30th July there is a huge open-air festival at Soroni to celebrate the arrival of St Saul who was a fellow-passenger of St Paul during his ship-wreck at Lindos. (A case of transferred names and attributes—as with ancient Gods and Goddesses, one wonders?)

The violet delphinium (*Delphinium junceum* DC.) in flower. Also in August.

The golden thistle (*Scolymus hispanicus* L.) shows its yellow flowers in all uncultivated places.

The mullein (*Verbascum undulatum* Lam.) shows its yellow flowers.

Some species are used by the peasants to make fish poisons.
The oleander is seen in masses of pink (occasionally white).

Prickly-pear still in flower.

The agave (aloe) rockets upwards after a flying start in May and shows its spike of yellow-green flowers. Also in September.

AUGUST

The jackdaw is the bird of the month, and August begins with the Progress of the Precious and Unifying Cross. This feast prepares one for another fast which is prelude to the Feast of the Repose of the

Virgin. On the 23rd the Feast of the Holy Merciful is celebrated; again on the 29th a feast for the Cutting Off of the Precious Head of St John the Precursor heralds more abstinence.

In general however August is the great dancing month, and pana-gyreias are held at Maritza on the 6th, while the big feast of the Virgin held on the 15th and 23rd at Trianda and Cremasto is the biggest event of the year, attracting islanders from Simi, Cos, Casos *et alia*, and highlanders from the brilliant hill villages like Siana whose costumes and dancing reminds one of the fastnesses of Crete.

The beautiful sand lily (*Pancratium maritimum L.*) shows its white flowers in the coastal sands.

The caper still in flower (until September).

SEPTEMBER

On the 14th there is a festival dedicated to the Cross at Callithies. Childless women make the weary pilgrimage to the top of the razor-back hill called Tsambika below San Benedetto—and here, in the chapel of Our Lady, they eat a small piece of the wick from one of the lamps which will make them fruitful. If the resulting infant is not named after the Virgin it dies.

The autumn asphodel (*Scilla autumnalis L.*) shows its *unbranched* spike of white flowers in all the olive woods. The peasants make a rat poison from its huge bulb.

The grapes are gathered (beginning.)

OCTOBER

A golden month which belongs to St Demetrius; at his feast on the 26th wine-casks are unstapped and the new wine tasted. Many weddings take place in this month, and an eagerly anticipated spell of fine weather which comes around the middle month is known as The Little Summer of St Demetrius.

Grape gathering in full swing.

The crocus-like *Sternbergia sicula* Tin. shows its bright yellow blossoms after the first autumn rains.

The autumn mandrake (*Mandragora autumnalis*) shows its purple flowers at about the same time (rare).

The cyclamen have just started their lilac flood.

NOVEMBER

In many places still called 'The Sower' because seed-time is beginning; St Andrew is the most popular saint of this month and his feast falls on the last day of the month. He is the bringer of the first snow (Popular saying: 'St Andrew has washed his beard white'). The feast of the Virgin on the 21st is sometimes not celebrated in Rhodes. On the 18th also St Plato the Martyr (whom popular ignorance has transformed into St Plane-Tree, the names being very similar). The weather which prevails on the 18th will last through Advent (The Forty Days). Now the Pleiades begin to rise, and the first sea-gales drive the long-shore fisherman to his winter quarters. The melancholy of the dying year is hardly cast off by St Andrew's holiday on which everyone eats 'loucumades'—a sort of doughnut-shaped waffle.

The autumn crocus (*Crocus laevigatus*) appears. Flowers white to mauve.

The saffron crocus (*Crocus cartwrightianus*) also appears. Purple blossoms. Bulbs used to make the condiment 'saffron'.

Cyclamen in full blossom.

The fruit of the orange and tangerine begin to turn golden.

DECEMBER

The saint of the month is St Nicholas, and rightly so; the seafarer needs his patron saint most at the year's end; but there are plenty more on the index of saints.

4th December	St Barbara
5th ,,	St Savvas
6th ,,	St Nicholas
12th ,,	St Spiridion

After Spiridion's day the days grow longer by a grain—a horrible pun in Greek.

Christmas Eve—Incense is burned before supper, and those flat hot-cross buns called 'Christ's loaves' are baked in the oven. After supper the cloth is not removed from the table because it is believed that Christ will come and eat during the night. A log or an old shoe is left burning on the fire: the smoke will ward off stray 'Kallikanzari' (see 'Kaous' in the text).

New Year's Day belongs to St Basil: a cake with a silver coin in it is made and cut and luck belongs to whoever finds the coin. After supper the family plays games of divination. A slice of new year cake under a girl's pillow will do for a Greek girl what a slice of wedding-cake does for an English girl.

Twelfth Day—The curious ceremony of diving for the Cross can be seen on Rhodes harbour where a dozen shivering lads contend for the prize, and duck the winner of the reward.

Cyclamen end; anemones begin.

Almond and Japanese medlars in flower towards end of month.

Oranges and tangerines ripe.

Snow-drops come out in bloom in some parts of the island.

Peasant Remedies

A few peasant remedies are given here, quoted by permission of the author, from a paper contributed by A. Raymond Mills to the *Bulletin of the History of Medicine*, Johns Hopkins University.

ABSCESS.

1. Crushed onions with mastika are put on hot as a poultice.

2. Scoop out the centre of an onion and fill with sugar, incense, powdered dried reed, olive oil, and a little soap. Cook in the oven and apply to the abscess hot.

3. Snails are gathered, taken out of their shells, ground up, and applied.

4. Baked potatoes without their skins are mixed with oil and sugar and used as a poultice.

BALDNESS AND FALLING HAIR.

1. Mix garlic, dynamite powder, and powdered roofing tile and make a paste with water. Shave the head and apply the paste. Cover the paste with cow dung.

2. The dung beetle is powdered, mixed with alcohol and dabbed on to the bald patches.

3. Two yolks of egg are added to powdered dry fig leaves. This paste is put on to the hair. It cures baldness and dandruff.

BIRTH.

This is often performed in the sitting position, and a chair cut away in the seat is used specially for this purpose. (The squatting position is now being tried by a London hospital.) In the Cyprus Museum there is a terracotta figure of a woman giving birth and being held up by the arms in the sitting position, with a helper delivering the baby. This figure dates from 500 B.C. and shows a strong Phoenician influence.

To bring on labour pains bran (píteron) is boiled and wrapped up in a cloth and applied to the abdomen hot. A hot tile (keramídi) is used in a similar way to apply dry heat.

Seven days after the birth of the child the midwife puts her bare foot on the vulva of the woman and pulls each hand in turn. A vaginal douche is then performed after which sexual intercourse is permitted. This treatment is supposed to replace the genital organs and its efficiency was vouched for by a woman who was the mother of fifteen children!

BURNS.
Ink is used in a similar way to tannic acid.

In the majority of cases mastika is applied liberally and a light dressing put on. Infection is said never to occur with this method.

COMMON COLD.
Crude sheep's wool is dipped into a mixture of paprika and mastika. The whole body is rubbed vigorously with the wool.

CONJUNCTIVITIS.
Wash out eye with sap of vine or tears. Or with cow's or human urine. An ophthalmologist friend of mine has seen bilateral gonococcal conjunctivitis as a result of this method. The child lost the sight of both eyes.

ERYSIPELAS.
1. Dissolve copper sulphate in mastika and massage into the area.
2. A piece of red cloth is put on top of the area of the rash. Seven pieces of resinous wood and seven small pieces of cotton wool are used. A piece of cotton wool is placed on top of the red cloth and a piece of resinous wood on top of the cotton. The wood is lighted and as soon as the cotton takes fire it is flicked off with the finger and the following words are repeated. The whole process is repeated seven times:

> 'káto stó gialó stín ámmo
> oí spanói zeygári kánoyn
> vázoyn tís psolés tón alétri
> kài t'archeídia tón zeygári.

195

Mi òspóros tón matiásei
míti fókio na rizósi.'

This may be translated as follows:

'Down on the beach, on the sand
the beardless ones are mating,
they use the penis like a plough
and their testicles like a pair of oxen.
Let not the Evil Eye fall on the seed (sperms)
nor the erysipelas take root.'

This is strongly suggestive of the ancient phallic ceremonies in which foul words and gestures were used to ward off evil spirits and at the same time, ensure fertility.

LACTATION.

An amber bead hung round the neck of a pregnant woman will ensure a plentiful supply of milk, as will wine and hot bathings. If the mother wishes to stop lactating, a key is hung down the back inside the clothes. Mud from flat roofs (patelía) is made into a paste and smeared on the breast to stop the flow of milk. (This is an interesting link with the Egyptian Arabs who use mud from the roof for the same purpose, the mud in this instance containing dung.) If a woman suckles her child she believes that she cannot become pregnant, during that time. I have seen children being suckled at the age of three and a half years.

PREGNANCY.

The desires of the woman for unusual foods at unusual times must be satisfied. If she does not satisfy her desire and happens to touch her body at the same time, the baby will be marked where she has touched herself. The birthmark of the child is also supposed to indicate the nature of the desire.

Indigestion during pregnancy is due to the unborn infant developing hair. The indigestion is cured by a spoonful of sesame seeds. Coffee is applied to the umbilicus of the newborn infant as an astringent and antiseptic.

A pregnant woman must not cross her legs on sitting down because the child will have the 'cord round the neck'.

Sex.

To determine the sex of an unborn child the following methods are used:

1. When the woman is seven months pregnant, a drop of breast milk is expressed into a glass of water. If the milk dissolves, the child will be a female. If the milk drop remains fibrous and upright in the water, it will be a boy. The latter is obviously a phallic symbol.

2. A knife and a pair of scissors are placed each on a seat and covered with a cushion. The expectant mother is sent out of the room while this is being done and she is called in to choose a chair. If she sits on the knife, it will be a boy; if she sits on the scissors, it will be a girl. The knife is another phallic symbol.

Smallpox.

The Greek name is 'evlogià'. This means 'she must be named with respect'. This is a reference to the fear of omnipotent destructive spirits. They must not be offended. Hence the respectful name. Compare with Evil Eye.

Select Bibliography

In English

Rhodes in Ancient Times	1885	Torr
Rhodes in Modern Times		
Aegean Islands	1887	Tozer
Travels and Discoveries in the Levant (2 vols.)	1865	Newton

In French

L'île de Rhodes	1881	Bileotti and Cottret
L'île de Rhodes	1856	Guerin
Description des Monuments de Rhodes	1828	Rottiers
Histoire des Chevaliers Hospitaliers	1726	Vertor

In Italian

Isola de Rodi	1688	Coronelli: Parisotti
Istoria del Sacro Militare Ordine Gerosolimitano	1602	Bosio

In Modern Greek

ΡΟΔΙΑΚΑ	1939	ΑΝΑΣΤΑΣΙΟΥ Γ. ΒΡΟΝΤΗ
ΡΟΔΙΤΙΚΑ ΤΡΑΓΟΥΔΙΑ	1939	ΑΝΑΣΤΑΣΙΟΥ Γ. ΒΡΟΝΤΗ
Ο ΑΓΙΟΣ ΣΟΥΛΑΣ	1934	ΕΜΜ. ΚΥΡΙΑΖΗ

DATE DUE

10-31			
DEC 1 1970			
JUL 23 1971			
OC 23 78			
GAYLORD			PRINTED IN U.S.A.